T0312350

How to Raise a Viking

Also by Helen Russell

Non-fiction
The Year of Living Danishly
Leap Year
The Atlas of Happiness
How to Be Sad

Fiction
Gone Viking

How to Raise a Viking

The Secrets of
Parenting the World's
Happiest Children

HELEN RUSSELL

4th ESTATE • *London*

4th Estate
An imprint of HarperCollins*Publishers*
1 London Bridge Street
London SE1 9GF

www.4thestate.co.uk

HarperCollins*Publishers*
Macken House
39/40 Mayor Street Upper
Dublin 1
D01 C9W8, Ireland

First published in Great Britain in 2024 by 4th Estate

2

Copyright © Helen Russell 2024

Helen Russell asserts the moral right to be identified as the author of this
work in accordance with the Copyright, Designs and Patents Act 1988

A catalogue record for this book is available from the British Library

ISBN 978-0-00-860272-7

All rights reserved. No part of this publication may be reproduced,
stored in a retrieval system, or transmitted, in any form or by
any means, electronic, mechanical, photocopying, recording or
otherwise, without the prior permission of the publishers.

This book is sold subject to the condition that it shall not, by way
of trade or otherwise, be lent, re-sold, hired out or otherwise circulated
without the publisher's prior consent in any form of binding or cover
other than that in which it is published and without a similar condition
including this condition being imposed on the subsequent purchaser.

Typeset in Granjon by Palimpsest Book Production Ltd, Falkirk, Stirlingshire

Printed and bound in the UK using 100% renewable
electricity at CPI Group (UK) Ltd

This book contains FSC™ certified paper and other controlled sources
to ensure responsible forest management.

For more information visit: www.harpercollins.co.uk/green

For the mini-Vikings
(Sorry about the bubble machine.)

For parents-to-be
(It'll all be okay and don't worry if you can't keep basil
alive. I can't keep basil alive. Or any houseplant, despite
following instructions. Green-fingered friends persist, buying
plants they assure me are 'foolproof'. These inevitably
brown and wilt, and we both look like fools. Houseplants?
No. But children? Yes! Three of them! So don't worry if
you can't do basil. You can still do parenting.
Here's how Vikings do it . . .)

Contents

Introduction:
The Accidental Viking

I KNEW I'D passed the point of no return when googling 'best axe for children' in a coffee shop while my babies slept outside in their pram. Munching on rye bread, jam and cheese (together . . . welcome to Denmark), I was feeling the creeping sensation of caffeine working its magic when an email pinged up from my son's Scout group. I was expecting pre-camp paperwork or an invitation to bake something. Instead, it read: 'On Wednesday we build bonfires! Bring daggers!'

No, he hasn't joined a gang: in the land of Vikings, children are regularly tooled-up fire starters. Something that could earn him jail time in the UK is normal for mini-Vikings, who are packing blades every Wednesday. By the age of six, the eldest already had his own 'dagger' and toolkit, complete with hammer, saw, screwdrivers – flat-head and cross-head. He couldn't read or write – Scandinavians aren't fussed about 'book learning' before the age of eight. But he was *killing it* at boat building and kindling campfires.

It wasn't supposed to be like this. The girl about town, convinced she couldn't have children, never expected to become a mother of three living in rural Scandinavia. I lived and worked for twelve years as a journalist in London, and I had no intention of leaving until, out of the blue, one wet Wednesday, my husband was offered his dream job working for Lego in Denmark. I was sceptical to start with. I had a career I'd worked hard for. We had a flat, good friends, close family – I had a life. Okay, so my husband and I both worked long hours, ran on adrenaline, and barely had time to see each other. We regularly had to bribe ourselves to get through the day and we'd both been ill on and off for the past six months.

But that was normal, right? We thought we were 'living the city dream'. In reality, we were burnt out. We'd also been trying to start a family of our own, with years of fertility treatment. Only it never seemed to work. So when this other-life possibility was dangled in front of us – the chance to swap everything we knew for the unknown – we stopped in our tracks.

Denmark had just been voted the happiest country in the world and I became fascinated by this – how had a tiny Nordic nation managed to pull off the 'happiest nation on Earth' title? Was there something in the water? Could beer, bacon and pastries really make life so much better? I discovered that Denmark had regularly been voted one of the happiest countries in the world – in studies going back to the 1970s. We visited one weekend, just to check the place out. And as soon as I stepped off the plane, I noticed that there was something different about the Danes we met. They didn't look like us, for starters, quite apart from the fact that they were all strapping Vikings, towering over me. They looked more relaxed and healthier.

They walked more slowly.

They took their time to stop and eat together.

Or talk.

Or just . . . breathe.

And we were impressed. My husband – an outdoorsy Yorkshireman, not shy of a cagoule – was sold on the idea. He begged me to move, promising we'd relocate for my career next time. And I found myself agreeing. I quit my job as editor of marieclaire.co.uk to go freelance and decided I would give it a year, investigating the Danish happiness phenomenon first hand. I would look at a different area of living each month to see what Danes did differently – from food to family life, from design to daycare and education. Each month, I would throw myself into 'living Danishly' to see if it made me happier – and if I could change the way I lived as a result. I would seek out sociologists, historians, scientists, economists, politicians, psychologists – everyone, in fact, to try to uncover the secrets to living Danishly.

So we emigrated, swapping the bright lights and bustle of the UK's capital for rural Jutland, in the middle of winter. I didn't know anyone, didn't speak the language, and had no job. My 'Lego Man' husband left to go to work at 7.30 a.m. and I was all on my own. Almost. Our dog – a woolly mutt of unknown origin (his mother being something of a local belle) had come along for the ride. But canine conversational skills are substandard, and I started to worry that I'd just made the biggest mistake of my life.

But that was ten years ago.

And I'm still here.

The cultural gap between the UK and Denmark has only widened since I wrote about my initial experiences in *The Year of Living Danishly* (2013). Since then, we've had Brexit, Boris and the Trump years. My first book ended with a newborn in tow: now I'm a mother of three.

Born here, my children – a redhead and IVF twins – have only ever experienced the Viking way. Despite their dad and I both hailing from the UK and planning on just a year of living Danishly, here we are, a decade later. Mostly because we're incredibly disorganised, time has flown by and it's all our children know. So I have an alarming amount of skin in the Viking parenting game, whether we end up staying or not.

Parenting Danishly is strangely anachronistic at times. Like an Enid Blyton book without the bigotry. And mini-Vikings are different from children back home. They eat differently. They learn differently. They play, dress, even sleep differently. They sing (All The Time), run, jump, climb, fall and get up again, out in nature, for hours a day. It's cold and wet and uncomfortable – often. But they cope.

In Denmark, children play outdoors, schools have no gates, and babies are left to nap outside in their prams. Because 79 per cent of Danes trust *most* people, a statistic I found extraordinary (I don't trust 79 per cent of my immediate family . . .).[1] Okay, so Denmark is a small country of just 5.8 million people. But that's about the size of south London, and I didn't trust everyone there, either.

In the UK and the US, levels of trust have fallen dramatically in the past sixty years, from around 60 per cent to 30 per cent.[2] I grew up in the 1980s and '90s with the full force of the 'stranger danger' campaign. Along with generations of school-children, we were taught to trust *less* – with annual police talks on the perils of people we didn't know. My American friends had McGruff, a hard-boiled crime dog with a gravelly voice who warned of danger at every turn. To be a child in the 1980s was to be acutely aware that you could be done for on any given day. But in the Nordic countries? Less so.

Trust in Denmark has always been high, and has actually been on the rise by a few per cent in recent years. Children are taught that the world is an essentially good place and most people are not out to get them. Which is ~~madness, delusional,~~ *liberating*. 'If you trust the people around you, you can be more relaxed,' as my oldest Viking friend puts it. She's a formidable flaxen-haired Nordic goddess with three children who 'gets things done', apparently effortlessly, and is surprised when others (i.e. 'me') don't. But she has a heart of pure Viking gold and has been helping me decode the Danish way ever since our arrival. And this much I learned early on: Vikings typically trust that children will figure things out, learn how to use their bodies, and manage their surroundings. Internationals always joke that there is no such thing as health and safety for Nordics (contrary to what Brexiteers would have us believe about Europe). Instead, there are lit candles everywhere, four-year-old children saw wood, and six-year-olds walk the family dog or bike to school by themselves. As my Veteran Viking friend says: 'Our children grow up free – because they trust.'

This trust seems to be a self-fulfilling prophecy: Denmark is the least corrupt country in the world and even politicians, notoriously untrusted in most countries, enjoy a relatively good reputation.[3] Nordic countries regularly top the UNICEF rankings in terms of happiness, education and equality.[4] And children in Nordic countries generally have the highest rates of well-being, globally.

By contrast, youngsters in the UK and US are more likely to suffer from mental ill health than in almost any other rich country, according to UNICEF.[5] A report from the Children's Society shows that the number of UK children who are unhappy with their lives continues to rise. In the US, a third of all teen-agers now have symptoms that meet the criteria for an anxiety disorder, according to Harvard data.[6]

The US and UK models aren't working. So, what are Vikings doing differently? What are the secrets to Viking parenting? And what can the rest of us learn from them? From pregnancy and birth to toddlerhood and school, I want to find out what it's like for children and their caregivers in Denmark, Norway, Sweden, Iceland and Finland.

'Wait,' I hear you cry, 'are Finns Vikings too? And is Scandinavia the same as "Nordic"?'

To which I say: 'It's complicated,' and, 'Not quite.'

There's often confusion about the Scandinavian countries, and conversations about my relocation regularly go something like this:

'How's the Dutch coming along?'

Me: 'I'm in Denmark. They speak Danish.'

'Oh. Okay then: how's the *Danish* coming along?'

Points to the middle distance 'Look! A bird!' (Danish is tricky and I still suck at it.)

But generally? The bewilderment runs deep. Google 'Is Denmark . . .' and the most-searched terms that come up are:

. . . *an island?*

. . . *English speaking?*

. . . *part of Sweden?*

(Answers: nope x 3.)

There are three Scandinavian countries: Norway, Denmark and Sweden, whose languages share common characteristics. But there are five Nordic countries: Norway, Sweden, Denmark,

6

Finland and Iceland. 'Nordic' is the term used to describe anything related to them, like Nordic design or Nordic cuisine. 'Norse' is used to refer to the ancient people who were native to these five countries and their common culture.

'What about those guys with the horned helmets and hipster beards?' friends ask.

Me: 'Do you mean Vikings?'

Friend: *Nods vigorously*

Despite every cartoon depiction ever, Vikings never wore horned helmets. We only think they did because of the German composer Richard Wagner. For the 1876 production of his *Ring* cycle, based on the Norse sagas, the costume designer included horned helmets. The show was such a hit that Vikings with horned helmets became standard.

So it's all Wagner's fault.

'Huh! Who were Vikings then?'

Well, Vikings were seafaring folk who roamed northern Europe from 800 to 1066 CE. The word Viking comes from the Old Norse *vikingr*, or 'to pirate'.

'So was it all marauding, sex and dragons?'

'Are you thinking of *Game of Thrones*?'

'Could be . . .' *adopts faraway look* 'Mmm . . . Jon Snow – not the newsreader . . .'

At this point, I bust out a portable projector for a *Viking 101*. Over the years of living Danishly I've done my fair share of Viking geekery, visiting burial sites and racking up more rune stones than I remember. I've ventured east, following the Norsemen's route to the Arab world, to see picture stones first hand – showing images of Viking life as it was recorded at the time, cutting out the guesswork. I've hung out with archaeologists and historians, who have attempted to school me. I've learned how Vikings travelled extensively on iconic longships (the ones with the oars and the big bendy sail) and how their impact on the history of Europe is widespread. Millions of Viking descendants exist today, many unaware of their genetic background (it could be you!). Even the names of our days come from the Nordic tradition. Sunday is named after Sunna, the Norse goddess of the sun. Monday comes from 'moon day', named after the god of the moon. Tuesday is Tyr's day, named for the god of war and law. Wednesday is Woden's day, named after the Norse god Odin. While Thursday is named after probably the best-known Norse god Thor (the one with the hammer). Friday gets a little hazy (doesn't it always?), but it's either named after the Norse god Freyr or the Norse goddesses Freya or Frigg.

'What about Saturday?' I hear you ask.

Well, they were tired from all the marauding by then, so Saturday is just named after the Roman god Saturn.

Vikings originated in what is now Denmark, Norway and southern Sweden. They travelled west to trade, spending time in Finland at ports along the southern coast en route to Russia. So the history of early Finland is surprisingly Viking-heavy. Denmark-based archaeologist Marika Mägi argues that the Baltic Finns were Vikings, too, but the world ignores this fact because Finns missed their moment.

Vikings really became popular in Europe at the end of the nineteenth century, when Scandinavians started writing about them. But Finns were busy being an autonomous grand duchy of the Russian Empire around then. It was only after Finnish independence in 1917 that they could start talking about their Viking ancestors – but by then it was too late.

'Gutted!'

'I know!'

The story was already being told, the souvenirs sold, and the t-shirts printed throughout Scandinavia.

'What about Iceland – didn't you mention Iceland?'

'I did!' I flick back through my PowerPoint and pick up the laser pen no one needs and only uses for teasing cats. I point at the volcanically active island in the North Atlantic and explain how the country we now call Iceland was unpopulated before Norse settlers arrived in 874 CE. 'Today, it has a population similar to that of Stoke-on-Trent, 100 words for wind and a restaurant that exclusively serves tomatoes. So Iceland is in the Viking club.'*

'Got it: Scandinavia = Norway, Sweden and Denmark. The Nordic countries = Iceland, Finland, Norway, Sweden and Denmark.'

At this stage, I put away my laser, lest local cats congregate, and send the newly minted Viking enthusiast on their way. I've got Scouts to shuttle, axes to sharpen and wood to whittle (the whittling never ends). All before another round of coffee and *kanelsnegle* (cinnamon swirls). But it's not all baked goods, hot drinks and *hygge*. The Nordic countries may be among the 'happiest' on Earth, according to the latest UN report, but Vikings face the same challenges as the rest of us.

The region has changed since I first arrived, in step with the rise of nationalism across Europe and the US. And my experiences won't be the same as everyone else's. But there are

---

* Greenland, however, isn't. Greenland's current population is descended from the Thule culture, arriving in the 1200s. The Faroe Isles are also not in the Viking gang, having been settled 300 years before Vikings arrived.

common trials and troubles that we face the world over. Because trying to 'do life' right is hard. Parenting-while-sleep-deprived-and-poorer-than-in-your-previous-life is hard. Relationships, once children come along, are *insanely* hard.

The latest figures from Statistics Denmark show that around 40 per cent of marriages end in divorce.[7] Getting unhitched can be done online in Denmark for just DKK 775 (£89) at the time of writing, so divorce tends to be less acrimonious. But there are also cultural factors at play. The Nordic countries are famed for gender equality, and female employment has long been a given. Since both sexes work and tend to be paid a liveable wage, women don't depend on their husbands for money. And Danes rank the highest in Europe for overall life satisfaction. So although no one sets out to get divorced, it isn't the end of the world if you do. And Danes are happy to give marriage another go. Denmark is the number-one country in Europe with regard to remarriages, and as my neighbour puts it: 'Danes really like getting married, so we don't mind doing it more than once.'

'The great thing about Denmark is that there are lots of different ways to be a family,' a fellow school mum tells me. In fact, there are thirty-seven different types of family unit in Denmark, according to the official government website, from same-sex couples to single parents and more. The wicked stepmother trope holds no truck in Denmark, where a growing majority of families include a 'bonus mum/dad/sister or brother'. As Rasmus Kjeldahl of Denmark's children's rights association, Børns Vilkår, puts it: 'You can have happy children *despite* the high divorce rate in Denmark.'

Sweden, Norway and Iceland have more births outside marriage than within it, and 67 per cent of Icelandic babies are born to parents who aren't married.[8] In the US and the UK, these family formations are associated with being worse off and can attract stigma. But in the Nordic countries, more flexible arrangements are embraced. Former Finnish prime minister Sanna Marin was raised by two female parents. She had a baby in 2018, came to power in 2019 and *then* married in 2020. Mette Frederiksen became Denmark's youngest prime minister in 2019 as a single mother of two. She has since married and now lives with her husband plus his three children in a household of five, ~~which must be total chaos~~ as a happy blended family.

Even those who aren't Danish see the appeal of raising Viking children.

The country famed for Lego, Nordic Noir and perfect pastries has another major export: sperm. Danes currently send their sperm to 100 countries worldwide. Shipments to the UK have been increasing year on year and now account for 30 per cent of all new imported donors in what's being termed 'the gentle Viking invasion'. A friend in the UK going through the process now with Danish sperm says, 'They make it easier to go it alone in the Danish system – and the idea of a Viking baby doesn't hurt, either.' It's not that everyone looks like Mads Mikkelsen or Nikolaj Coster-Waldau in Denmark, it's just that, well, a fair few do . . .

But there's more to it than that, I think, watching my children scale trees and generally maraud, fearless, free . . . and *happy*? Here's hoping. I want to find out the secrets of Danish parenting and what I can learn from the Nordic approach.

Some aspects of Viking parenting can be applied wherever we are. Some can act as inspiration. Some may be an insight into a different way of living – exotic, even, in some cases (see 'jam and cheese'). So this is a tale of fish-out-of-water parenting. With me – clueless in both parenting *and* the Viking way.

Because let me be clear: I have no idea what I'm doing.

Forget 'conscious parenting' – I'm more of a 'lurching parent', ricocheting from one calamity to the next. My most commonly used emoji is the face-palm. My most commonly used phrase is: 'Oh shit, I forgot about *insert relevant item or event here*.' I drop balls *daily*. Despite a decade of living Danishly, I still have an outsider's perspective, albeit with insider information from friends who take pity on me, regularly, and explain what on earth is going on.

When raising small people, every phase is new. Each life stage brings distinctive difficulties and rewards. I am learning all the time. There's plenty of talk about 'self-parenting' these days, but if we weren't raised with an inner core of Viking grit, is it something we can learn as adults? I want to find out. With you. And snacks, preferably. Sitting comfortably? Then let's begin.

1

Congratulations! It's a Viking!

I'M PEERING DOWN a microscope at what looks like a party. Single and ready to mingle, densely packed shapes move about. Women in lab coats and squeaky Crocs navigate tanks of liquid nitrogen and fridges graffitied with tadpoles. Nearby, straws of 'genetic material' are poked into pastel-coloured tubes before being sent to fertility clinics across the world.

'We send them by DHL usually,' one Croc-wearer tells me as she places vials of semen in a smoking vat of liquid nitrogen. 'Or, if it's only a short distance, via UPS in a Ziploc with ice packs.'

'Ice packs? Like in a cool bag for lollies?'

'Sort of, but chilled to minus 196 degrees. And for sperm.'

This is Cryos, the epicentre of the international sperm trade. And it's just up the road from me. I'm not exactly a regular visitor, but I first took tea with the man responsible for 70,000 babies in 2015. No, not the reincarnation of Genghis Khan, but Ole Schou, the business student turned sperm magnate who in 1987 set up Cryos in the Danish city of Aarhus.

'I had a dream,' he told me when we met.

'That one day every valley shall be exalted . . . ?'

'No: about frozen sperm. I could just see it, as clear as I see you now, and so I started reading all I could about the process of freezing sperm. I got a business loan, and here we are!'

The market developed and demand increased, helped by the supposed 'virility' of Danish men and their unusual willingness to donate sperm. Cryos isn't the only sperm bank in Denmark, but it's the biggest. And demand is so great that all of Denmark's sperm banks are kept busy. Cryos currently sends its seed to 'every continent except Antarctica', says Ole, but some countries import more Viking genes than others. In the UK, one in three donor-conceived children have biologically Danish fathers. There's a limited supply of the home-grown stuff since 2005 legislation outlawed anonymous donation in the UK, putting off many would-be donors. But Vikings are less easily deterred.

Denmark holds the world record in fertility treatment, thanks to generous state funding that made reproduction a national project rather than just an individual endeavour. Since 2007 in Denmark, women without children have been granted access to state-funded IVF regardless of marital status or sexuality.

Today in Denmark, one in ten children is conceived in a fertility clinic, a statistic I've contributed to. After failed fertility treatments in the UK, I was finally helped to start a family by the Danish system. Thrice. The first picture I have of my twins is two cells in a Petri dish. But whereas I made my babies with boring old British sperm, the Viking variety is rampaging far and wide.

To find out why, I'm back at Cryos, on the fifth floor of an unassuming building on a busy street. In reception there are fridges of bottled water, glass bowls of free muesli bars and Post-its reminding me to 'Be Awesome!' It's the hottest day of the year, so I'm delighted to see they're also serving ice cream (vanilla, mango or salted caramel).

It feels inappropriately intimate to be sitting on a plush grey sofa just a couple of metres from the 'donor cabins', with lights above the doors that glow red when occupied. Each has a rack of porn mags, excellent internet and virtual-reality goggles. Cryos was the first sperm bank in Denmark to invest in 'virtual-reality porn' at a cost of about DKK 20,000 per headset (£2,300), after studies showed that users experienced 'a strong positive effect on the number of motile sperm in an ejaculate'.[1] Also: the longer they take to create their sample, the 'better the quality', I learn from the literature.

A steady stream of Vikings passes through reception, each picking up a sample cup, then hovering until the light turns green on one of the rooms. I try very hard to be a grownup but catch the eye of a twenty-something Alexander Skarsgård-alike. We exchange an awkward smile, then I glance at my watch to appear busy, ignoring the fact that he's off to beat one out before a mango sorbet.

Only 5–10 per cent of applicants are accepted onto the donation programme, 'But getting turned down doesn't mean you can't be a father: it just means you can't be a donor,' Ole told me. Sperm is divided into IUI (intrauterine insemination) or ICI (intracervical insemination) straws according to the motility and quality. For IVF, you need fewer good sperm in each sample, since you're injecting it directly into an egg. For IUI, it's more of a scattergun 'send 'em up and set 'em free' approach (and I should know: I've tried both).

Donors apply online, then give a sample. This is analysed and, if approved, donors discuss family history and rule out any serious hereditary disorders. Doctors take blood and urine samples, analysed by geneticists. All before a 'psychosocial interview' to assess the 'maturity and mental state' of the donor.

From getting to know donors at Cryos and other Danish sperm banks (for 'research', I hasten to add), I've gleaned that Vikings spreading their seed can loosely be divided into three groups: Family Guys, Donor Disciples and Young Bucks.

A third of donors already have their own family. 'My girl-friend and I tried for 18 months before we got pregnant the first time,' says one Family Guy, 'so I know how hard it can be. After I experienced becoming a parent, well . . . it just does something to you. I think that everyone who wants kids and can take care of them should be able to have them.'

Then there are Donor Disciples, those with first-hand experience of donor families. 'My sister has a little girl by a donor,' one tells me, 'so when I was talking to my mum about getting a job when I started university, she said: "Have you thought about donating sperm?" My sister was inseminated because she wasn't interested in finding a husband or a boyfriend but she wanted a baby. So I wanted to help other women like her who wanted a family.'

The third group are the Young Bucks: carefree men in their early twenties who may not be mad about babies but are happy to help out and assure themselves that they're virile.

'"Is your sperm good enough?" was the headline that first got me interested,' one Young Buck tells me. 'It was a leaflet for the clinic saying, basically, "Are you 'man enough' to have good-quality sperm?" I came here really just to see how my sperm was. I didn't expect much after I heard how only the top 5 per cent actually have the quality of sperm to be a donor, but I went through all the tests and got to thinking it would be a good thing to do. And get paid for it.'

How much a donor is paid depends on the quality of the sperm and whether or not they have an anonymous 'non-ID-release' profile or become an open 'ID-release' donor. Remuneration starts at DKK 250 (around £30) for a basic profile with low motility – fewer forward-moving sperm in a millimetre of semen. It goes up to DKK 500 (£60) for an ID-release profile with high motility. But studies show that it's not about the money for most Danes.

'Donors tend to have more altruistic motivations,' Ole told me. 'Perhaps it's something about being raised here – we do things differently.' Denmark has a world-famous welfare state, tax-funded healthcare and education, and high levels of trust and volunteering (42 per cent of Danes do volunteer work in their spare time[2]). There's a strong tradition of being community minded – 46 per cent of the Danish sperm donors also donate blood.[3] And there's no stigma to being a donor in Denmark. 'I'm pretty open about it and know other guys who do it, too,' says one Young Buck. 'I ran into a friend when I was donating once. It was a bit funny, but we found it pretty easy to talk about it. I'm currently seeing someone, and I talk to her about it. I think it's something you want your partner to know, because if it turns serious, she might be surprised when you turn forty and all of these biological donor-kids get in touch. It's difficult to say how you're going to feel when that happens – I can't even imagine being 40!'

'Same.' *Side eye* It occurs to me that although I could technically be his mother, it would have caused a great deal of family strife and societal judgement in the 1990s Home Counties. *So there's that . . .*

Those who elect to become non-anonymous are encouraged to carefully consider how they'll feel when children conceived with their sperm come knocking.

'I could have twenty kids on my doorstep within the space of four years,' another Young Buck who has chosen to be an open donor tells me. As he talks, I get the sneaking suspicion that he quite likes the idea. 'It's a lot,' he admits, 'so it's something I think about.'

When children conceived with non-anonymous donor sperm turn eighteen, they are given the name, address and birth date of their donor. Then, it's up to them – Cryos doesn't facilitate meetings.

There's been a debate in Denmark about whether anonymous donors should still be allowed. Many children conceived with anonymous donor sperm have spoken in public about the disadvantages of knowing just half of their genetic make-up.

'That affected me,' says a Young Buck who decided to be non-anonymous as a result. He tells me how he was raised by a solo mother, 'And it's strange, not knowing half of what made you.'

I understand this. Not having a relationship with my own dad means that when I look in the mirror, I wonder how much of him is in there. It's the same with my children. One of them has olive skin that definitely didn't come from my Irish, blue-hued maternal side, nor my Lego Man husband's Milky Bar Kid complexion, honed by a misspent youth in sunny Middlesborough.

So is the olive skin from my father? A man my son's never met?

'It makes you wonder,' says the Young Buck/potential father of twenty. 'And I have no doubt at all that these children are much wanted and will be looked after to the best of these parents' abilities. If there is any confusion when they meet me, I'll say: "Hey! You have a great family already! The ones that love you most are over there!"'

All the donors I have met over the years are, as my grandmother would have said, 'thoroughly nice boys'. So nice, in fact, that knowing where to begin when choosing between 800 hopefuls vying to spread their seed on the Cryos website seems impossible. A friend in the UK who has been through the process of buying Cryos sperm for her own 'Project Baby' tells me: 'It's a lot like online dating. You start with the basics, so looks, height, eye colour, etc., then nose around at their hobbies.' These are extensive, but a brief browse informs me that:

Nikolas likes diving and jiu jitsu.

Emil enjoys Frisbee.

. . . and:

In his free time Kasper enjoys most things.

'Most things', Kasper? *Pick a lane! Commit!*

Badminton is wildly overrepresented in the sperm-donor community (know a Great Dane who's fond of a shuttlecock? Chances are he's shuttling sperm in his spare time), and profiles also cover favourite holidays and films as well as 'staff impressions'. Here, the Cryos team share their thoughts on donors – a bit like Waterstones' staff picks. You can learn that:

Ulrik is chatty.

Svend has kind eyes.

Lars resembles a mix between the American actor James Franco and the singer Joe Jonas.

Or this gem:

Aksel has good muscle tone in his arms. He has an attractive triangular body shape, and a roughness to his appearance that adds a lot of charm. Aksel has sparkling green eyes and a flirty smile. The sun is giving him crow's feet around his eyes, which adds a pinch of wisdom to Aksel's appearance . . .

Dear staff member: I think you should date Aksel.

If you're looking for a donor with a specific facial feature, like a curve of the nose, you can ask for a manual photo match.

'Generally, people want a better-looking, smarter version of themselves,' says Helle Sejersen Myrthue, CEO at Cryos following Ole's retirement.

And are some donors more popular than others?

Helle laughs: 'You'd be surprised! Sometimes we get people in, we'll see the photos or their profiles, and someone might say, "I can't sell him." But then someone else in the office will love them. There really is someone for all of us!'

Prospective parents can also see personality-test results, handwriting samples, donor baby pictures and adult photographs. The latter are behind a paywall – 'to stop their friends browsing just for fun' – and there's a lot of interest in the adult donor photos from the UK. 'It is by far the European country with the greatest number of people who have paid to access the images on our website,' says Helle.

Once you've picked a donor, you click to buy a straw of sperm to be FedExed to your nearest fertility clinic. Each country sets its own rules on the number of children a donor can father. American guidelines recommend twenty-five children per population of 850,000, although there's no enforced national limit. In Denmark, donors are subject to a twelve-family limit. So families can have multiple children by the same donor, but a donor can't donate to more than twelve different families. And in the UK, there's a ten-family limit. As long as a donor hasn't exceeded his country quota, he's all yours.

So who are the women opting for Danish donors?

'We're seeing an avalanche of educated older women,' Ole told me. 'Eighty-five per cent are aged between thirty-one and forty-five and half have a master's degree or higher. More and more of them are going it alone.' Cryos exports 96 per cent of its sperm internationally and the sperm-shopping demographic is made up of 15 per cent heterosexual couples, 35 per cent same-sex couples and 50 per cent single women.

I wonder about the resources needed to raise children alone, as a single mother by choice in the land of Nord where the cost of living is dizzying. 'It's actually easier to be a *solomor* – or single mother – in Denmark than elsewhere because society accepts and supports you,' says Karin Erb, lab director at the fertility unit of Denmark's Odense University Hospital. 'If you have a good network, babysitters and family nearby willing to lend a hand, then there are ways to make it work.' There are currently 135,000 households headed up by single women with children in Denmark (and just under 32,000 headed up by single men, according to Statistics Denmark).[4]

Becoming a solo parent via donor conception isn't most people's Plan A, and 90 per cent of women surveyed wanted to have a child with a partner, according to a study by Copenhagen's University Hospital.[5] Lone Schmidt, professor at the University of Copenhagen Department of Public Health, tells me: 'Two-thirds had a partner with whom they wanted to become pregnant, but their partners weren't ready.' The average age of couples seeking help for fertility problems in Denmark is thirty-three, while the average age of single women is thirty-six. 'In other words, women are waiting it out, and when it becomes clear that there isn't going to be a man in the picture, they're taking action themselves,' says Lone.

Back in 2015, I interviewed a series of elective single mothers in Denmark for the *Guardian* newspaper and have kept up with a few over the years. One of the growing tribe says: 'I was so focused on finding the man and then having the child. The possibility of turning the order on its head hadn't crossed my mind.' When it did, the choice became simple: 'Having a child without a man and then hoping for a man to enter my life later became a rational solution.' Another shared: 'I'd always dreamt of having three or four kids, but the man I was in a relationship with in my thirties wasn't ready. I wasn't anti-men: I adore men! I just couldn't find one who wanted kids. I saw lots of friends choose to become pregnant with boyfriends they knew wouldn't last – purely because the desire to have a child took over. I also saw "traditional" families breaking up all around me, so I thought, *Maybe I should just make this happen on my own.*'

These women asked themselves 'all the hard questions', like: 'Does the world need more people? Couldn't I adopt?' And most looked into it, but adoption is an expensive, lengthy process with no guarantee of a positive outcome – in Denmark those over the age of forty-two aren't allowed to adopt babies.[6] Many considered a one-night stand – not a big deal in Denmark – but felt this would be somehow dishonest, 'stealing' sperm from someone. This left donor conception.

The cost for the women looking to conceive with donor sperm varies based on circumstances and donor choice. A straw of sperm from an 'anonymous' donor might cost the equivalent of £630, including donor costs, extensive screening and shipping. You might pay a local fertility clinic £600 for an IUI and get pregnant for £1,230 all in. Costs rise to £1,590 for a straw of sperm from an ID-release donor with an extended profile – and upwards of £1,050 for sperm micro-injection in an IVF cycle. In this scenario, the total costs will be upwards of £2,640 *per try*. It's a lot. But it's less than you'd pay elsewhere. In the UK, even IUI procedures cost between £700 and £1,600 per try, excluding donor sperm.[7] And same-sex couples must go through six attempted inseminations before they can receive government support. 'So it's just much harder,' says one British woman who has elected to be inseminated in Denmark instead.

Henriette Cranil got lucky first time. A striking woman with piercing blue eyes who also happens to be a *solomor* by donor sperm, says: 'I was in my thirties, my relationship ended, but I wanted kids – and to be a single mum has been an available option in Denmark for a long time. I was at a party with a lesbian couple, and one was pregnant, and I thought, *I could do that too*.' Henriette had a successful insemination with an anonymous donor, but during her first scan, the nurse looked confused. 'She could see two tiny flashing hearts. Twins.' There was a moment of concern about how Henriette would cope with two babies as a single mum. 'I could see the worry in the nurse's eyes – and the doctors' notes! We all knew this was going to be hard. But I felt really looked after.' She had weekly scans and the babies were born at thirty-six weeks. 'We were in hospital for two weeks, then we went home, and my parents came to babysit for an hour every day so I could sleep.'

An hour of uninterrupted sleep a day is hardly ideal, but it's better than no hours. Any newborn is hard. Two newborns? Psychedelically so.

'I was *extremely* exhausted for the first seven . . .' – she corrects herself – 'eight . . . no: *nine* months. Then I went back to work as a psychologist, and they went to a very good daycare. I was totally knocked out, but I got used to it.' Henriette recommends baby-proofing your life as a single mother: 'Finding other adults who you can share the small moments in life with is key.' The hospital where she gave birth had a Facebook group for single mothers, 'So from day one, I've had a community.' There are around 20,000 donor-conceived children in Denmark today.[8] 'And we hang out with other donor families – so it's normal for us.' The only real difficulty? Dating. 'Being a single parent locks you in, romantically speaking. There's a window of time [when] you can go everywhere you want with a huge pram, but it's not ideal for dating.'

No . . . Talk about intimidating: my twin transporter was the size of a tank and just as menacing rolling towards you. Shoppers would scatter in anticipation.

Henriette is now married to a former colleague. 'Early on, he was aware we needed to make some big decisions – everything is more complicated with children involved. Of the women I know who are single mums, life is primarily work and children,' she says. 'I'm sure if they could have had their children with a great love, they would have preferred that. But not to have had their children? That would have been far worse.'

This I understand. When baby fever began to consume me, age twenty-six, the idea of a 'great love' became far less important than my preoccupation with procreation (sorry to my boyfriend at the time: I get it, I was A Lot).

The solo mothers of donor children spend years researching the pros and cons of single parenting before starting treatment – including the psychological impact on a child. There's a traditional idea that children of single parents suffer. But this tends to be based on lone mothers bringing up children post-divorce or after unplanned pregnancies, says Professor Susan Golombok of the Centre for Family Research at the University of Cambridge in *Modern Families: Parents and Children in New Family Forms.*[9] 'Unelective' single mothers may be statistically more at risk of mental health struggles, due to the stress of a split, conflict with a former partner or financial anxiety. But single mothers by choice are spared all this. Children conceived through medically assisted reproduction (MAR), such as IVF, are at no more risk of developing emotional or behavioural problems than those conceived naturally according to London School of Economics (LSE) research.[10] A collaboration between University College London and the University of Helsinki looked at 280,682 children born between 1995 and 2000 and found that children conceived by MAR actually did better at school.[11] This could be because parents who elect to pay for fertility treatment tend to be highly educated themselves and so prioritise education. But still, researchers agree that donor children are likely to be 'okay' – as long as they're told the truth about where they come from.

Henriette has been honest with her twins from the start. 'We've always talked about it and I haven't tried to take away the sadness at not having a dad – that's just how it is. Life isn't perfect.'

Twenty-six-year-old Emma has known she was donor-conceived for as long as she can remember. 'Mum and Dad made me a children's book when I was two and explained how they loved each other very much and wanted a child but couldn't have one. They went to a doctor and found out that Daddy didn't make enough sperm, so a nice man gave us some of his to put on Mummy's egg. They read this to me as a bedtime story and I could ask all the questions I wanted.' And she did. 'Mum still has the drawings of the egg and sperm cells I did when I was five, explaining it all to my classmates.'

Goodness . . . how did that go down?

'They were fine about it!'

I wonder whether she's ever felt different as a donor-conceived child.

'Never. Donor-conceived children are the most wanted and hard-won. I've always felt super-loved.'

This is wonderful to hear. Any assisted reproduction is tough, I know – with daily injections, painfully invasive treatment, a tsunami of hormones and 75 per cent of all fertility treatments failing. It's never the easy option.

Many of the sperm donors – even the young ones – realise this. A Young Buck with sandy hair says: 'I know parents will have given it a lot of thought and will give all their love to this donor child.' A Family Guy agrees: 'There's been prejudice against lesbian couples and single mothers in the past – but if it's two women or one woman, then I don't think that should decide whether or not you have children. We're liberal in Denmark and we're not going to stand and giggle about it. If I told someone in the street that I was a sperm donor, they'd say, "Great! Good for you."'

At the end of my time at the clinic, I'm back in reception when Alexander Skarsgård-alike finally emerges from the donation room. *Blimey*, I look at the clock: *he's been in there a while*. I remember what I was told earlier: 'The longer it takes, the better the quality.'

Wow . . . good job.

Skarsgård and I exchange a smile and both pretend that he hasn't been furiously masturbating for the duration of my inter-view. He's walking towards me and for a moment I contemplate a '*hej!*' or even a high five, then I see him reaching for the hand sanitiser and think better of it.

Instead, I pick up a packet of Post-its reminding me to 'Be Awesome!' and make my way down ten flights of stairs, back out to the busy street.

What I've learned about how to raise a Viking from cell-cluster onwards

1. Embrace science when necessary. Nature is great. We all love nature. But isn't it amazing that humans can give it a helping hand once in a while? Without science I wouldn't have two-thirds of my family. I am exceedingly grateful that fertility treatments were a) accessible to me and b) worked. Thank you, science.

2. Be honest about where your small person has come from. For much of human history, 'brushing things under the carpet' was the modus operandi for many parents. Adoptees weren't told they were adopted. Children conceived with fertility treatments or surrogates were kept in the dark. But now we are (allegedly) enlightened – and children are pretty liberal and accepting. Tell a child their origin story early and they're unlikely to blink an eyelid.

3. Keep an open mind: a loving family comes in many forms. Baby Mette may have two mums; Svend may be raising his son single-handedly; Lars and Ingrid may have used donor sperm. Each of their families will have strengths and flaws – just like ours. Learning more about the Nordic approach to family has shifted some deep-seated private shame that I had no idea I'd been carrying around with me for the past forty years. Growing up the only child of a single mum, I was often made to feel that my family was 'lesser' somehow. So I internalised this. Believed it, even. But it's not true. It can't be. What matters is how much we're loved. We

27

know enough by now to appreciate that the 'traditional' set-up is no guarantee of future happiness. And normcore couplings don't have the monopoly on well-adjusted children.

2

A Viking is Born

I N A SCANDI modern glass house with the Danish flag
flying outside and a view of the Baltic Sea, it finally
happened. After years of trying came two blue lines. And life
changed for ever.

Thanks to a centralised healthcare system and a handy yellow
ID card, after the first doctor's appointment I was officially 'in
the system' and on autopilot. I was assigned a midwife, my
appointments were scheduled, and I was 'enrolled' at the local
hospital. My progress was tracked in a yellow journal, used by
every expectant mother in Denmark. And I learned early on
that Danes use fewer needles, tests, exams or any other medical
procedures than elsewhere. Because Vikings go old school – as
typified by visits to my midwife.

Following a cursory chat about how I was doing and a good
deal of linguistic creativity (my gynaecological Danish being
below par), she came at me with an ear trumpet.

'Now, we listen for the heartbeat!' I had been expecting a
scanner, but apparently a 'Pinard horn' worked just fine. And
aside from encouragement to eat a vegetable once in a while,

dietary and lifestyle advice was minimal. Consequently, other internationals expressed horror at some ('all') of my life choices during pregnancy.

'Coffee! You're drinking coffee? What about the baby?'

The blood rose in my cheeks. *Had I mistaken 'coffee' for 'crack'?* I checked the guidelines in my yellow journal: 'Coffee: No more than 2–3 cups a day.'

'I think a single-shot latte is probably okay . . .'

'In Denmark, maybe . . .'

The following week, lumbering to a Japanese restaurant with friends, I was ambushed by the judgey international again.

'Sushi? You're eating sushi?'

I got out my yellow journal to show him how pregnant women are advised not to eat sushi made from fish that has not been frozen. But in Denmark, all fish has been pre-frozen, 'So it's safe to eat sushi when pregnant in Denmark.' *Actually.*

The only restrictions – other than alcohol and smoking – are around two major Danish food groups: *leverpostej* (liver pâté) and *lakrids*, or liquorice. The former contains too much vitamin A, while the latter can increase blood pressure and cause fluid retention. I don't know about you, but I retain plenty of fluid all by myself, so I steered clear. But Danes confine themselves to the smallest smear of pâté and limit liquorice to 50 grams a day in pregnancy. Then, for the most part, it's business as usual.

Vikings don't change their lifestyle just because they're pregnant. They don't blast babies with Bach or Gregorian chants in utero. There's no pressure to do daily affirmations or burn a candle that smells like your vagina (just for instance). Danes are happy to cycle, run and swim up until birth. In Norway, they also ski. 'Until around six months pregnant at least,' a mother of two in Oslo told me. Despite looking like I'd been inflated with a bicycle pump by the second trimester, I did my best to keep up with my Nordic neighbours.

Whereas friends in the US and the UK increasingly 'shower' mothers-to-be leading up to birth, Vikings simply assemble a few essentials themselves. It's normal to welcome hand-me-downs or buy pre-loved baby gear, and Danes are a thrifty bunch. There's no eBay or Amazon in Denmark, but sites such as dba.dk and reshopper.dk are popular for all manner of secondhand items, from toys to car seats.

Since 1938, Finland's expectant mothers have been offered a baby shower by the state in the form of a 'baby box'. This contains a mattress, sheet, blanket, sleeping bag, insulated mittens and bootees. 'There's also a hooded suit, socks, a knitted hat and a balaclava,' says mother of one, author and journalist Katja Pantzar in Helsinki. 'There are bodysuits, romper suits, a hooded bath towel, nail scissors, a hairbrush, a bath thermometer, nappy cream, a washcloth, nappies, muslin squares, a picture book, bra pads, condoms—'

'Condoms?' *I think that horse has bolted . . .*

'—basically, everything you need – for free!'

The contents of Finland's baby box have changed over the years, offering an insight into Viking parenting norms. In the 1970s, with more mothers working, disposable nappies and easy-to-wash baby clothes in colourful patterns replaced white non-stretch garments that took an age to launder. Then in 2006, cloth nappies were reintroduced to assuage environmental concerns, and the bottle was left out to encourage breastfeeding.

Once Finns have unpacked their boxes, the new arrival can sleep in it. Since the 1990s it's been recommended that parents don't sleep with babies due to the increased risk of SIDS – or sudden infant death syndrome. My sister died this way in the

1980s, so this has always been an issue close to my heart – and one I worried about from the moment I discovered I was pregnant. The risk of SIDS is highest in the first six months of life, when parents are the most exhausted and the least equipped to make safe sleep choices. So Finns figured out that giving families a portable place to put sleepy babies made parents more likely to follow guidelines. Finland now has one of the lowest infant mortality rates in the world – two deaths per 1,000 live births, compared with a global rate of thirty-eight in 1,000, according to the UN.[1]

But this isn't just about a box. Finland's baby kits were introduced at the same time as prenatal care, so pregnant women had to attend clinics to qualify for the package. At the start, the baby box was only for Finland's poorest families, and just 31 per cent of pregnant women received prenatal care. By 1949, the package was offered to all expectant mothers, 'And coverage has been 99–100 per cent in recent decades,' says Professor Mika Gissler of the Finnish Institute for Health and Welfare. The baby boxes are symbolic of Finland's wider health-care system and dedication to combating inequality – something the UN Secretary-General Antonio Guterres called one of the four biggest challenges facing the world today (along with the cost of living, 'crumbling' trust levels and the fact that our 'planet is burning'. Good times).[2]

Finland's baby boxes spawned imitators in England, Canada, Australia, India, Scotland and South Africa. But these initiatives can't make up for the structural inequalities outside of the Nordic countries. 'You're always taken care of here,' is how one Swedish friend puts it, 'you feel safe. However much you earn, however rich or poor your parents are – you get looked after. So in pregnancy, you can just, well . . . relax.' This was my experience.

'Hello, darling!' my mother FaceTimed in a frenzy a month from my due date. 'You look tired.'

'Thanks.'

'Have you *nested*? You must *nest*! Defrost the freezer! Deep-clean the bathroom! Get it all done now and you'll thank yourself later!'

I won't.

'What about your hospital bag? Have you packed your hospital bag? It could be any day now!'

It wasn't. My firstborn was eleven days overdue.

'Pack your hospital bag – today!'

I walked to the bathroom, picked up my electric toothbrush and dropped it into my handbag: 'Done.'

'That's it?'

'That's it.'

The hospital-bag packing list in Denmark is:

✓ *Toothbrush*

End of list. You *can* pack more if you like. But there's nothing you *need*, since the hospital has it sorted.

'What about a birth plan?' my mother asked. 'Sarah from work had a paddling pool with U2 playing! Would you like a paddling pool with U2 playing?'

I would not.

'I don't think they do birth plans here . . .' They didn't, at the time.

'About as close as we get is a white scarf in the car,' says my oldest Danish friend and mother of three, Veteran Viking. She tells me this while rustling up dinner for five and watching a YouTube tutorial on how to fix a U-bend (like I say, 'gets stuff done').

33

A white scarf? Surely labour is no time for Hollywood glamour? Or a Marilyn Monroe tribute?

'Traditionally you'd hold a white scarf out of the car window if you were having a baby, then it was accepted that you could skip the traffic.'

'Was that *legal*?'

'Sure. Still is, as long as it's an emergency and you get police permission.' This is so entrenched in Danish life that it's illegal to dangle anything white out of your car, except in a crisis.[3]

Which all meant no Marilyn Monroe chic for me. 'I couldn't face the fashion police and labour on the same day.' I wasn't sure I could face labour at all. I already knew from friends that Viking childbirth tended to be au naturel. Everyone seemed to agree that it was a good idea to take birth-preparation classes, but these weren't an option where I lived (Sticksville) back in the Middle Ages (2014). So instead, I talked to my midwife.

Me: 'What are my pain-relief options?'

Midwife: 'What would you like?'

Me: 'Everything?'

Midwife: 'We will write "oxygen as a last resort".'

I had rather assumed 'oxygen' as a given – something I enjoyed on a daily basis.

'You could also try a heat pad.'

'A hot-water bottle?'

'Or a bee-sting? This is where water is injected under the skin with a very small needle so that you're distracted from the big pain by a smaller, different pain.'

'Does it work?'

'For around half of all women giving birth, yes!'

I didn't love those odds. 'What about an epidural?'

'The "princess stick"?' This, it transpired, was Viking for 'epidural'. 'A princess stick is serious—'

'Isn't "having a baby" serious?'

'Ha ha ha ha ha!' she laughed. I did not.

Veteran Viking told me matter-of-factly that having a baby was 'like being kicked by a horse', before adding: 'But I've done it three times now, so it can't be so bad.'

'What if I don't want to be kicked by a horse?'

She shrugged: 'It's not always optional.'

She was right: it wasn't.

Baby number one emerged after eighteen hours of labour, with a shock of red hair and the biggest lungs in the hospital, so the nurses told me. Second time around with twins, I had a C-section at thirty-eight weeks.

'I'll be with you every step of the way,' Lego Man told me, before fainting at the glint of the surgeon's knife.

I was grateful to swap eighteen hours of labour for a seven-minute C-section, but recovery was agony.

Nanna Schultz, founder of the Danish pregnancy and birth community Momkind, described her experience of new mother-hood as 'shellshock'.

'I loved my new baby, but I was surprised by how difficult I found it all. I felt like, "I'm brave! I'm adventurous!" and then I had this kid and suddenly, I didn't feel like I was any of those things. I didn't feel like I was doing anything right.'

Feeling out of control conflicted with the idea Nanna had of herself. 'Here in Denmark and the Nordic countries, women are supposed to be "strong". We have careers; we can do everything; we are Vikings! So suddenly, when I felt like I couldn't do everything, when I didn't feel strong . . . well, it was a real shock.' Nanna felt inspired to share the lows of parenting as well as the highs, setting up Momkind to help other Danish parents through the process.

I wonder what makes a 'good Viking birth', and so get in touch with Louise Simsick, midwife and mother of three, including my son's *second*-best friend from kindergarten (when you're small, these things matter). I make her tea and she tells me, 'I think many women here find it difficult to be out of control – and having a baby can feel very out of control.' So what should we do? 'I want women to have thought through what they expect, what they're scared of and what they look forward to,' says Louise. And when she speaks, women listen. Midwifery is notoriously competitive to get into in Denmark, requiring the highest grades in the country for just a few prized places, so midwives enjoy a phenomenal level of respect in Danish society. I had my babies in the same hospital where Louise works, and experienced first hand the expertise of her colleagues.

Once a baby has been delivered and the professionals have made sure everyone's okay, there is the ceremonial new-baby breakfast tray, with bread, jam, cheese, juice and a Danish flag on a wooden stand. This isn't purely a sign of patriotism, but of celebration – used to mark every birthday in Denmark.

After I'd been fed and watered, I was given my own room and Lego Man was invited to stay over on a spare bed. 'But if you're going to be here, you have to help,' an excellently brusque Danish nurse told Lego Man after the birth of our first. She handed him a leaflet entitled: 'A partner's role during hospitalisation'. He read aloud: 'Responsibilities include changing bed linen as needed; picking up clean clothes and towels; collecting food and drink; and "fetching things" . . . ?'

'Like what?' I asked.

'Anything you need,' said the nurse.

The Corridors of Power in Viking maternity wards are lined with cupboards containing clothes, nappies, flannels, industrial post-birth sanitary pads, sick bags, breast pumps, vases for flowers and mysterious-looking packets marked 'fishnet panties'.

'You haven't worn these before?' The nurse took in our surprised expressions.

I looked at Lego Man. Then the nurse. Then at Lego Man again.

'I mean, I may have, one time . . . '

'They can be very useful if you soil yourself,' the nurse went on.

What? I'd have thought 'fishnet' would be the very last fabric advantageous in any sort of accident. It's basically a sieve . . .

'Because then you just toss them away.'

'Oh!' Lego Man was quicker off the mark. 'You mean disposable pants?'

'What did you think I meant?'

'Just that . . .' I mumbled.

Next time the brusque nurse was passing, she brought me several enormous pairs of ruched-leg pants, definitely more surgical mesh than Ann Summers. I thanked her profusely.

During my time in hospital, nurses and midwives were unfailingly patient and generous in teaching me to care for my new baby.

'How do I clean . . .' – I stared at a tiny bottom covered in what looked like curried yoghurt – '*this*? Are there wet wipes? I'm sure I've seen people using wipes.'

'No. We use *skumvaskeklude*!'

'Scum—? What did you say?'

'*Skumvaskeklude*!' These turned out to be small sponge 'slices' to be run under water, then used to wipe away whatever it is you need to wipe away, without chemicals.

Okay, I told myself, *I can do this! Bring on the skum!*

I got the hang of changing, but struggled with breast-feeding, resulting in a chest that became so full it turned square. Two stony-faced nurses in their fifties took turns pummelling me like bread to encourage 'let down'. Because Vikings, I learned, are big on nursing. Icelandic hospitals even import supplies of breast milk from Denmark for preterm babies whose mothers are unable to breastfeed. This is great for babies, but can be tough for the Nordic mothers I speak to who feel that their worth and identity are tied to their ability to breastfeed.

New mothers who are ready to leave hospital but are experiencing lactation issues have an opportunity to stay on at the 'Stork Hotel' or 'Patient Hotel' for around DKK 300 a night (£32) with a nurse on call. A friend who gave birth in the US was incredulous at this when she called to compare war stories of the 'miracle of birth'.

'Wait, so you can just . . . *stay*? Being *looked after*? With someone else doing the cooking and cleaning and newborn poopsplosion laundry? With professionals on hand for any emergencies or existential crises at 1 a.m. because your baby won't latch and you've never felt more alone in your life? For the price of a trip to the movies? Tell me you're staying?!'

I had to disappoint her here, too. Once my son was out of special care and I could urinate without a catheter, I elected to go home. But whereas new-parent friends in the US left hospital with a hefty bill, in Viking land childbirth is free.

'Presumably you pay for it with your crazy taxes, though?' asked incredulous US friend.

'Yes and no,' I told her.

The average Dane pays 35.4 per cent of their income in taxes, compared with the Organisation for Economic Co-operation and Development (OECD) average of 24.6 per cent.[4] But the average monthly salary is DKK 45,500 (£5,244).[5] This means Danes are taking home an average of around DKK 31,000 a month after tax (£3,573).[6] Back in the UK, the average monthly wage is £2,773 before tax (DKK 24,000).

Yes, the cost of living in Denmark is around 15 per cent higher than in the UK. But house prices are, on average, 15 per cent lower than in the UK.[7] Danes also get free healthcare, free education and free dental treatment up to the age of twenty-two. Oh, and although the official working week is thirty-seven hours, OECD figures show that the average Dane is only putting in thirty-three hours a week.[8]

'So, you know,' I told incredulous US friend, 'it's not bad.'

The high tax and the redistribution of wealth makes for less inequality, too. Which, in turn, makes Danes happier. Americans are also happier when there's more economic equality. Psychology professor Shigehiro Oishi from the University of Virginia studied General Social Survey data from 1972 to 2008 and found that Americans were – on average – happier in the years with less national income inequality.[9] He found that happiness remained stable until the 1990s, then began to drop as income inequality grew.

Social epidemiologists Professors Richard Wilkinson and Kate Pickett believe that: 'Trying to maintain self-esteem and status in a more unequal society can be highly stressful,' and that growing inequality worldwide is even leading to a rise in addiction.[10] Whereas in Denmark and the Nordic countries, where tax is high and there's less inequality, there's less animosity between the (relatively) rich and the (relatively) poor. And I can leave hospital without paying a thing.

'I shall have to try very hard not to punch you in the face next time I see you,' incredulous US friend told me.

'I love you too,' I told her.

Bag packed, disposable underwear in place, I stood and prepared to leave, held together by stitches and codeine. We were going home. To somehow take care of a brand-new baby all by ourselves.

'And I can't even keep basil alive,' I murmured.

'Nobody panic . . .' muttered Lego Man as he tried to navigate an ISOFIX child seat and the small pink thing started hollering. 'No need to panic . . .' But his eyes, very clearly, said: 'Panic!'

What I've learned about how to raise a Viking . . . from the inside out

1. There is no easy way to get a baby out. Worse luck. Pregnancy and birth are unpredictable, regardless of best-laid plans. There may not be whale music or scented candles or U2 playing a private concert in a paddling pool. But that's okay. We'll have some impressive new scars, mesh underwear and war stories to share instead.

2. There's no need to buy all the 'stuff' advertised to new parents. We are a captive, scared, susceptible market, making babies in a madly capitalist age. There are plenty who seek to exploit us. But just because a schoolfriend on Facebook bought a Bugaboo doesn't mean I need to.

3. It's worth reframing 'high taxes' as 'reducing inequality and investing in the next generation', Nordic-style. Sharing really is caring and a baby is not a commodity; it shouldn't arrive with a price tag.

3

Baby Dane

W E BEGAN LIVING like moles, blackout blinds drawn, a wooden stork outside the front door – as is the custom in Denmark – warning the postman to tread lightly for a while. I experienced moments of pure joy, visceral love, and a lot of laundry. The basil plant on the windowsill shrivelled and died. Time bent and particles suspended as I heaved my broken body through a new world of erratic sleep and mind-blowing responsibility. I noticed parts of the day – and night – that I had somehow skipped for the preceding decades.

'Bloody hell, *owls* are loud, aren't they?'

'Mmm,' Lego Man made a noise into his pillow.

Two hours later.

'Blimey, dawn's bright, isn't it?'

'Uh-huh.' A thick, muffled sound came from under the duvet.

When the redhead cried in the night, one of us would slide heavily out of bed, wondering whether the other had heard or noticed. Resenting. Forgiving. Then resenting again. Delirious with exhaustion. When the health visitor came to visit, I dissolved:

'I didn't know days could be like this! I didn't know love could be like this!' I told her about the smell that came off my newborn's head and how it was the most phenomenal sensory explosion that had ever existed and, 'Did people *know* about this? *Everyone* should know about this! This stuff could stop *wars*!'

She smiled and said gently: 'I know.' Then: 'Do you need a hug?'

I did.

Extra help was offered, from 'baby physiotherapy' to psychotherapy and lactation consultants. One friend was assigned a male lactation consultant who brought his own puppet 'to demonstrate' (a frog, just FYI). Another friend had a lactation nurse called 'Lone Wolf' – to this day, my favourite Danish name ever ('You never forget Lone's Latch!' is still a catchphrase round my way). But there was less attention paid to the mothers' physical recovery post-birth. In the early days of parenting, I asked my Veteran Viking friend about postpartum pelvic-health options, only to be met with a look of disdain.

'We're not *French*!'

Intrigued, I took to Google and read with envy how France's state-subsidised 'perineal re-education' programme helped strengthen a new mother's pelvic floor. But Vikings, I discovered, were more about the 'hearts and minds' of new parents.

'Do you have enough support?' my health visitor always asked. I didn't. But then, do any of us? The upheaval of a newborn is like nothing else, and today we're expected to manage it within the four walls of our home. This is why the next part of the Danish set-up works well, usually. When new parents are at their most vulnerable, sleep deprived and eating peanut M&Ms like it's their last supper, a health visitor sets them up in a mothers' group.

Four or five other mothers who've given birth at roughly the same time meet weekly to support each other, with some municipalities offering fathers' groups and family groups, too. The health visitor joins the first gathering to encourage parents to tell their 'birth story' and how it's all going so far. Basically: therapy. Talking about the birth ~~trauma~~ *experience* helps to develop a narrative around it and so begin to process it. As the psychotherapist Julia Samuel explained to me: 'In annunciating the words, the feelings emerge.' So a chatty mothers' group is a pretty good plan. Some work better than others. Embarking on friendships purely because you had an amniotic explosion around the same time isn't always successful. In my first mothers' group with the redhead, everyone else's babies slept like logs, waking only occasionally to guzzle clotted-cream-grade breast milk. Mine did not sleep. Instead, he cried and thrashed continuously, refusing both milk and sleep. One of the other mothers asked: 'Have you thought about swaddling?' just as I was in fact swaddling, to the best of my ability. I went home soon after for a cry.

'It's pot luck,' says my Danish friend Camilla, a tall, willowy artist and mum of two. 'My first group was a lot of talk about *bleer* (nappies or diapers in Danish). But the women I was with for my second baby were a lot more fun. The day we all peed our pants with laughter, I remember thinking: 'I've found my people!' We talked about everything from life, men, work, and "by the way, I had a baby!"'

It was second time lucky for me, too. We'd moved house, away from Sticksville on Sea to the Porny Pony town,* where

---

* The prominent local landmark being a stallion on two legs bearing its full-frontal glory, surrounded by cats with breasts. When I see you, I'll show you pics.

there was more going on and a bigger pool of new mothers to be matched with.

Capes flying in the wind, legs askance, with dry ice pumping out of every possible nook, my mothers' group after twins were Grade A superheroes. We talked about everything, and even on days when we collectively had breath like stale milk and armpits that smelled of crisps, we were there for each other. The day the twins got a stomach bug and the dog ended up chin to tail in chunder (the bathroom looked like a Jackson Pollock painting), the Superheroes dropped off lasagne. When another told us, 'I'm so tired, I might be sick—' then was, we rallied with *skumvaskeklude,* the sponge 'slices' I'd been surprised to find Danes use instead of wet wipes.

We tended to meet in coffee shops, late morning since it took hours to pack all the baby gear. Fortunately, there was no need to pack light, with plenty of space for nappies, dummies, food, muslins, if not a weekly shop, under Danish baby transit. Viking babies don't do strollers – they are wheeled around in huge Mary Poppins-style prams or *barnevogne* ('child-wagons'). This is because it's considered crucial for Vikings to be able to lie down flat, rather than bent banana shaped in a buggy or car seat.

'Isn't it rather cumbersome?' asked a sceptical bachelor friend who never knowingly wears a shirt without unbuttoning it to his navel. He pointed with horror at my huge Mary Poppins pram on an early visit from London: 'How are you getting *that* in a restaurant?'

I explained that parenting in rural Denmark involved remarkably few restaurants. He held my hand and looked sad for me. Deep V thinks all babies look like potatoes and would tolerate no such sacrifice. 'Okay then, a *café*? How are you getting *that* . . . in a *café*?'

'I'm not.'

Danes trust each other so much, they're happy to leave their babies outside in a pram to nap while they pop in for a flat white or to grab a sandwich. Families living in apartments – especially in Copenhagen or the big cities – even leave babies sleeping in communal courtyards. And yes, when I first heard about this, pre-parenthood, I was shocked, too.

'Won't it take you a long time to get down there, if the baby needs anything?' I asked a new-mum friend as we sat drinking coffee on the balcony of her fifth-floor walk-up.

'Yep,' she nodded, taking a long, slow sip of her latte.

It sounded insane. But Finnish researchers found that babies sleep longer when they nap outdoors,[1] and all the Nordic countries are big believers in the importance of fresh air. Giving mini-Vikings great gulps of it from around two weeks old at every opportunity is thought to help lungs develop. There's no 'cry it out' approach in Denmark. Viking babies always have their needs attended to, with new parents schooled in the principle that 'you can't spoil a baby'. But when it comes to napping? They're out in the cold. Often literally, since babies are allowed to sleep outside until it's around minus 20°C. Wim Hoff has nothing on Viking babies.

'Isn't it dangerous?' I hazarded, early on. 'What if someone ... *takes* them?'

'No one steals babies in Denmark,' Veteran Viking assured me.

In fact, the last reported case was in 1966 and came as such a shock that it made the *New York Times*. The baby was returned alive and well four weeks later, and since then? Nothing. Today, putting babies outside to nap is still common practice in Denmark. But not so elsewhere.

45

A Dane in New York was famously arrested for placing her baby outside in her pram to nap. On a May evening in 1997, Anette Sørensen parked her baby daughter outside a restaurant in Manhattan's East Village while she and the baby's father, a New York-based playwright, were inside. Both parents were arrested for child-endangerment. The episode sparked outrage in the US, with Americans astounded at the idea of parents leaving a child alone. But Danes were equally stunned by the concept of criminalising alfresco naps. All charges against Anette were eventually dropped, but the case is symbolic of the cultural differences between the Nordics and North Americans.

I get in touch with Anette, now fifty-five, who has the same wide smile, large eyes and brown curls as the young mother in the press clippings I've read from the 1990s.[*]

'The whole thing was . . . a shock,' she tells me, with characteristic Danish understatement: 'I just didn't think about it – leaving babies outside to sleep in their prams was very normal to me. But the US press were all against me. And although the Danish media was on my side, it was overwhelming.' Anette grew up in the Danish countryside, the daughter of farmers, and so was used to a lot of freedom. 'We played outside all day long – and were trusted to do so.' Because that was the Danish way. 'I always go back to this idea of *tillid*.' This is a Danish word that translates as both 'trust' *and* 'faith'. 'The whole society in Scandinavia is based on *tillid*,' says Anette. 'Our parents had faith in us and we had faith in ourselves. But the opposite of trust and faith is anxiety, and I don't want to live like that. Of

---

[*] And her book, *Ormen i æblet: En barnevogn i New York* (*The Worm in the Apple: The Pramcase of New York*).

course, we shouldn't be naive – it's important that we are awake and can be critical. But at the same time, I still believe trust and faith have to be the headline in our lives.'

After my first year of living Danishly, I already felt more trusting and happier – with faith, even, in a more equal society. But I still couldn't imagine leaving my tiny, squalling redhead outside in his pram to sleep. I wasn't quite 'there' yet. Then one day I did. And it was okay.

And then I had twins.

And as Henriette, the psychologist and *solomor* found out, getting a twin pram in anywhere is nigh on impossible. So if twin babies were sleeping, they stayed outside and I'd take a window seat, keeping an eye out for twitching blankets. Some of the Superheroes had baby monitors ('a new-fangled idea' according to my neighbour), but many relied on their ears or the kindness of strangers to alert them to any stirrings.

And then, at a time when many parents are thinking about childcare provision and returning to work, Vikings elect *not* to.

Parents get fifty-two weeks of parental leave in Denmark. Mothers take four weeks before the birth, then each parent has eleven weeks of non-transferable, use-it-or-lose-it leave, with the remaining twenty-six weeks to share.

In Norway, parents are also entitled to a year, with mothers getting three weeks before birth and six weeks after. Then there's a 'shared period' (*fællesperiode*) divided between parents, and a 'paternal quota' (*fædrekvote*). Parents in Iceland are entitled to six months each, with one transferable month, so one parent could take seven months and the other five. But a major chunk of the leave is non-transferable, with both parents encouraged to be actively involved. Finns get fourteen months, with the 'parent who has been pregnant', as the inclusive legislation terms it, getting forty days more to recover than the 'parent who has not been pregnant'.

Want to know who's 'winning' on parental leave? Sweden. Swedes have *480* days paid parental leave and Swedish fathers use the most parental leave in the world – 120 days per child on average. 'Today, 90 per cent of all Swedish fathers use some parental benefit, and the term "housewife" doesn't exist any more,' says Niklas Löfgren from the Swedish Social Insurance Agency (Försäkringskassan). 'In the late 1950s there were one million housewives in Sweden. Now the term is obsolete – and there is no desire from women to go back there.'

Sweden was the first country in the world to give both parents the same opportunities to be at home with their child back in 1974, with ninety days of parental leave for the mother and ninety for the father. 'But you were allowed to transfer them from the father to the mother, so everyone did. Men were *very* reluctant indeed,' says Niklas. It would take another twenty years to reach a point where men would use even 10 per cent of it. In 1995, the first *pappamånad* – 'daddy month' – was introduced, with thirty days of leave reserved for the father on a use-it-or-lose-it basis. 'Almost every father spends time at home now. If you don't, it's thought of as a bit strange.' There's even a nickname, *latte papas*, used to describe the well-turned-out dads hanging out in coffee shops with a baby in tow.

I ask how Niklas persuaded the men of Sweden to get on board with this plan and he laughs: 'Well, there weren't protests on the street with men holding signs! It's important to stress that this was *not* a change driven by fathers. Men had to be encouraged to take this time; they haven't chosen to do so from the start. It was because politicians dared to push for this change, even though they may have lost votes.'

Brave politicians? Making unpopular decisions for the greater good? Now there's a thought.

Politicians weren't prompted purely by a sense of fair play, however – there was an economic imperative, too. Educated women have always been a major resource and losing them from the labour market makes poor financial sense. So shared parental leave and childcare in Sweden is a no-brainer. As Niklas says: 'If you help women to be in the workforce, you get more taxes.' The OECD, the European Union and the World Economic Forum all encourage member nations to guarantee their workers paid parental leave and subsidised daycare because shared parental leave has been unequivocally proven to be good for economic growth (let's get t-shirts printed! Or tattoos! Who's in?). The Norwegian government recently valued the contribution of working mothers to the country's GDP at £626 billion – equivalent to the value added by its oil reserves.[2]

'Plus, if you make it doable to have a career and a family,' says Niklas, 'you increase future tax income.'

But are these rights subject to the whims of politicians? Could a new government turn back the clock?

'Not now,' says Niklas. 'We're seeing that the policies just make sense, so no one is going to argue with the bottom line. Even though there are political parties today that want to take away the "use or lose days", it isn't high on the political agenda.'

That's not to say that the Nordics have it nailed. Even with all the emphasis on helping mothers back to work, they're still less likely to work as CEOs than their male counterparts. An unintended consequence of generous leave is that while it allows women to stay at home without giving up work, it also keeps women out of the workforce for an extended period. Something that can set anyone back in their careers but may be a particular problem for those in high-powered corporate careers.

Women make up almost half of all the workforce but only 36 per cent of managers in Finland, 34 per cent in Norway, and 29 per cent in Denmark. In the UK, it's 32 per cent.[3] But in the US? Where there's no parental leave? Women make up 40 per cent of managers, according to Catalyst research.[4] American women may be stressed and in need of a rest, but they *are* making it up the slippery corporate pole (apologies for the phallic analogy).

So can career success only come at the expense of family life?

Well, no. Turns out it is possible to 'have it all', with Swedish women making up 43 per cent of managers.

'This is largely down to Sweden's use-it-or-lose-it policy having been in place for the longest,' says Lise Johansen, advisor on gender equality and family policies at the Danish Confederation of Trade Unions, since for parental policy to work, governments need to effectively force men to take time off. One study showed that a woman's earnings rose 7 per cent for every month of leave her partner took.[5] And researchers have found that paternity leave also improves maternal health, because women have support and can take time to heal.[6] This is better for women, babies, and the economy. British dads typically take very little paternity leave, so new mothers are left holding the baby when they're at their most vulnerable. One in ten mothers will experience postnatal depression in the UK, but even those who swerve this wrecking ball are likely to experience anxiety and low moods after birth (80 per cent).[7] The charity Birthrights found that depression and anxiety in new mothers costs an additional £17.5 billion in England alone.[8]

Denmark may lag behind the UK and the US on the CEO count, but with the introduction of use-it-or-lose-it paternity leave in 2022, it's hoped that the percentage of women in management roles will rise. And for decades now in Denmark, parents have been able to *have a life*, as well as get on in life. Only 1 per cent of employees work very long hours in Denmark, compared to the OECD average of 10 per cent.[9] And yet Danes are the second most productive workers in Europe – more productive than those in the USA, Canada and Japan.

'There are still challenges,' says Niklas, 'like the "sickness gap".' A long-term study of men and women in Sweden showed that before becoming parents, there's no significant difference in terms of illnesses, poor health and lower immune systems between the sexes. 'But after the first child, women take much more sick leave – and this comes at a cost to society,' says Niklas. This 'sickness gap' carries on until a woman's youngest child reaches the age of ten, according to a study from Uppsala University.[10]

Is this just a Swedish thing?

'There hasn't been research from other countries to my knowledge,' Niklas tells me. But I begin asking every mother I meet, and it rings true: we are worn out. And the parent-who's-had-a-baby has also, you know, HAD A BABY. Something now proven to take the same toll on the body as an ultramarathon or doing the Tour de France.[11] At the very time bodies are recovering from growing and pushing out a human, we're at our most sleep-deprived. On returning to work, we pick up every bug going at playgroups and daycare. I had the constitution of an ox pre-parenthood. Now I'm down with something most months. And my youngest are only five. Am I condemned to another five years of this? I'm not sure I can cope.

'I hear this a lot,' Niklas sympathises.

'Why aren't things . . . well, *better*? Even in Sweden?' What with all the shared parental leave and hot latte papas . . . ?

'Women still tend to be the project leaders of the family,' says Niklas. 'They stay home unpaid a lot more before kids go to daycare.'

So what's the solution?

'More paternity leave!' says Niklas.

The Danish Fathers Association found that many men who would like to go on parental leave don't feel able to – if they earn more, for example. But this is short-sightedness, says Lise from the Danish Confederation of Trade Unions: 'Because about twenty years from now they'll realise that fathers have missed out on time with their kids, women have missed out on promotions and companies have missed out on all the skilled women who could have created more wealth for society.'

'There also used to be the argument that kids can only attach to one parent, and that parent was "mother-shaped",' adds Niklas, who raised his two children single-handedly. 'We know now that this isn't true, but the cultural hangover remains.' It's something he's working on. Now, Niklas speaks about the Swedish model around the world. 'I've been to Korea, South Africa, Argentina, Ukraine, Moldova, Croatia – all over. People from different countries all have different starting points, but in common is the idea that we should be able to work and have children at the same time.'

'What about the US?' I'm curious.

'I haven't been there – they haven't invited me.'

'And the UK?'

'Same.'

I tell him this is depressing. He tells me to hurry up and spread the word.

'I think what's most important to point out,' says Niklas as I prepare to say goodbye, 'is that for fathers it's a *fantastic* opportunity to be at home with your children. I would urge anyone to use it. It's a short time in your life, so if it's possible, you should go for it!'

Lego Man took ten weeks off back in 2014, fully paid, to care for the miniature redhead while I went back to work. Something he couldn't have done in the UK at the time, when paternity leave was a mere ten days (UK parents are now entitled to share thirty-seven weeks paid). Suddenly, I could drink coffee and wee whenever I wanted. Once, at the same time. I could regain a sense of self and navigate this new identity of 'working mother', then go home to a fat-cheeked cherub who I could really enjoy spending time with. It was nice to see my baby, too.*

Dads throughout the Nordic countries change nappies, cook and do the daycare run, 'So much so that it's like you're not a real man if you haven't done your share of diaper duty,' says photographer and Finnish father of three Johannes Romppanen.

There's nothing inherent about women that makes us 'better' at parenting. Neuroscientists from the University of Tel-Aviv analysed 1,400 MRIs and found no discernible difference between male and female brains.[12] A study from Bar-Ilan University in Israel studied eighty-nine first-time parents and found that primary caregivers develop neural pathways in their brains that make them more responsive to the emotional cues of children in their care – regardless of their gender.[13] Brain

---

* Joke.

scans show an increase in grey and white matter in the regions linked to nurturing, affection and threat detection. Thanks to neuroplasticity, the same pathways develop in fathers who are primary caregivers. It's loving care and putting in the hours that counts. Men who take parental leave tend to have better relationships with their children and are more likely to muck in with extra childcare once they return to work, according to a Swedish study.[14] Sharing the burden keeps everyone sane. Advisable, since you need your wits about you in the first six months of a Viking's life to avoid committing a crime. Let me explain . . .

In the Nordic countries, you must choose a name for your child from a preapproved government list. 'If you really want something that's not on The List, you need special permission – and "creative spellings" are rejected,' the Veteran Viking instructed me. The official list is available at borger.dk, but many parents take to Google as a first port of call to see if a name they're considering is legal. Some of the results that appear when you search *Can I name my baby* . . . in Denmark include 'Batman', 'Disney' and 'Shrek'. To which the answer – I'll save you the trouble of searching – is 'no'.

Thankfully there are 7,000 other names that you *are* allowed to call your child (this is generous; in Iceland, it's only 3,500). If you want a name that isn't authorised, you have to justify it in an application to the local priest or choir director.

Who gave choir directors such power? I marvelled. *It's like Gareth Malone is king of the world!*

If the name is approved, it's written on The List of approved names and can be used freely by anyone in future.

'I could become some sort of Shrek trailblazer!'

The baby looked livid.

'That'll never happen,' Veteran Viking assured him. 'The idea is that the name must not disadvantage the child. A kid's life shouldn't begin badly because their parents have bad taste.' This seemed fair, though the rules can appear arbitrary, disallowing some perfectly inoffensive monikers (incidentally, 'Monica' *is* allowed). One Icelandic couple faced fines for calling their child 'Alex'.

Being too tired to operate the TV remote, let alone face legal action, we stuck to The List. And then came twins. And we lost the remote control for two months and just watched an iPad through glazed eyes while feeding squalling babies day and night. The List came through for us again, none of my children accidentally got called Batman, and then there were five of us. A family. Come what may. Only the 'may' part turned out to be rather a lot. As we're about to find out.

What I've learned about how to raise a Viking . . . from birth

1. Dads can do this parenting lark too and shouldn't be treated like buffoons – or 'babysitters'. Having grown up without one of these fabled 'father' creatures, I struggled slightly to know what to do with one when my own children came along. I've had to learn to 'share' – everything from the parenting load to big decisions. It's a work in progress, but I'm trying. ('*Trying*?' You're "exasperating"!' Lego Man tells me. I throw a satsuma at him. And so it goes on.)
2. *Tillid* is . . . everything. Parenting is a largely thankless task, so trust and faith in the future – in humanity, even – is advised.

3. A gang of other new parents helps. Friends at a similar life stage keep us sane, when all around us are losing their shit (mostly babies, but once, me). Fellow parent friends can remind us to have a shower/sandwich once in a while. They can offer a counterbalance to the simmering resentments of parenthood. Fact: everyone hates their partner at some point in the trenches of new parenting. Friends to vent to are essential.
4. Taking time to choose a name is smart. Shrek might have been called something sensible like Simon had his parents not been quite so sleep-deprived with a newborn at home.

4

Bringing Up *Børn**

I'M STANDING IN a field, staring up at a tree. The tree contains several mouldy apples, a broken bucket and my youngest son. It is a blustery Tuesday, and I would really like to go home. But the universe has other plans.

'How long's he been up there?'

'He was with us for lunch . . .' offers a student helper at my son's *børnehave*, or kindergarten. It's 3 p.m., so this isn't much help. I thought something might be amiss when he wasn't in the sandpit with his favourite mini-Vikings. Neither was he etching on walls with chalk. Nor cooking up a feast in the 'mud kitchen'. This is because, it now emerges, he managed to find his way up a tree. But, like cats in every *Fireman Sam* episode ever (or *Brandmand Sam* in Danish), he cannot, it seems, get down.

'*Kom nu!*' calls out Student Helper, meaning, 'Come now!'

He does not move.

'*Kom nu!*' she tries again.

He still does not move.

---

* 'Children' in Danish.

57

'*Kom*—' she goes for a third round.

'I think', I stop her, 'if he could *kom nu*, he would have *kom nu* by now . . .' I look around for assistance, but all the other adults have children hanging off them like human monkey bars. These are *pedagogues* or early-years educators – highly trained daycare staff, with a three-and-a-half-year bachelor's degree in social education, who are used to children hanging off them like human monkey bars. They are less used to children stuck up trees. So this one's on me.

I try coaching my son down ('put one foot there, the other here . . . ') but to no avail. I'm going to have to go up, I see now. I'm going to have to hitch my skirt and scale a tree. For the first time in thirty years.

The lower branches are easy enough, if an inelegant spectacle. The next are trickier. *Fair play*, I think, impressed that my five-year-old managed it. From my elevated vantage point, I see sunshine bouncing off glossy roof tiles and several dads ambling up the road to pick up offspring.

'Oh, *hej*!' I wave and almost lose my grip.

'Are you okay?' one of them calls out. It's the one Lego Man always swears is 'the spit of Peter Schmeichel'. After googling 'Who is Peter Schmeichel?' and learning that he was a footballer and famous goalkeeper for Manchester United, back in the day when Manchester United won things, I refuted this ('He's just tall and blonde – like everyone here!'). Also: my husband wears thick glasses and has shocking facial recognition. But he insisted, so the name stuck.

'Would you like help?' asks the Peter Schmeichel lookalike.

I would like help, actually. But a small girl dressed as Elsa from *Frozen* is looking up at me with saucer eyes.

I can't let Elsa down . . . We've only just started getting good

Disney female leads. What would Mirabel do? Or Moana? They would NOT, no way, wait for a strapping Viking to come along and save them . . .

'*Nej tak*, I'm fine,' I tell him in my now trademark Danglish (Danish-English), then manage: '*Jeg kan gøre det selv*' or 'I can do it myself' – the phrase all good Danish Vikings learn from approximately age two.

'Sure?' Peter Schmeichel asks.

'Uh-huh . . .' I waver in response. *Damn Nordic egalitarianism, making all damsel-in-distress action impossible!* '*Jeg er OK!*' ('I am okay'), I lie.

There follow a few standard swears and minor splintering, but one grazed knee later, I make it down with my son. Tights laddered, pride intact. Ish.

'*Flot!*' a pedagogue with three children hanging off her calls out, which means 'nice!' And then: '*Tak for en rigtig god dag!*' or 'Thanks for a really good day!'

This is daycare, Danish-style. All children in Denmark attend high-quality, state-run daycare five days a week from around ten months until they turn six, when they (finally) start school. And I mean 'all'. Even Prince Christian, the future king, attended public daycare. Parents may opt for a child-minder or *dagplejemor* ('daycare mother'), who can look after up to four children, although *vuggestue* (nursery) and *børnehave* (kindergarten) are the most common options.

Whatever has happened in the preceding hours, no matter how battered, bruised or mud-caked your child appears at pick-up, the response to the question 'Did he/she have a good day?' will inevitably result in the answer: '*Ja, rigtig god!*' ('Yes, really good!')

Your child may have a black eye and a fractured collarbone, but the response is still likely to be, '*Rigtig god!*'

'Are you sure?' a concerned parent may then ask. There will usually be a pause, as they wait for more information about how the day was 'really good' when their child now has Viking battle scars. But no explanation is usually forthcoming, unless a visit to the hospital or the emergency dentist is needed. And I write from experience here.

Very occasionally, things go (more) awry. 'My daughter found a hole in the fence and escaped,' one dad tells me. 'Mine got locked in daycare after it shut,' says another. And a pedagogue who will remain anonymous tells me first-hand how a child went AWOL during 'forest time'.

'A mother called the *børnehave* and said, "Have you got Thunder Bear with you?" (Thorbjørn is a hugely popular name in Denmark, from Thor, God of thunder, and *bjørn*, meaning bear. I know. It's too much. *Immediately changes name by deed poll*) So Thorbjørn's mum was on the phone and the daycare staff looked around, did a quick headcount, and had to admit, "Actually . . . no: we haven't got him with us." "No, you haven't," the mother replied, "because he's found his way home and he's outside my window."' Remarkably, everyone was able to 'see the funny side' by Friday and commend the boy on his resourcefulness.

Vugguestue or the 'nursery room' for under-threes is fractionally less perilous, although with ten-plus children ranging in age from ten months to three years, it can be quite the kid-soup. When little Ingrid or Svend are first dropped off aged ten months, they have to be very lucky indeed not to be trodden on by a hulk of a three-year-old. The month of their third birthday, toddlers graduate to *børnehave*, where they will be expected to ~~avoid being crushed alive~~ *hold their own* with children up to the age of six.

'It's fine, though,' a lovely pedagogue named Pia assured me after my son's first black eye, 'because we have the "step by step" programme, which teaches them to read each other's emotions. Presumably so that they can ~~avoid being crushed alive~~ *hold their own* and survive the elemental clashes of toddler versus toddler.

Despite my scepticism, this approach has precedent. Anthropologist Abigail Page studies hunter-gatherer communities, and found that mini-'alloparents' – individuals other than parents who care for young – provide about a quarter of all young children's care in some places.[1] Psychologist Sheina Lew-Levy found that in central Africa, child-to-child teaching is much more common after infancy than adult–child teaching.[2] It's thought that multi-age playgroups are important for helping children expand their horizons, gain social and emotional skills, and learn how to function in society. Other children tend to be better teachers and playmates than adults, since children naturally integrate play into learning and have skill levels closer to each other. So that's all lovely – as long as they can ~~avoid being crushed alive~~ *hold their own*.

'Teachers also practise being "actively passive",' says Lise Hansen, a smiley blonde pedagogue who works at Valhalla Børnehave in Vejle (her Australian husband calls her 'the Viking from Valhalla'). 'We sit on our hands,' she tells me. I assume she means this metaphorically. She doesn't.

'So if a child joins a group where everyone's sitting on a chair and there's no chair for them, and they're about to get upset or have a tantrum, you sit on your hands. *Literally*. To send a signal. You might say something like: 'Oh, sorry you can't find a chair. What can we do about that?' The nudge is to make other kids go and pull up a chair.' Instead of 'fixing it', pedagogues expect that children will handle it themselves.

'It works with the really little kids, too,' says Lise. 'In nursery, if a baby is crying, you might say to the others, "Oh, Anton is sad! Do you remember what we used to do when you were sad?" And a two-year-old might say, "We would get a *sut*?" – a dummy or pacifier in Danish. I'd then say: "Great! Can you find Anton a *sut*?" And this way, we're teaching them empathy, too.'

Whereas in the UK and Australia, where Lise has also worked, 'It's less about developing them as a person and more about reading and maths – even from the age of four.' Nadine, a Danish mum of two in my town, spent ten years in Silicon Valley and recalls nurseries that specialised in Mandarin and extracurricular activities to get kids 'Stanford-ready' – aged two.

But for Vikings? 'We prioritise play and time in nature,' says Kitta, a statuesque Viking pedagogue who has looked after all three of my children. Kitta, fifty-one, started work in a kinder-garten when she was eighteen years old and has worked her way up ever since, 'Apart from the three years I spent in prison.'

I wonder whether I've misheard: 'Prison?'

'Yes! I spent so many years in kindergarten, I felt I should try something else. So I became a prison guard.'

Jail, she tells me, is actually a lot like kindergarten.

'You're looking after people; you have to earn their respect and you have to find a way to communicate.' This makes sense. I once interviewed an FBI hostage negotiator who told me how everything he learned on the job could also be applied to toddlers.

So why didn't Kitta stay in prison, so to speak?

'Too boring!' she says. 'I'd work from eight until four and nothing really happened. Whereas kindergarten . . .' She holds her hands wide and blows air out of her cheeks: 'It is never boring with children.' In case a dozen mini-Vikings weren't enough to contend with, Danish pedagogues actively encourage their charges to go berserk every now and again. 'It's important for them to run wild and have *ramasjang* ['hullabaloo' in English],' says Kitta, 'so we let them run up and down hills and make noise. How they move is how they learn to talk. If they don't use their body the right way, it's harder for them to learn speech.' Studies show that while motor development does not *cause* language to emerge, they are related, and new motor skills can contribute to language development.[3]

The goal of daycare in Denmark is to promote children's well-being, give the family flexibility, and prevent negative social inheritance, according to Denmark's Daycare Services Act. Swedish childcare is similarly based on the principle that early-years education is as a form of poverty prevention. The OECD now advises that a better quality of childcare service contributes to a better start in life for children. And three decades of research shows that what happens between birth and the age of five lays the foundations for our future health and happiness. This window of opportunity is when our brain is at its most receptive and adaptable. If we miss it, we pay down the line. LSE researchers estimate the remedial steps to tackle mental and physical health issues in children 'that might have been avoided through action in early childhood' cost £16 billion.[4] A year. In England alone.

Which, we can all agree, is daft. In the Nordic countries, they take a different approach. 'You notice from the very beginning that the pedagogues are not "babysitting", they're bringing up people,' says Finnish mother of one Katja Pantzar, 'so they'll show kids how to bake, help out, put their dishes back on a tray after meals – kids learn to participate.'

'Participation is key,' agrees pedagogue Lise. 'We have to

make sure that all children can participate in all of the activities at the same level.'

I don't mean to come over all Maggie Thatcher, but doesn't this mean *no one* gets to thrive? Aren't some children held back when everyone is treated the same?

'No,' Lise tells me (firmly), 'it's the opposite of everyone being squashed down and treated the same – they are all treated *differently* to get to the same level. Each child is treated as an individual with individual needs.'

This sounds brilliant, but what does it look like in practice?

'Kids participate in the planning of the day, and we follow their interests, so if they love farms, we might read books about a farm or arrange a visit.' Children are also offered any extra resources or help they might need. 'You just have to snap your fingers and you can get a psychologist, a speech therapist, a physiotherapist, four different experts, even translators, to be with you for an hour-long meeting in a couple of days,' says Lise.

'In Finland, if you are highly sensitive, or have a speech impediment, or you're scared of loud noises, or find it tough to play with others, you get practical help to address the issue,' says Katja.

How does this work with the idea of Viking spirit or Finnish '*sisu*', often translated as 'grit' or 'resilience'? Isn't there a conflict here?

Katja wrote the book on *sisu*, twice (*Finding Sisu*, 2018 and *Everyday Sisu*, 2022), so she should know. 'But actually,' she says, 'no – there is no conflict. You don't want to wait until you have a situation on your hands; you look at the early signs and you find a solution. It's worth doing, to ensure that there aren't bigger problems later on. This is part of the Nordic approach of helping each child fulfil their potential, regardless of income or birth circumstances.' As the former director-general of the Finnish Ministry of Education Pasi Sahlberg writes in *Finnish Lessons:* 'Kindergarten in Finland doesn't focus on preparing children for school academically. Instead, the main goal is to make sure that all children are happy and responsible individuals.'[5]

So how much does all this cost? Well, in Denmark, the state pays 75 per cent of the cost of childcare. For under-threes, parents pay around DKK 3,588 (£420) per month and for ages three to six, it's DKK 2,036 (£239). If your collective household income is lower than DKK 576,799 (£67k), your childcare will be cheaper and if it's below DKK 185,701 (£22k), daycare is free.[6] There's also a sibling discount, so if you have more than one child using childcare, you pay full price for the most expensive daycare and half price for the other(s) – a lot like a WHSmith's Richard & Judy book deal.

In Iceland, daycare can start when a baby is six months old if you're a single parent, or nine months for cohabiting or married couples. Monthly costs start at around £430 for a full-time place.

Norwegians attend daycare from the age of one and parents pay around £265 a month. Daycare in Finland is free for low-income families, with costs capped at £253 per month. The gold medal goes again to Sweden, where parents pay just 10 per cent of the actual cost of daycare, around £112 per month, with the rest financed through taxes.

At the time of writing, full-time nursery for children under the age of two in the UK costs almost two-thirds of a parent's weekly take-home pay in many areas. Britain has the second highest childcare costs in the developed world.[7] 'I basically hand over my salary each week so that my son can bring home a new bug,' says one friend with a particularly Petri-dish child.

It's changing, slowly, thanks to trailblazing work from the likes of Stella Creasy MP and campaigning charity Pregnant Then Screwed. In the 2023 budget, the government acknowledged the impossibility of growing the economy *without* affordable childcare. By the end of 2024, children aged between nine months and two years will get fifteen hours a week of free childcare. From September 2025, every working parent of under-fives will have access to thirty free hours. And by September 2026, the chancellor has pledged funding for all primary schools to provide wraparound care from 8 a.m. to 6 p.m. But as many friends say, 'I'll believe it when I see it.'

In the US, there is no national childcare programme. Which is bananas, since studies show that for every dollar invested in early childhood education, the broader economy gets back between $1.50 and $2.80.[8] In the Nordic countries, the high proportion of working mothers (82 per cent in Denmark[9]) means more tax revenue to fund the welfare state – including tax-subsidised, high-quality childcare. Childcare pays for itself. Even better, in Viking land it's automatic, and you don't have to be a Mensa member to navigate it.

'Whereas the process of arranging childcare in the UK is administratively laborious,' says British mum of one Lydia Wright, who has a degree in early childhood studies, heads up Horizon Childcare in Exeter, and also happens to be my cousin. There are currently seven categories of childcare eligibility in the UK that even the government website doesn't appear entirely clear about. 'Many parents don't understand what they're entitled to or how best to apply for it,' says Lydia, 'and so childcare professionals are also expected to be accountants and coaches to help parents through the process.'

For new parents juggling the world of work with raising a

human being, this is an onerous ask. In the Nordic countries, government-subsidised childcare is affordable, easy and organised by the municipality. Childcare institutions only close for a couple weeks over the summer, so parents can manage around their own annual leave – usually five weeks' paid holiday a year.

High-quality, state-run institutions heavily subsidised by taxes are now the norm, and the Danish ethos is that it's verging on child cruelty *not* to let your small person socialise from ten months. The same is true in many hunter-gatherer societies. For the Maya people of the Yucatán Peninsula in southeast Mexico, not letting others love your children is considered mean-spirited. The indigenous people of Kugaaruk, Canada, believe that just as parents need breaks from their offspring, toddlers get sick of their parents and should socialise regularly.[10] Kitta agrees: 'You have to learn to be social – when children are at home for too long, it's so difficult for them to play with others. So it's important to start early.' This isn't a sentiment you hear in the UK or the US. At least, not these days.

During the Second World War, it was seen as a patriotic duty for both men and women to work in the UK and the US, so nursery education was presented as being beneficial for children. By 1943, 80 per cent of married women were working, and both Britain and America provided nursery places to every child. But after 1945, men returning from war needed jobs – and women lost theirs. Nurseries were seen as an expensive wartime legacy and so closed. In 1950 the World Health Organization commissioned a report by British psychologist John Bowlby on children separated from their parents as a result of war.[11] In the report, Bowlby condemned institutional care in France, the Netherlands, Sweden and Switzerland, describing large orphanages as incapable of meeting the needs of individual children. He extrapolated from this argument, claiming that *any* maternal separation would adversely affect a child to some degree (Bowlby doesn't bother about fathers – he left the care of his four children entirely to his wife, Ursula). In response to Bowlby's 'findings', the World Health Organization claimed that nurseries and daycare caused permanent damage to the emotional health of children. Only his 'findings' showed no such thing. Quite apart from the fact that his research methods have been largely discredited, he was looking at the results of huge orphanages, filled with deeply unhappy children who had suffered conflict, loss or abuse. Not *daycare*.

US anthropologist Margaret Mead and the British psychiatrist Michael Rutter were among many to dismiss Bowlby's ideas in subsequent years, only by then, 'attachment theory' had taken hold in the UK and US.

But not in the Nordics. There, governments wanted women in the labour force to contribute taxes, so they needed good childcare. Psychologist Henriette Cranil doesn't think this has done Danes any harm either. 'There's a lot of attention to attachment in Danish daycares,' she says, 'and the focus should really be on the quality of care that children get. You could be with your child all day, every day, but it may not be quality time if they're in front of a TV for large chunks of this, for example. Daycare is good for helping children to learn self-regulation with the warmth of highly trained pedagogues.'

Alarmist headlines regularly claim that working mothers risk damaging their children, but Harvard studies since 2015 categorically debunk this. Researchers analysing data from twenty-four different countries found that daughters of working mums have better careers, better pay and more equal relationships than daughters of stay-at-home mothers.[12] And they're just as happy in adulthood as the children of mothers who stayed at home. A study from the University of North Carolina found that children develop better with a mother who is happy in her work than with a mother who is frustrated by staying at home.[13] By all means stay home with children if you choose. But if you don't choose it, you shouldn't feel obliged to. Because a parent permanently seething with resentment isn't much fun for anyone. As the economist Emily Oster put it in *Cribsheet* (2019): 'The weight of the evidence suggests the net effects of working on child development are small or zero.'[14]

My mother worked while I was growing up out of necessity. But most mothers didn't. We are all products of our upbringing, so at the beginning of my parenting path, I had all sorts of 'rules' for myself to make it okay to put the mini-redhead in daycare. First, I decided he had to have more daylight hours with me each day than at *vuggestue*. When I realised that daylight was minimal in Denmark between October and March (we're talking Mordor), I modified this to: more *waking hours* with me each day than at daycare. It's an ongoing tussle, but I know by now that I am a nicer, more fulfilled member of the human race when I have a work life and a home life.

'In Denmark, we believe that others can care for your children – you don't need to be on guard *all* the time,' says lovely pedagogue Pia from my children's daycare. 'It's good to let grandparents, friends or pedagogues take over sometimes.' Also: men.

'My son goes to a daycare with all male pedagogues,' says Lise, the Viking from Valhalla. 'This would be considered weird in the UK, but my son loves it. It's very outdoorsy, very physical.' Mini-Vikings spend their mornings running around the nearest forest, playing tag, building forts, making 'art' with leaves and sticks, catching bugs and generally rolling in mud. They'll break for lunch, then the older ones might do it all again in the afternoon. 'I'm really grateful my son is getting that experience,' says Lise. 'The stigma around men working in childcare helps no one.' *Hear, hear.* My twins are currently dazzled by a man at their daycare called Simon who can do a fishtail braid and draw a killer unicorn (when requested). He isn't a trained pedagogue; instead he's a student helper, seeing if he might want to work in the field.

'Every kindergarten will have one or two student helpers,' Kitta explains. 'They may not have the experience or the same training, but they bring energy and new ideas'. All Danes have a criminal-record check before working with children, but there is far more trust that people are essentially 'good'.

Whereas British and US friends tell tales of biometric finger codes to enter nurseries and even CCTV, when my son started daycare we used a 'magnet system'. And the word 'system' is doing a lot of heavy lifting here. Each child had a magnet that parents could move along a whiteboard to show when they planned on swinging by later. If a grandparent or babysitter was picking up, parents could notify carers via a Biro dangling from a string. Over the last couple of years, they've gone high tech, with an electronic system to 'check in' and 'check out' your child daily. But we *all* miss the magnets. 'I think it's amazing the trust this puts on the children, too,' says Lise. 'We don't always even have gates on daycares, so we're relying on a three-year-old not to cross an imaginary line.'

Although for a good deal of the day, littler ones *can't* escape. Under-threes nap outside in their Mary Poppins-style perambulators under a shelter or in a 'sleeping shed'. The sight of row-upon-row of prams was startling when I first visited a Danish daycare, before I had children of my own.

I'd met an American. A mother of three, with perma-glossy hair and distinctly North American dentistry who'd also found herself living Danishly. One afternoon, I joined her on the daycare pick-up. First stop? Swinging by the prams to check if her smalls were still sleeping.

'They're strapped in so they can't "escape",' American Mom friend explained, pointing out the rein-like harnesses wrapped around still-snoozing infants. 'And some prams even have hinged wooden bars over the opening, so they stay put until a pedagogue comes to get them!' She demonstrated, lifting and lowering a small square. 'Like baby cages!'

My eyes widened. 'And, err . . . what's with the ladders?'

'Ah! Well, some Viking babies are . . . you know . . . *Vikings*,' she explained. The three-foot ladders leaning against some prams help sturdier toddlers make their own way up to sleep, thus saving pedagogues a trip to the chiropractor down the line. The whole thing looked archaic, but as American Mom put it, with a flash of a Whitestrips-bright smile: 'They nap like a dream!'

Babies are frequently checked on by pedagogues and there's a monitor in the sleeping shed, so the grown-ups can hear what's going on. Under-threes cosy up under a duvet and possibly extra blankets before being covered with a fly net.

'In winter?' I asked, surprised: 'Do they have some kind of badass Viking flies here?'

'Well, no,' American Mom told me, 'but they do have cats . . .' True story: one child woke up with a cat on his face before the year-round bug-net policy was implemented.

Most children are dropped off before 8 a.m. and collected between 3 p.m. and 4 p.m. The working day in most Danish offices is 8 a.m.–4 p.m., but two-parent families often tag-team, so that one will work an hour later while the other picks up children. On a Friday, everyone winds down even earlier. I once had to collect the redhead at 4 p.m. on a Friday and he was the only child left. Pia was ready for the weekend and I was consumed by guilt. I never did it again. But there's generally a lot of love both ways between parents and pedagogues. Kindergarten staff in central Denmark even offered parents two hours' free childcare on a Thursday evening, so that the parents could have 'special adult time'.[15]

It's pretty great. But there are challenges. 'It used to be one pedagogue for every four kids in *børnehave*,' says Kitta, 'now it's one for every seven or eight.' This issue was brought to nationwide attention in a 2019 TV documentary by the Danish public-service broadcaster DR. *Hvem passer vores børn?* or 'Who is looking after our children?' showed one institution where three members of staff were left to care for thirty-one children. After the programme aired, protests took place and a nationwide parents' movement was set up called '*Hvor er der en voksen?*' or 'Where is there an adult?' Campaigners began fighting for one adult to every three children in *vuggestue* and one to every six in *børnehave*. In 2020, the government agreed to meet the demands . . . in theory. But when a pedagogue is ill and a substitute comes in, Statistics Denmark registers this as two separate employees. The daycare manager and kitchen staff are also counted. 'We need more help,' agrees Pia. 'We need to attract more people to the profession and keep existing pedagogues working.' But the real threat to the Danish daycare system is admin.

'The toughest thing that has happened in my industry since I started is that we have to document everything now,' says

Pia, from language accumulation to motor skills and the ability to share and communicate new ideas. She explains how the Danish government likes to have a handle on how its mini-Vikings are faring, 'But that time comes away from the kids.' Kitta agrees that it's a problem: 'Almost half want to leave the profession as there is now too much paperwork.'

There's also a nudge towards the more central European and US approach of 'goals', says Pia. 'Around everything from social skills to language and more admin – which means less time with the children.'

'And who is this coming from?'

'The government in part. And actually . . .' Pia hesitates.

'Go on?'

'Parents.'

Oh.

'Expectations among parents are higher than they used to be,' agrees the Viking from Valhalla, Lise. 'We are slowly becoming consumers in Denmark – just like everywhere else. I think the influence of American TV and culture can really be seen here.'

So how do we get back to a more balanced place?

'Well, what sets us apart is that we have equal opportunities,' says Lise. 'We need to hold on to that.'

'And boundaries,' adds Pia, ominously. 'I'd say parents under the age of forty are pretty bad at setting boundaries.' *Ouch*. 'But as adults, sometimes you just have to be firm, like when it comes to wearing the snowsuit in winter.' This is the Maggie-from-*The Simpsons*-style zip-up padded onesie that all Danish children wear in varying sizes from birth until they're about ten. 'You have to wear the snowsuit, because it's cold.' There's no debate here: it's Baltic.

Boundaries are crucial for Kitta, too. She's famed for her no-nonsense, firm-but-fair approach, inspiring awe and envy in all. (Why, when *Kitta* asks them to put their shoes on, do they actually put their shoes on? How come when *Kitta* says 'wash your hands', they actually wash their hands? When *Kitta* says 'no throwing rocks', they ACTUALLY stop throwing rocks!) I beg Kitta to tell me her secrets. ('Is it magic? It's magic! Isn't it?')

'Maybe it's because I'm bigger? Maybe I'm older?' she suggests.

That's not it.

'Okay, then: I know what I stand for and when I say something, I mean it. I don't move from A to B; I am consistent.'

That's it.

'Also,' she adds, 'I really like the kids. It's very important to say how much we get from them as well. Some days it can feel like too much, then one of the kids will give you a hug and say "thank you" and it's all worthwhile. We get so many hugs. I missed that in prison. There wasn't so much hugging.'

'No.'

'And with the bigger kids, you can have a dialogue. They are so kind and funny.' I hear her here. My youngest (by two minutes) is currently indignant that 'every Easter, bad guys peg a man called Jesus to a wardrobe!' while my daughter, having learned 'how we all come from monkeys', is telling everyone that her elder brother has orange hair: 'Because *he* came from an orangutan.'

'It's a really good age,' smiles Kitta.

I'm glad to hear her say this, since the twins have a birthday coming up and I'm about to ask if she wouldn't mind leading a field trip for an hour's cake 'n' chaos. This is the Danish tradition whereby the pedagogue arrives with the class to the home of the birthday girl or boy (or, in my case, both) to go mad for an hour before the teacher takes them away again. There's no hanging around, no small talk, no social one-upmanship, or infringement on evenings or weekends. And the whole thing costs no more than the price of a few snacks. It's an inexpensive, efficient ninja birthday squad: in and out.

'Not like in the US,' says American Mom. 'There we're talking professional cakes, entertainers, puppeteers, Disney princesses, a creepy snake guy—'

'What?'

'Oh, just this guy who did the party rounds back in the US,' – she waves a hand in dismissal – 'but the point is, in Denmark it's easy! The kid-party production values here are *very low*. As you'll find out . . . '

I can't wait.

The following week, Kitta, two colleagues and eighteen mini-Vikings between the ages of three and five bumble up the road in high-vis vests for an hour-long game of *du kan ikke fange mig!* (you can't catch me!) before demolishing 1kg of carrot batons, twenty-five *pølsehorn* (Danish sausage rolls), twenty sticks of cheese, three red peppers, four cucumbers and two casserole dishes of popcorn. After what feels like the longest and loudest hour of my life, Kitta claps her hands. The children line up in pairs, pull on their fluoro-yellow tabards (that my daughter already views as an affront to her personal style), and they're off. As am I: for a lie down in a darkened room.

Give pedagogues a medal. Give them anything they want. They deserve it.

What I've learned about how to raise a Viking . . . in daycare

1. Embrace the chaos. Yes, it's loud, but it's doing them good (probably). Mixing up ages happens in families anyway, with bigger children stepping in to look after smaller ones (or, rather, I'm hoping this is what happens).
2. Children need boundaries. Denmark is a rules-based society and Danes tend to follow these in the name of 'community'. No one crosses the road until the green man/woman/Viking flashes up (Danish pedestrian crossings are more inclusive). And 'freedom *within* boundaries' is something I've come to appreciate. Within a structure, I feel free and secure (oh yeah, and my children do, too).
3. Danish-style children's parties are the way forward. I'm wondering whether I can lower the bar still further next year. Perhaps just a: 'Join us in the park for a play on Saturday morning! No presents please, but bring snacks.'
4. Small people and their carers romp outdoors all year round in Denmark. Regardless of rain, freezing fog and general end-of-days weather. *What? How? Why? Wait and see . . .*

5

No Such Thing as Bad Weather (Just the Wrong Clothes)

R AIN HAMMERS HARD and water bubbles up from
the drain. It's been wet all week in my town and the river
running through it has churned into a thick stew of swirling
sand. Winter comes sooner in Denmark – 22 September to be
precise.

In England I'm sure we had 'autumn' . . .

In Denmark, it's cold and dark within a week. We've only
just left the house for a walk and already my feet are sodden.

'Might come back early,' I message Lego Man: *'rotten out.'*

Infuriatingly, he sends a smiley face in response and a splash
emoji. I make a note to tell him that this doesn't mean what
he thinks it means. Especially after he sent that aubergine to
a colleague in a restaurant recently ('What? I wanted baba
ganoush.')

Just as I'm composing a response, my children begin splashing
in puddles and ricocheting off wet bushes. *For 'fun'? How are they
having a nice time when the weather's so dire?* I wonder, perplexed.

'*Lucky the kids are dressed for it!*' Lego Man texts again.

Oh yes. That's why.

During my first year of raising Vikings, I sent the miniature redhead to daycare in a woollen duffel coat like Paddington Bear. Only with marmalade-coloured hair rather than a sandwich under his hat. In my defence, I came from London. Plus I wasn't a Viking yet. Within hours, the woollen coat smelled of wet dog (it drizzles daily) and his toes had frozen.

'These are no good,' one of the pedagogues told me at pick-up, gesturing with disdain at my son's Stinky Paddington ensemble. 'He needs proper outdoor clothes. Otherwise? He will freeze.'

In some places, they put up posters to remind parents exactly what children need for each season. In my place, Vikings are just expected to *know*. I did not know. So I threw myself on the mercy of my oldest Danish friend and mother of three, Veteran Viking.

'We'll make a list,' she told me: 'Come for coffee at 16.00.'

Coffee? At 4 p.m.? Crikey, Danes are hardcore . . . Still, grateful, I accepted and arrived as instructed, notepad in hand, ready to be schooled.

'Number one, you need a *flyverdragt*,' Veteran Viking told me as she marched around the house, dodging cats, picking up stray clothing and sending texts simultaneously.

'A *flyverdragt*?' My rudimentary Danish had taught me that *flyver* was the verb 'to fly' and *dragt* meant 'suit'. 'My son needs a "flight suit"?' Were we staging a *Top Gun* prequel?

'*Flyverdragt* is the all-in-one snowsuit for winter.'

'Oh!' I scratched this into my notebook.

'Next: winter boots! Gore-Tex.' She banged together two weighty pieces of footwear to illustrate.

Having long evangelised about the virtues of technical outer-wear, I knew Lego Man would be thrilled by this.

'Boots they can get on and off easily – no laces.' This is because children have to have a good crack at dressing themselves for outside play from the age of two, she told me.

'Two?!'

'Two. Now, you need an *elefanthue*.'

'An . . . elephant hat?' I stared at Google Translate doubtfully.

'Yes.'

'Does it have a trunk?'

She looked at me as if I were an idiot, and not for the first time. A cat slunk past with a similar expression of disdain.

'What then? Flappy ears? Tusks?'

She rummaged in her youngest son's kit bag and pulled out . . . a balaclava. This is the 'elephant hat' all Danish children wear much of the year round in varying thicknesses – from cotton in spring to wool in winter.

'He needs *fingervanter*.' This translates to 'finger gloves'. As opposed to toe gloves, obviously . . . 'As well as thermals and, in spring and autumn, *termotøj*.' She wrenched out a nana-style quilted jacket and matching trousers. '*Termotøj* translates as warm clothes' – Danes like to be literal – 'not waterproof but *wind* resistant, so you may hear it called a "wind suit".'

I try not to snigger.

'Then there's *regntøj*,' she goes on. This translates as 'rain clothes'. 'Waterproof jackets and trousers for wet-but-not-freezing weather. Used all year around.'

Wet-but-not-freezing weather all year around? Great.

'From the supermarket is fine. And while you're there you can also get *gummistøvler*—'

'I know this one! Wellingtons!'

'That's right.' She gave me a brief smile, as though congratulating a child who's mastered a knife and fork. 'A pair for home and a pair for daycare is a good idea.' Some daycares have a drying cupboard – where you can hang up wet clothes between outdoor playtimes for a quick blast with a few dozen built-in hairdryers. Our daycare has nothing so fancy: we dry out our clothes with *air* and Viking spirit.

'Lastly', Veteran Viking told me, 'children needed *løbesko'* – which translates as 'running shoes' – 'for the few days of the year when it's not raining or cold.'

'Okay. And what about summer?'

'Just *less* of everything.'

'Sunhats?'

She shrugged. 'You can send one in but you can't make kids wear one. Plus pedagogues have a lot on' – she downs the rest of her coffee – 'so you're lucky if they get sunscreened.'

All these fair-haired children! Prime sunburn candidates! Future melanoma! I made a mental note to slather the redhead in factor 50 from April to October.

I looked at my list: a mere nine new items to procure and pack for the daycare run. It's fortunate second-hand shops rule in Denmark.

Once satisfied that I'd fully absorbed her sartorial schooling, Veteran Viking and her cat waved me off with a parting gift: 'We have a saying in Denmark: there's no such thing as bad weather, just the wrong clothes.'

I managed a weak smile. Vikings of all nationalities have variations on this mantra and calling the Nordics 'outdoorsy' is an understatement. In Norway, *friluftsliv* – or 'free air life' – is the most popular self-reported leisure 'activity' nationwide, with higher participation than all other sports activities combined.

During my last trip, I was alarmed to find Norwegians getting their *friluftsliv* on in weather so cold, my eyelashes froze.

Swedes love being outside so much that 25 per cent of the population are members of an official outdoor organisation, Friluftsfrämjandet, and many five-year-olds attend Saturday 'nature school'. Here mini-Swedes learn about life cycles, insect identification, forestry care and how to stay warm and dry outside in all weathers. 'Plus the more you know about nature, the more you care about the environment,' says Per Nilsson from the Swedish Environmental Protection Agency.

Studies have long shown that spending time outdoors can improve mental well-being, reduce stress, help with concentration and cooperation, and even out differences between low-achieving and high-achieving children.[1] 'And, most kids just do better outside,' says Pia at my children's daycare. 'They get outdoors and everything is easier for them. They transform.' In the wild, children have to use their imagination to create play, as there are no toys. Researchers in Norway have found improved motor skill development and less conflict when children are out in nature. 'Because kids don't have to fight for resources or equipment,' says Karen Marie Eid Kaarby from the Faculty of Teacher Education and International Studies at Oslo Metropolitan University: 'There are enough stones and twigs to go around for everyone.' So children are happier – and grown-ups are, too. 'Pedagogues are much more relaxed being out in nature,' says Karen Marie, 'so now we have more and more forest kindergartens, welcomed by parents and taken seriously by academics.'

Just as prison-guard-turned-pedagogue Kitta noted how playing in nature helped children learn how to use their bodies, the act of moulding and kneading nature's squelch – like mud or sand – can help develop the senses and movement. Francesco Vitrano, a child neuropsychiatrist, psychotherapist and lecturer at the University of Palermo, Italy, found that what's known as 'sensorimotor development' helps children to understand their bodily signals.[2] And then there's the pure unalloyed joy of just getting muddy.

When I was growing up, 'Don't get dirty!' was a popular parental catchphrase. Playing in mud, or sand, or getting grass stains, or climbing trees, or anything that might involve 'ruining' our clothes was a no-no. I never wore white growing up as it would 'only get dirty' (I was strongly discouraged from black, too – 'doesn't do our complexion any favours . . . '. Instead I grew up in pastel shades, which made me look like a boiled egg). So I'm determined to let my children get mucky if they want to. And it turns out that mud is good for our immune systems, as well as our souls.

Mud-loving researchers in Finland even 'transplanted' soil and vegetation from a forest floor to the playgrounds of four daycare centres. A month later, children showed signs of heightened microbial diversity on their skin and in their gut, as well as improved immune function.[3] In future, it may be possible to enrich the soil in playgrounds worldwide with beneficial organisms. But for now, parents and teachers work with what they have: the forest and homemade mud kitchens – in our case a few old pots and pans filled with soil and water. Or rather, just soil. The rain comes soon enough in the Nordic countries. But that's okay, too.

'Did you know,' I geek out at dinner after a day's research into the glories of 'weather', 'that raindrops release special, err, compounds that combine in the air we breathe? And inhaling these compounds improves our mood?'

'Why?' Lego Man is a details man.

I tell him I'll get back to him on this. After pudding, and consulting my printout, I announce that 'as water and air molecules collide, they create negative air ions'.[4]

'What are air ions?' the redhead demands.

Bugger.

'Um, well, air ions,' I read from the scientific paper with more confidence than I feel, 'make a molecule with an extra charge, and this can improve respiratory health and immunity, apparently . . .' The main take-home, I insist, is that Austrian scientists found walking in heavily ionised air boosted levels of a vital antibody in the lining of the mouth, nose and gut. 'So rain is "good". In fact, all weather is pretty good.'

'Thanks for that, Michael Fish . . .' Lego Man comments before loading the dishwasher like a racoon on meth (i.e. 'as normal').

Growing up, my aunt would send my cousins and I outside to 'run in the wind', which all felt rather *Wuthering Heights* on a blustery day. I always suspected that this was just to get us all out of her hair. But a 2021 study suggests she may have been a medical visionary. Scientists found that wind actually disperses bugs – so we're all better off being outside on a windy day than cooped up at home. During Covid-19, when we were only allowed to socialise outside, researchers from Stony Brook University had a hunch that slower wind speeds might be associated with increased risk of transmission. They studied Covid cases and average wind speed. And what do you know? It turned out people weren't nearly as susceptible to catching the virus when it was windy out.[5] Wind = nature's air purifier. Fortuitously, it's often windy in Denmark. And wet. And grey. But that's okay.

'You can't wait for a sunny day in life,' says Lasse Heimdal, formerly of Norway's Friluftsliv Association. Lasse is now harnessing *friluftsliv* to help people through the challenges of modern life in Norway's answer to the Samaritans. 'When it's snowing and rainy, we still go outside – we had to historically to survive.' He tells me how, for hundreds of years, this instinct has been honed: 'Those who fell in love with someone strong would survive in nature. Their children would survive in nature. So even today, for example, being super-skinny is not the goal in Norway: the goal is to be fit and strong.' He looks at me, then adds: 'You'd survive!'

'Err, thanks.'

'Let's see your arms?'

I flex him the gun-show.

'There you go! You could stretch a bow or swing a club if you had to.'

This is the strangest compliment I've ever received. But I'll take it.

'Survival in nature, whatever the weather, is a big part of our culture,' Lasse goes on. 'You learn how to dress, how to handle the cold and dark, to walk long distances and live in a rough climate. Even kindergartners learn to use a map and compass, to light a fire and be outside all year around.'

From childhood, Nordics develop what Stanford University social psychologist Kari Leibowitz calls a 'positive wintertime mindset'. 'Because if we have this negative idea of winter and feel a sense of dread, we're not only making winter less enjoyable, we're also making the preceding season less enjoyable, too,' she tells me. A positive wintertime mindset, by contrast, frees up mental energy that might otherwise be spent 'dreading'. Instead of sitting indoors and cranking up the central heating to wish away winter, we'd be better off welcoming it. Because winter's coming – to all of us, every year, whether we want it to or not. Learning to *dress* the part is the first step – for parents as well as their small people, says Kari. 'In much of the world when it's cold, people still dress normally to go out, then wonder why they're uncomfortable.' But Vikings make no such rookie errors.

Since my first technical-outwear training session with Veteran Viking, I've had two more children. That means two more sets of flight suits, elephant hats and wool-based products. But I've still been reluctant to walk the walk myself. When I moved from the world of glossy fashion magazines to rural Denmark, I bought wellies. This was a big step. Since then, Lego Man has been slowly trying to kit me out in appropriate footwear, wet-weather wear and snow gear, but I have resisted, repeatedly. Until now.

Learning more from Lasse and Kari about the importance of dressing the part to truly #goviking, and aware that I haven't got a leg to stand on, asking my children to wriggle into winter suits while I prance about in a pleather jacket, I submit.

'Will you', I take a deep breath, addressing Lego Man, 'help me to get all the right outdoor kit?'

He looks like it's Christmas.

'I thought you'd never ask!' He swivels his laptop and opens several tabs that appear to have been bookmarked, possibly for years. 'Shall we start with outdoor trousers?'

'Must we?' I look down at my jeans. 'Won't these do?'

'No.' He clicks 'add to cart': 'You want hard-wearing, quick-drying and synthetic.'

'Aren't there any . . . nicer-looking ones?' I ask, still hopeful.

'Nothing looks as good as comfortable feels!' he tells me.

'I don't think that's what Kate Moss said . . .'

'Now you want an under layer. Not cotton.'

'Why?'

'GWSW,' he says, not looking up from his screen.

'Sorry?'

He sighs as though I am the most infuriating human that has ever lived. 'Gets wet, stays wet! No. What you need is something else—'

'Is it a spa day?' I'm really hoping it's 'a spa day'. Or 'cake'. It is not.

'Wicking'!' says Lego Man. 'Something synthetic to take sweat away from the body. Then you need a warming intermediate layer . . .' He's in his element. 'A good outer shell against wind and rain. Then some good hiking socks . . . you know what they say!'

'No.'

'No?'

'No! What do "they" say?'

'"Abrasions are a hiker's worst enemy"!'

'I've never heard anyone say that.'

He looks at me as if to say 'your loss', and the order is placed.

A week later, packages arrive and I am kitted out with wicking layers, waterproof trousers, a waterproof yet breathable jacket, hat, socks and walking boots. I look like a ~~bellend~~ walking North Face shop, but my children approve, and I notice there is far less griping over pulling on their own weather-appropriate gear now that I'm wearing it, too. Not everything is new – dba.dk and Reshopper have offered up some prize pre-loved items and Vikings can also *rent* technical outerwear. Almost every Norwegian has access to an 'outdoor library' to borrow anything from skates to skis, cooking equipment and tents. Katja in Helsinki tells me that dressing the part is obligatory in Finland, too. 'One friend has her own "sock bar" in the hallway – with multiple pairs of wool socks in all sizes, on pegs, so everyone can take a pair and be ready to go on a hike. It's part of everyday life!'

I promise to fully commit to the ethos of 'no such thing as bad weather', despite crossing my fingers behind my back. This pledge is instantly put to the test when my family unanimously vote on a last-minute road trip to 'test' my new look in 'the great outdoors'.

As a rule, I do not like camping (because: camping) but my children love it. So, sometimes, there is tent action. This is one of those times. Camping in Denmark is perfectly safe, there are no dangerous animals apart from ticks, and you can often camp for free or stay in one of 2,000 wooden shelters dotted around. There are rules attached, naturally – so you can only spend one night in the same spot, must steer clear of roads and buildings, must take your litter with you, and when nature calls, you dig a hole. But other than that? You can roam wherever you like. This felt wonderfully liberating when we first began living Danishly. But in the other Nordic countries, this freedom is even more entrenched. 'The land belongs to all' isn't just a pithy slogan in Sweden – it's part of the constitution. *Allemansrätten,* or 'the right of public access' allows everyone to roam freely by law, and the Norwegian government has funded a campaign to increase awareness of the right of public access and promote *friluftsliv* for everyone. 'Parents not born into this culture may not be as comfortable getting dressed up to go outside in all weather,' says Bente Liers, now general secretary of Norway's Friluftsliv Association, 'so we create many initiatives to invite people in, to show how helpful *friluftsliv* can be and the benefits it can bring for whole families.'

Exposure to 'green space' has been shown to lower cholesterol, reduce stress and spark creativity, while sunlight boosts serotonin and melatonin to improve sleep.[6] And yet, three-quarters of UK children spend less time outside than prison inmates.[7]

I was one of those 'indoor kids'. I liked books. And TV. And walls. And sofas. Only if I want to raise Vikings, I have to overcome my natural impulse to burrow under a duvet when it's wet and windy out. But how?

Lego Man is no help here: *adopts hearty Yorkshire accent* 'Just strap on your boots and get out there,' he tells me, not saying but strongly implying: *'you big southern softy!'* He likes to think of himself as an honorary Viking, since 'Yorkshire and the River Tees were very significant in the Viking period'. Which is great, for him. But it doesn't help me.

Fortunately, Norwegian friends have a better idea: bribery.

'I always recommend chocolate, nuts and raisins for a hike,' says Lasse. 'Food is a big motivation for many,' agrees Bente. 'When we talk to kids who aren't so keen on the idea of *friluftsliv* – or people from cultures where this isn't the norm – as soon as food comes into the equation, they're big fans.' Several packs of trail mix and emergency 'motivational chocolate' later and we're on our way.

There's a citrusy tang of pine and the birdsong is louder out here, in no-woman's land. While Lego Man is driving, I look at the scant details available about our destination and read:

What's included: firewood.

What's not included: essentials.

Skylarks flutter as we drive – me, Lego Man, the redhead,

the twins, the dog – and I transport about 150 down jackets, wicking layers, a camping stove, several sporks (spoon-forks), pasta and porridge oats.

We hike for thirty minutes from the car to where Lego Man decrees is 'the perfect spot' to pitch a tent. But blisters? Not one.

Appropriate outerwear: check.

In the forest the air is clear. The children throw sticks and balance along fallen tree trunks.

Nature's playground: check.

We graze on wild blackberries as we go, stopping to feast on chocolate rations whenever morale is flagging.

Food as friluftsliv *motivation: check.*

There is an emergency 'outdoor bathroom break'. Once we've dug, buried, wiped, etc., we go on our way.

Call of nature: check.

A child complains of itching. There is an inspection to reveal . . . a tick. With the aid of a phone torch and Swiss Army knife tweezers, I remove a tick from somewhere unmentionable.*

Roughing it, contrary to indoor-kid 'southern softy' disposition: check.

Since becoming a parent, I've slowly realised that I'm stronger – mentally and physically – than I ever believed I could be growing up. Not only can I push an *actual human being* out of an impossibly small orifice, I can raise one, too. I can leave the house without wearing a vest if I want to (though it's Denmark: why would I?). I can get dirty and survive without a shower for twenty-four hours. I can neglect Netflix or my

---

* A bumhole. I had to remove a tick from a kid's arse. My life is non-stop glamour.

fancy coffee machine for days and no one dies! This has been a self-parenting revelation. Someone hire a blimp! Tell the world: I am tough! I can even handle ticks now *fights wave of nausea at the memory, wins, just . . .*

When we arrive, the twins experience a sudden surge of energy, running up and down forest slopes enjoying 'nature's parkour'. Then it rains. We get the tent up. Or rather, I think we do. Only apparently, I've done one of my poles wrong.

'It's structurally unsound!' Lego Man tells me.

'You'll be structurally unsound in a minute,' I grumble as rain lashes down.

He fixes the faulty pole. ('It's not the pole that's faulty, it's your assembly,' he tells me. 'How's the air up there on your massive high horse?' I manage through gritted teeth. He flicks mud at me. I fling a whole clod at him. He tells me I'm being 'unreasonable'. I tell him he smells like a teenage boy's car. We call it quits.)

The rain stops. And then there is mud. Lots of mud.

My daughter makes mud pies.

'Old friends' and health-promoting microorganisms: check.

The rain eases off, we cook over the campfire, wash up in fresh rainwater and sing, inexplicably, the title track of UB40's 1986 album *Rat in the Kitchen*.

We sleep like logs and make it home in one piece, loaded with good ions. And possibly roundworm.

But were we cold? Not once.

'Because you dressed the part!' Peter Schmeichel nods approvingly when I recount our adventure. He's a huge admirer of Lego Man's outdoorsy exploits, although we both agree that my husband must never find out, lest he become insufferably smug. 'Do you know, we have a saying in Denmark: "There's no such thing as bad weather, just the wrong clothes"?'

'Yes,' I tell him. 'A few people *might* have mentioned this . . .'

What I've learned about how to raise a Viking outdoors, in all weathers

1. The weather's often awful, so we might as well get out there. Hippos were right: mud is marvellous for multiple modern malaise; rain makes magic; and wind blows away bugs as well as cobwebs.
2. I might be an indoor girl at heart, but there's plenty of science to show that getting outside is good for us. When in Viking land, I've resolved to do as Vikings do (and even *like* some aspects of it now).
3. Dressing the part helps. 'You enjoy it so much more and stay out for longer if you're well prepared and comfortable,' says Kari. 'Enjoy' is a strong word but I'm certainly more comfortable. Ordinarily, I run cold. Combine this with 'wet' (see Danish weather) and 'bugs', and it's a recipe for misery. But if I'm warm and dry? Turns out I'm a different person. Whole pieces of what I've taken to be my personality-jigsaw up until this point are gone. Am I . . . 'hardy' now? Outdoorsy, even? I am Viking, hear me roar! Turns out Gore-Tex is the new black.
4. Still, pack snacks. 'It's important to bring food that gives you a lot of calories,' Lasse tells me. But what food fuels Vikings? Well, loosen your belt . . .

6

Foraging and Family Meals

I'M SHELLING PEAS with salty hands. Sweet and salt combine as I squint in the sunshine to watch five-year-olds – buckets dangling from elbows, ankle-deep in cold Baltic water – scanning for mussels. The eldest has gone up the lane with a twenty-kroner coin to buy a punnet of strawberries from the honesty stall, and it occurs to me that this is a far cry from the snacks of my youth.

Not a salt-and-vinegar Hula Hoop in sight . . .

I grew up in the 1980s and 1990s in a household where the main food groups seemed to be Frusli bars and All-Bran. No child needs All-Bran. But fibre was king and what was I going to do? Hula Hoops, though, were ('are') the holy grail. Whenever I could find a classmate to do swapsies ('Who wants a Frusli bar? Anyone? Anyone?') Hula Hoops would be my goal. It was also the era of the Pop-Tart. Squeezy cheese. Findus Crispy Pancakes. All the processed delights. But not in Denmark. Danes ate real food. And they still do, for the most part.

'We like to think we're pretty healthy,' my chatty neighbour tells me – and food is good here. My friend Tracii from Los Angeles calls it 'basic with sauce' – 'everything is fresh so it tastes so good and goes bad so fast'. He's right, it does. All fresh produce in Denmark is like an avocado: delicious for a day. Two, max. 'After that? Screwed.' This is because Denmark has the highest per capita consumption of organic food in the world[1] (Sweden and Norway also make the top ten[2]). An agricultural nation until a couple of generations ago, there's still a connection with the earth for many. Since 1889, Denmark has celebrated 'potato week' every October, when children were kept home to help with the harvest. Although far fewer work on the land today, the tradition persists, and schools shut in week forty-two of every year (Danes love a week number).

Once we've survived another Nordic winter and the sun begins warming the land in May, everyone eats Danish strawberries and peas. June means new potatoes, often sold by the roadside (before harvesting the 'old potatoes' in autumn). And there's a year-round culture of stick-to-your-ribs food, starting young.

My first lesson in how to feed a Viking came when the miniature redhead started *vuggestue*. All under-threes are given daily meals that are 90 per cent organic. I was never sure what these consisted of, and my son couldn't tell me much, so I usually guessed from the colour of his clothes what had been on the menu that day. A weekly 'food diary' looked something like this:

Monday: brown
Tuesday: green
Wednesday: red
Thursday: pink
Friday: yellow

Eventually I asked Pia the pedagogue for the foodie lowdown.

'Any child arriving before 7.30 a.m. is offered breakfast or *morgenmad* – normally oats with milk.'

'You mean porridge?'

'No: oats. With milk.'

This, I discovered, is A Thing in Denmark. 'But there's a technique to it,' says Trine Hahnemann, legendary Danish chef and owner of Hahnemann's Køkken bakery and cooking school in Copenhagen. She confides in me the secret to this most hallowed of children's breakfasts: 'You make a mountain of oats, and then you sprinkle a little sugar on top to be the snow [my daycare skips this part]. Then you make a river around it with milk and slowly fold in the raw oats. Kids love it.'

'Mid-morning snack' is served around 8.30 a.m. (yep: 8.30 is 'mid-morning' in Denmark. Vikings have been up for *hours*) and consists of fruit, crudités and homemade bread rolls, or rye bread in neat triangles. Lunch is served at around 10.45 ('10.45 *a.m.*?' ask my in-laws, for whom this is too early even for breakfast). This might be fish or meat with potatoes and vegetables, soup, pasta, *frikadeller* (meatballs) or *fiske frikadeller* ('fish meatballs' – Danish is a direct language). A couple of days a week, it's a more low-key *smørrebrød* open sandwich with egg, salmon, mackerel, beetroot (aka pink clothes and 'alarming pee day') or *leverpostej* (liver pâté). Yes, when American kids are having PB&J, Danish children are munching on a thick slab of pork liver and lard.

'Since the Second World War, liver pâté has been kid food in Denmark,' Trine explains. 'Pork-production industries have had huge advertising behind us all eating the meat in Denmark and there's a lot of fat and liver leftover.' Denmark tends to export the more expensive meat, 'But Danish Crown paid for advertising to make us think the rest of it was a good idea, too,' says Trine – thus the pâté.* The most dedicated Danes make their own. 'You grind the liver and add the fat, then you boil this down to make a roux, and bake it in water,' Trine tells me. I'll take her word for it. Trine lived in London when her son was an infant but imported a lot of Nordic customs: 'To bring Denmark with me!' Top priority was making her own rye bread.

'I couldn't find it in the UK then and felt like rye bread was the core of being Danish – so I baked it.' A few years later, Trine moved to the US, where she had a daughter. 'Suddenly there were these great supermarkets and all this choice, but I still wanted rye bread, so I had to be part of a co-op in Virginia to buy my own cracked rye and make it.' It's impossible to overstate the importance of rye bread in Denmark. It is a staple. It is delicious. It is, in the words of Oprah, 'like eating a slice of the earth'. Give us this day our daily bread and let it be rye.

When a child reaches *børnehave* age in Denmark at around three, many parents enter the dreaded (for me) lunchbox territory.

'My parents were very good at packed lunches,' says Nanna from the parenting community Momkind. 'Dad would make my lunches and put in a little drawing each day; it meant a lot to me. I always had freshly baked bread, but some of my friends would have the same thing every day: *ostehaps* (Danish soft-cheese portions), *spegepølse* (salami), *leverpostej* (pâté) on rye bread, carrots, peppers and cucumber.' It's the same in our

---

* Danish Crown, a pork-focused food company, also paid for advertising that made us think a rasher of bacon was an essential part of the British breakfast, says Trine.

house. The monotony of daily lunchboxes is a ~~slog, pain in the arse~~ challenge. I can't even make up for my pitiful culinary abilities by slinging in a pack of salt-and-vinegar Hula Hoops in Denmark, either. I mention crisps as a lunchbox staple of my youth, only to be met by snorts of derision.

'You British and your potato chips!' daycare dad Peter Schmeichel shakes his head.

What?!

I speak to Line, a Danish mum of three married to a Brit. I ask how the two food cultures compare and she says, straight off the bat: 'English kids get given a lot of snacks on the way home from school – like crisps! That is unheard of in Denmark, at least, if you want to be a good parent . . .'

Ouch!

I ask my friend Rikke, who has two children, a full-time job, a microbrewery and a mischievous twinkle in her eye at all times. Rikke also spent a decade in the UK. Her overriding impression of children in the motherland?

'I remember thinking they ate a lot of crisps . . .'

What is going on? Can our reputation for salty potato snacks really precede us?

I ask Trine what she noticed about the way UK parents fed their children and she answers instantly: 'Crisps! I saw them all eating crisps in the playground!' I blush the colour of Walker's Smoky Bacon. 'We don't do that here,' she breaks it to me gently.

In Denmark, you can't even buy individual bags of crisps (believe me, I've tried). This makes it a less easy snacking option – 'Because what are you going to do?' asks Peter Schmeichel. 'Open a family-sized packet and eat them all?'

I take longer than is optimal to say: 'No. Of course not . . .'

In truth, my approach to snacking (especially pre-menstrual snacking) is very much 'Everything Everywhere All at Once'. But Danes prefer three solid meals a day.

'For Vikings, lunch has to contain proper filling food,' says my friend Andreas, a ridiculously kind and gentle deputy head-teacher and Scout leader in Denmark, who works a lot with exchange students throughout the Nordics. He tells me how American or British children often turn up with a packed lunch of white bread and shiny square cheese sandwiches – 'And they can't last the day! There's not enough energy in that to keep going!' White bread is made from refined wheat flour, has a high glycaemic index and can lead to blood-sugar spikes. After which, we experience a sugar crash and feel awful. Rye bread, on the other hand, has a lower glycaemic index, takes longer to digest and doesn't cause our blood sugar to rise as rapidly. 'Despite all the clichés about rye bread and herring, at least Viking kids have fuel,' says Andreas, 'and children who are well fed can participate and concentrate.'

With this in mind, Sweden and Finland provide free school lunches for all pupils. Sweden introduced daily cooked meals in the 1940s and began charting the impact that this had. Researchers from Lund University found that both boys and girls who received school meals during the entire nine years of compulsory school grew almost 1cm taller, were more likely to go to university, and even had a 3 per cent higher lifetime income – purely because they could concentrate more and so got higher-paying jobs. Children from poorer households bene-fited the most from the free school meals, achieving a 6 per cent higher lifetime income than those without.[3]

'We've got it good in Sweden,' agrees Jacob Holmström, father of two and Michelin-starred chef, formerly of Gastrologik.

'There's a cooked breakfast at school, a healthy snack and lunch cooked on the premises – which is really important for me.' Despite shipping and global culinary trends, many Swedes stick to the seasons and eat according to what's growing – something that filters down to school lunches, too.

'The Swedish approach is about seasonal, local and organic,' explains Uppsala-based food writer and mother of two Liselotte Forslin. 'We love to forage; picking nettles and wild garlic in spring; blueberries and cloudberries in summer; and mushrooms and lingonberries in autumn. It's totally normal to spot a family in the woods with plastic buckets picking berries and mushrooms.' There's a respect for food and nothing is wasted. The National Food Agency's website actively dissuades Swedes from throwing away food, with thrifty tips that include freezing leftover pasta and 'using shrivelled vegetables in stew'.

Mmm . . .

Finland takes food equally seriously. 'Kids get proper hot food every day, *for free*,' says Katja, who is now raising her son in Helsinki but grew up in Canada. 'You wouldn't get that in North America. But in Finland it's taken for granted. People still like to complain, but we're talking real First World problems, like, "Oh, my free school lunch isn't as varied as I'd have hoped!"? We know we've got it good, too!'

What's more, Vikings learn their way around a kitchen from an early age. Once a week, there is 'Food Lab' and the mini redhead can now muster up scrambled eggs and porridge by himself. 'Then from around the age of around nine or ten, many kids cook once a week at home,' says Nanna. 'That's what I did growing up and so did my brother and sister.'

This is excellent news. With three children, I might only have to cook twice a week soon. At present, I am the reluctant weekday chef, with a selection of underwhelming dishes on rotation. Lego Man bakes (dangerously well) and does occasional weekend dinners, when it doesn't matter if we don't eat before midnight. He makes delicious food, but it takes a while and involves a lot of swearing. Something I now blame partly on his schooling.

'Boys all learn to cook properly at school in Sweden,' chef Jacob tells me. 'Each classroom had a kitchen outside; it was tiny but built for purpose. So once a week we cooked. It was normal – we loved it.' A UK study found that getting kids involved in cooking can help encourage healthier eating habits, since 14 per cent of British five-year-olds are now obese. By the age of eleven, this rises to 25.5 per cent in the UK.[4] In the US, it's one in five across the board.[5] In Denmark? It's 5 per cent.[6]

But things may be changing. Researchers from the University of Copenhagen have found that having overweight parents makes children more prone to weight gain,[7] and in Denmark, adult obesity has doubled in the past decade to 18 per cent (though for scale, in the US it's 42 per cent).[8] When I moved to Denmark in 2013, there were far fewer prepackaged snacks available. But there's been a rise in ultra-processed foods on Danish shelves in recent years – just as elsewhere. And a diet high in ultra-processed foods has been shown to lead to weight gain.[9] A 2022 study found that 13 per cent of Danish children were now overweight (but not obese).[10] There isn't currently World Health Organization data on childhood obesity in Finland or Iceland, but in Norway 6–7.5 per cent of children are obese and in Sweden it's 6–10 per cent.[11] 'It's something we're keeping an eye on,' says Peter Schmeichel, who, fittingly, works in fitness. 'Though it's more about staying active and eating proper food than dieting or carb-cutting crazes. No Dane would let you take away their rye bread!'

Rye bread makes a second appearance in the daily diet of Danish children as an afternoon snack, provided at around 2.30 p.m., along with crudités and fruit. And then? Everyone goes home to eat dinner together as a family.

'I think this is one thing Denmark really gets right,' says Trine Hahnemann. 'Everyone goes to kindergarten growing up, there are certain opening hours, and these have defined the way we work in Denmark. So even the CEO of Lego is allowed to say in a meeting at 4 p.m., "I have to leave now to pick up the kids." And they can just go home, to eat together as a family – every day. In Denmark we have created family time – between picking up the kids by 4 p.m. until around 7 p.m. After children have gone to bed, you might do more work then, or do sports – but family time is sacred,' says Trine.

'Meals are something you have sitting together, to talk about the day,' agrees Nanna. 'We would never, ever eat in front of the TV. We always ate around the table growing up – so I do the same with my kids.' Finns, Icelanders, Norwegians and Swedes also prioritise family mealtimes. 'Having dinner with the whole family is key to the Swedish way of life,' confirms Liselotte. 'Men cook, too – my husband just opens the fridge and makes something terrific out of leftovers. Whoever has time just *does* it. We share the cooking and eat together around a table. Every day.' Unlike back home.

In our old life, Lego Man or I would regularly be shovelling something into our mouths with one hand while clutching the remote or a phone with the other. Dinnertime conversations would run along the lines of: 'Want food?' 'No thanks, I ate earlier. At the fridge . . .' But this won't do in Denmark, where 'life around the table' is prized. 'At dinnertime, you leave your phones in another room, shut your laptop and sit down together to eat,' says my Veteran Viking friend. She tells me this while confiscating an iPad from her youngest and texting her middle child to lay the table, but the point still stands: Vikings believe it's vital for all children to be part of family mealtimes. And it starts from birth. Most Danish homes are centred around a dining table for the express purpose of prioritising family mealtimes. A large wooden table that fits eight diners is the norm, accompanied by the ubiquitous Stokke chair.

'What's a Stokke?' I hear you ask.

Great question. Take a seat – pull up a Tripp Trapp in fact.

Tripp Trapp is the highchair designed by Norwegian industrial designer Peter Opsvik back in 1972 – now in thirteen million homes worldwide. He wanted something to help his toddler son to sit in a natural way at the grown-ups' table. Tricky, since a three-year-old is half the height of an adult. So he created a chair with an adjustable seat and footrest to grow with the child, from eight months to twelve years. Sitting at eye level with adults at the table helps children interact as 'equals', strengthening connections and a sense of belonging to the family 'team'. Conventional highchairs tend to be fitted with a harness and tray, suggesting children are 'too messy' to share a table with the grown-ups. 'But having a tray is actually less safe,' Peter tells me, 'since a child has to climb over the tray to get in it.' So the Tripp Trapp encourages independence and autonomy, 'Because why shouldn't children be allowed to get up and down?' This approach is at odds with many parenting practices, and Stokke was forced to make a tray for the US market, where the legislation demands both tray and harness. But Peter isn't a fan: 'Safety belts are used in case of a collision or sudden break in speed – adults do not use a harness when sitting in chairs. So why strap a child into a seat? A child that objects to sitting does not become calmer by a harness.'

This much is true. I've witnessed great brutes of three-year-olds being hauled up and placed inside vast plastic contraptions back home, strapped in, kicking and screaming.

But in Denmark, everyone opts for the Tripp Trapp instead – with many homes having more than one. 'I inherited one and bought one for my kids,' Nanna tells me. 'They last so long and they're such high quality that there's no shame in passing one down or buying second hand.' Travelling around Norway, Sweden, Iceland and parts of Finland, I see the same trend play out. The design hasn't changed since 1973 and Tripp Trapp chairs are always listed under the 'wanted' column in the classified ads. In fact, the greatest competition facing Tripp Trapp in the Nordic countries is second-hand Tripp Trapp chairs. So when I became a parent, there was only one option. And thanks to the hand-me-down culture, I ended up with three Tripp Trapps. There's also a baby unit for newborns now – meaning that my three have been at the dinner table since they were a week old.

As well as making over mealtimes, the Tripp Trapp transformed daycare centres. Nurseries and kindergartens used to be furnished with low tables and small chairs. But in Scandinavia, most institutions now have grown-up sized tables and Tripp Trapp chairs. 'This improves the relationship between adults and children – of all different sizes,' Pia tells me. 'And an added benefit is that we don't have to bend down to the level of low tables all the time, so it saves our backs!'

The iconic design – minimalist, angular and 1970s-cool – also helps mini-Vikings develop an early appreciation for aesthetics. 'I think in the Nordic countries children grow up with design literacy – it becomes normal,' says Nanna. In Denmark, your average home looks like something out of an interior-design magazine, with white walls, wooden floors, uncluttered surfaces and smart, designer touches (not mine: mine's a mess).

Furnishings tend to be made from natural materials, tactile to the touch, with lots of wood, leather, wool and sheepskin – aka *hygge*. This is the strange, untranslatable word Danes have been using for centuries that the rest of the world has finally caught on to. Because cosiness matters in Denmark. Lighting is a key component, and Danes burn the highest number of candles per head in Europe. It's always someone's job to light them. 'From about the age of three, we got the kids to do it in our house,' Veteran Viking tells me casually.

Toddlers and matches – what could go wrong?

Pre-dinner, someone will light candles, someone else might set the table – napkins, knives and forks, crockery, the lot – and then you'll all come together. Probably on a Tripp Trapp. And everyone's at it.

'In the UK and the US, so much of food culture is defined by class,' says Trine, 'but Denmark has been so homogenous for so long that people eat the same way. Many still have a connection to farms, growing up with grandparents who had two pigs and a cow – a trend that only started disappearing in the 1980s.' Meat still rules for modern Vikings, with pork and potatoes daily staples in much of Denmark. The Swedes love a meatball (obviously) and there's the running joke that 'Icelanders drink so much because the food's so bad'. Having tried *hakarl*, or fermented shark, *hrútspungar* – sour ram testicles – and even *svið*, or sheep's head, I can see where they're coming from. Though to be fair, Iceland has a landscape so barren that nothing grows. Finland, Iceland and Denmark have been ranked third in a global meat-eating table – and in Norway, consumption of meat has doubled in forty years. What's more, Vikings LOVE a hotdog – or *pølser* in Danish.

Wagons selling *pølser* in pre-sliced white buns or hollowed-out baguettes attract lines of Danes, perusing a 'menu' of sauces, all milked out of dangling rubber teats. These range from your standard ketchup, to 'klassisk brown' and *remoulade*, a Danish condiment that Whitestrips-bright American Mom describes as 'like mayonnaise but gross'. And yes, these are about as appetising as they sound. But *pølser* are available at every petrol station, every kiosk, every IKEA, and every child's birthday party – grilled outside in summer and cooked inside in winter. There's no time when a hotdog *isn't* appropriate for Vikings. Icelanders like a *pylsur* or lamb-based version. Swedish children are raised on *falukorv* – a firetruck-red hyper-processed mixture of miscellaneous meats. Danes and Norwegians have *ventepølse* – or 'waiting sausage' – eaten around the grill while you wait for the main-event sausage to cook or in line at the *pølsevogne* or 'sausage wagon'. Finns even have a special term for the queue to buy their processed-meat snack from one of the ubiq-uitous stalls: the *grillijono* or 'grill queue'.

Lego Man is delighted by all this.

'Who doesn't love a "waiting sausage" in the "grill queue"?'

'Err, cardiologists?'

There have been attempts to wean Danes off their wieners. In 2011, Denmark introduced a tax on saturated fat in foods – the first country in the world to do so – with a planned tax on foods with added sugar. Lego, the bastion of Danishness, even had a 'sugar sheriff', purging the company of sweet treats and replacing them with crudités and rye bread. But the company expanded, sugar standards slipped and *snegle* – delicious snail-shaped Danish pastries – won out.* The fat tax was scrapped and today, Lego has its own in-house *konditori* selling Denmark's world famous *wienerbrød* (aka Danish pastries) for all the *hygge* coffee breaks (or *kaffepause*). Coffee with cake is part of daily life in Denmark and even the smallest conurbation in Denmark will have a bakery. Over the past decade, I have selflessly conducted extensive pastry 'research'. In addition to *snegle*, I can recommend rum balls, made out of all the cakes that bakers haven't sold the day before, and Napoleon's hat – a chocolate-bottomed, marzipan-filled cake that dates back to 1856, when Denmark sided with Napoleon (and so made a marzipan hat to celebrate). But Danes don't just eat a lot of buns, they bake them, too.

Sales of yeast and flour continue to grow year on year in Denmark, and while the rest of the world stockpiled toilet paper during the pandemic, Danes went wild in the aisles for *yeast*. There were no lengths Danes wouldn't go to in search of the grey stuff, and bumper stickers spotted during this time summed up the feelings of a nation: *Keep Calm and Carry on Baking*. Whereas fresh yeast is hard to come by in the US and the UK, in Denmark it's everywhere – from the biggest supermarket to the tiniest corner shop (or 'kiosk').

But does it make a difference? Can a squishy grey square that smells like old shoes really make buns taste better?

Lego Man looks affronted: '*Categorically!*'

---

* There is still a 'chocolate tax' with cocoa delights, as well as marzipan and liquorice, all weirdly liable. But this hasn't done much to dissuade sweet-toothed Danes.

'How do you know?'

He holds up his favourite book. Forget *The Great Gatsby* or *Catch-22*: Lego Man loves Trine's 2014 classic *Scandinavian Baking*. A more well-thumbed, batter-splattered tome you cannot imagine.

'Just because Trine says so?'

He gasps as though I've suggested selling our firstborn for *snegle*: '*Just*? You take that back!'

I tell him I won't, but that he should bake something 'to prove it . . .'

Before I've finished the sentence, the oven is on and bags of flour are being slammed on the kitchen counter, sending up puffs of powder. The redhead volunteers to crumble a square of grey old-shoe-munge into a bowl, and I watch as my daughter measures out butter and sugar. The resulting dough is left to rise, and I peek at intervals.

'Is it . . . *bubbling*?' I ask, perturbed. Is the dough coming to life? It looks like we're about to recreate a scene from *Ghostbusters*. Am I going to be stuck with a Mr Stay-Puft on my hands?

But no, this is 'normal', I'm told. Once the fresh yeast has worked its magic and the dough has risen, cardamom, cinnamon and more sugar are combined. The children take turns to spread the brown paste over the dough, the kitchen surfaces and themselves. The dough is then rolled into a long sausage and sliced into discs, which, I'm assured, in ten minutes will puff into the lightest, most delicious cinnamon buns (*kanelsnegle*) imaginable.

Before we can eat them, Lego Man insists that we go on what he calls a 'nice long walk' to 'earn' our cake. I'm tasked with cajoling cinnamon-smeared children into rainsuits and miss the final alchemy whereby 'dough and munge' become 'buns'. But the smell is phenomenal. The children are buzzing and the dog is beside himself at the prospect of a walk. He starts whimpering, tail wagging, until we can get him out of the door, and we walk. Reluctantly (me), striding ahead with purpose (Lego Man) or oscillating between the two (the smalls). After an eternity, we reach the spot that has been designated 'snack time'. And then, from Lego Man's rucksack, comes a large Tupperware box, fogged up with condensation.

'Ta da!' My children are near purple with pride as they snap off the lid. And there, with the smell of sunshine after the rain in our nostrils, we feast. And honestly, I'm not sure anything has ever tasted so good. Not even Hula Hoops . . .

What I've learned about how to feed a Viking

1. Don't skip carbs. Or protein. Or fruit. Or veg. Danes eat three times a day, with a couple of snacks in between. There are still fewer fast-food options available in the Nordic countries than there are back home. Although it's far from one huge Wholefoods Market, my adopted countryfolk have taught me to eat more of the food our grandparents would have recognised, rather than ultra-processed fare.
2. . . . with one caveat: hotdogs. A weird wiener obsession unites all the Nordic countries. The next time I'm peckish pre-BBQ, I'll demand a 'waiting sausage', explaining that it's 'a hallowed Nordic tradition'.
3. Eating together and making it *hyggeligt* matters – we're talking candles, place settings, cutlery, crockery, the lot. Living on adrenaline for the first three decades of my life combined with the palate of a toddler means that

I've often overlooked the fine art of dining. I viewed refuelling as something functional, to be raced through. But since raising Vikings, I've learned the pleasure of lingering over a meal with friends and family. I'm even learning to appreciate the art of 'table-scaping' (even if I don't quite have the yearning or headspace to do it myself, yet). I am, as American Mom observed: 'Growing up, getting some self-respect and not eating cereal for dinner.' (Who, me?!) Welcome to culinary Valhalla.

7

Singing, *Samfundssind* and the Social Brain

THE WAVERING SOUNDS of a piano scale and a lot of throat-clearing greet me as I enter the hall. People huddle like penguins, my son among them, his red hair making him instantly identifiable in any crowd. After a preparatory chord, the pianist gives a nod and voices start up, of varying ability, tune and timbre. Little voices blend with bigger ones and the group exchange occasional smiles across the circle.

'Now earth and sky are still . . .' I can just make out the words, '. . . only the croaking of the distant frogs, and . . .' *What are they saying now?*

'"The lowing of the cows",' a woman in a parka helps me out. It's cold in the hall, but fortunately we're warmed by collective good cheer and the 3,000 calories we've just consumed at a local bake sale (it's Denmark: there's always cake).

'Thank you for the day . . .' They sing on as I attempt to join in, unsure of both tune and words: 'For the days to come and for those that lie behind.'

I look up to fully appreciate the moment, but everyone's already moved on. This happens a lot with me and Danish. I have little clue what's going on, but group singing is so big in Denmark that locals know all the lyrics by heart. Parka Woman, who turns out to be a history teacher, informs me after the final chord that I did 'quite well, for a foreigner'. I thank her and we get talking about why Danes are always breaking into song like they're in a musical (and I mean *always*). She tells me that this is a legacy of the late, great Danish poet, politician and clergyman, Nikolaj Frederik Severin Grundtvig (N. F. S. Grundtvig to his friends).

At the beginning of the nineteenth century, old N. F. S. decided he wanted to create a feeling of cohesion among Danes by giving public talks. During one of these in 1838, he talked about the Battle of Copenhagen and the heroism of his friend, the naval hero Peter Willemoes. N. F. S. Grundtvig had previously written a poem about Peter (he really liked Peter) called *Kommer hid, I piger små!* or, somewhat creepily, 'Come here, you little girls!' The poem was intended to summon ladyfolk to celebrate Peter, who was a 'friend of all beautiful girls' (we *all* know a Peter). A composer came up with a melody to accompany the poem and the crowd got so excited that they jumped off their seats and spontaneously started singing. And the Danish institution of group singing was born.

'Today it's quite common to sing together at schools, offices, community events, voluntary organisations or sports associations,' says Kristian Kongshøj, a political scientist from Aalborg University, when I get in touch to find out more. 'We do it as a way to begin a meeting. Or end a meeting. Or both.'

Well, this sounds jolly! I think. Many schools still have group singing every morning for ten to fifteen minutes, with parents invited to join in. 'My mum and dad would always come for this,' says my friend and fellow twin mum, Annika. 'It was a lovely way to start the day.'

But it serves a purpose, too. 'When we all sing, we experience a feeling of togetherness,' Kristian tells me. 'We are involved in something larger than ourselves. We are present, in a "flow state", and we feel that the world speaks back to us in some way. This is what singing is – being in tune with others in a social activity that goes beyond ourselves.'

All Danes are familiar with the *Højskolesangbogen*, or *High-School Songbook* – a collection of 601 total bangers, which regularly tops Denmark's bestseller list. Old songs deemed irrelevant are occasionally phased out, with new ones added to reflect modern Denmark. Now in its nineteenth edition, the most recent songbook includes 'Ramadan in Copenhagen' by rapper Isam B, as well as songs about climate change, existential crises and divorce.

Less jolly, but still . . .

'All this helps build community,' says Kristian. Joining together in song has been proven to release the bonding hormone oxytocin, which lowers stress, while the synchronicity of breathing together creates feelings of connectedness, according to studies from Oxford Brookes University.[1] Some argue that group singing is also an exercise in democracy, since several voices can express themselves at the same time without conflict. Plus the voice is free, unlike other instruments, and everyone has the same access.

The role of community singing in national identity has long been recognised in Denmark, and a study from Aarhus University found that singing not only helps strengthen feelings of community, but also *constructs* community and feelings of social cohesion.

During the pandemic, Danish choirmaster Phillip Faber led daily singalongs on DRTV to boost morale (I told you choir leaders were all-powerful in Denmark). In his book *Den danske sang,* Phillip describes how all Danes have a collective repertoire of around 100 songs and hymns that nearly everyone can sing – even if they haven't sung them in years. So I meet Phillip to find out more. On a rainy afternoon when all I want to do is curl up with a cup of tea. And he is human sunshine.

'I always took it for granted that a group could just start singing in unison,' Phillip tells me, 'but it's actually a really special thing in Denmark. Neighbouring countries don't have this, I discovered.' In every choir concert Phillip leads, there is a community singsong in the middle where everyone joins in. 'If I have guests from overseas, they always ask at this part, "Is this your national hymn?" "No," I tell them. Then they'll ask: "Is it the second most loved song in the country?" "Nope, it's just one of many that everyone knows." The next question they'll ask is: "Do all Danes read music?"'

Do they?

'No!' Phillip laughs. 'It's just that everyone in Denmark can stand up and sing from a pond of 100 or so songs.'

Danes sing all the time – from around the Christmas tree, to around the bonfire, at school, at university, at work, and to get children to sleep. 'So there's this treasury of melodies that everyone knows, even in kindergarten.' Many of these are written by Denmark's national composer, Carl Nielsen, so they aren't simple 'children's songs'. But they are familiar to all.

This doesn't mean that everyone in Denmark sounds like Adele.

'Many confuse "group singing" with "beautiful-sounding choirs",' says Phillip, 'but it's the experience rather than the outcome that matters. It doesn't always sound good, but that's okay. It doesn't have to. That's not what it's for.'

What *is* it for, I wonder?

'It's about disappearing,' he tells me. 'In a world where everything is "me me me", singing together is like a starry night where you can see the Milky Way. You feel small and insignificant, but also not alone and as though you belong. It's the best feeling in the world.'

I used to sing in choirs, pre-children. Singing helped me through breakups, bereavements and the more banal bits of modern life.

There is a tradition of gathering to sing in times of crisis in Denmark, notably during the Second World War, says Phillip: 'So the tradition is there when we need it.' Televised *morgensang* – or 'morning song' – united Danes with a fifth of the country joining in daily during the pandemic, including the prime minister and Crown Princess Mary. 'It was a good fit, as group singing is about community spirit and we were all trying to pull together for the greater good – you didn't wear a mask for yourself: you wore it to protect someone else.' And at this most delicate of times, Denmark's PM Mette Frederiksen emphasised another lynchpin of Danish togetherness: *samfundssind*. A compound noun of *samfund* (society) and *sind* (mind). The term *samfundssind* was first reported in the 1930s but fell out of use until 'someone somewhere fascinatingly decided to dig it up again to use in the prime minister's speech ahead of the first lockdown,' says Kristian. *Samfundssind* became the cornerstone of Denmark's response to the pandemic, named Word of the Year 2020 by the Danish Language Board.

There have been many discussions about why this term gained so much traction. 'It basically means "solidarity",' says Kristian, 'so why didn't we just say that?' He pauses. I'm hoping the question is rhetorical. I'm in luck: 'Well, "solidarity" is a bit left-wing; it has socialist overtones – even for Danes – and it suggests common interests, but in the pandemic, old people and young people *didn't* have the same interests. Young people had to stay in to protect old people. Whereas *samfundssind*, or community mindset, meant doing something that isn't necessarily best for you, but for the sake of others. For the greater good.'

And 'for the greater good' is the ethos behind another popular Danish institution: the Scouts. You may think you know Scouts from your youth, your children or even from books. But Viking Scouts is something else (just wait until Chapter 10). If the average Dane loves singing and *samfundssind*, then Scouts are *samfundssind* fundamentalists.

'There are expectations about what it is to be a good human, and Scouts agree to do their best to follow a pledge that includes being a good friend, being considerate and helping others, both in the family and in the wider society,' my friend Andreas the Scout leader tells me in the woods the following Wednesday (after a Scout meeting, I should add – this isn't a prerequisite for interviewees). 'It's a lot to ask of children as young as six, but kids learn to strive and be aware of other people as well as the world around them.'

I've been impressed and surprised by the new badges available for the redhead and his fellow Scouts to earn. Back when I was a Brownie and a Girl Guide, I was encouraged towards badges such as 'housework' (depicted by a broom), 'cooking' (a pan) and 'hostess' (a cup and saucer . . . kill me now . . .). But my son's patrol can work towards their 'rights' badge (a raised fist), or their 'comforter' badge (a crying eye), 'earned by developing their soft skills', I read from the website.

'As well as their "knife skills"?' Lego Man clarifies.

'The two aren't mutually exclusive in Denmark,' I tell him (because this is what Andreas told me). Despite the emphasis on being strong Vikings on the outside, on the *inside*, Danes are often *whispers it* soft. Not in a bad way, but in a gentle, caring, attuned-to-humanity way.

Danes have a *fri for mobberi* or 'free from bullying' programme for children up to nine years old, led by a purple bear who teaches tolerance, respect, care and courage. They learn to stand up for themselves and speak out when they see someone over-stepping boundaries. From birth, they're taught to care and be an ally.

Almost every adult Dane I know has been off on stress leave at one point – often as a preventative measure before they hit 'The Wall'. This isn't because work is particularly stressful in comparison to elsewhere (oh *hej*, thirty-three-hour working week!), but because everyone's at it. There's no shame in taking time out and returning after six months. Danes look after themselves (wieners aside) and I discover that the average Dane is in contact with doctors, dentists and medical specialists eleven times a year.

'Eleven?! That's practically a relationship,' Lego Man points out.

So are Vikings just armadillos? A tender heart concealed beneath a rugged exterior?

I call on Marie Helweg-Larsen, a native Dane turned professor of psychology at Dickinson College in the US, to find out more. I settle down with a tea and watch swans flying in a V-shape out of the window as Marie explains to me how Danish culture is governed by 'predominantly feminine ideals'.

'The genders are more equal in Denmark, and Danes in

general tend to agree with more feminine ideals – as do people in all the Nordic countries,' she explains. The Dutch social psychologist Geert Hofstede developed a framework for assessing different cultures and found that whereas countries like the UK and the US tend to rank highly on 'masculinity' as a cultural value and approach to life, Nordics typically *don't*. Sweden is ranked as the most 'feminine' society in the world, with Norway a close second. This means that the softer aspects of culture are valued and encouraged, like consensus, cooperation, collaboration and compromise. Taking care of the environment is also important, as is a good work/life balance.

The welfare safety net and Nordic culture as a whole is considered more caring and 'feminine' (whether we like this definition or not). More caring cultures look out for each other, as seen in the famous 'wallet study', where researchers dropped 17,000 wallets in cities around the world to test how often they were returned.[2] The Nordic countries came out top. In Denmark, more than 80 per cent of wallets with money in them were returned. And more caring countries are also happier, according to the World Happiness Report – with an understanding that we all have to play our part to build social connections.

Samfundssind is baked in to living Danishly. All activities, clubs and associations rely on the goodwill, time and effort of the community. Whereas UK or US clubs are often exclusive, Danish clubs are run by volunteers. 'Everyone is invested, so children grow up seeing their parents get off their butts and help,' explains my friend who looks like Peter Schmeichel. 'We don't just *tell* children to contribute – we show it.' But he can't hang around chatting: 'I've got basketball coaching later today, then toddler trampolining!'

Him, too? I can barely keep my head above water and I'm doing bugger-all for the local community. The seemingly never-ending list of stuff that needs doing exhausts me on a daily basis. How do people have the time?

'They prioritise,' Peter Schmeichel tells me, buckling his daughter onto the back of his bike. 'Rather than slumping in front of the TV or scrolling their phones, parents make a point of getting out there!'

I'm sure the thirty-three-hour working week helps . . .

'You'd be surprised,' he says. 'People do it even if they work longer hours. Even if they have big jobs.'

Like Diana.

When I mention to Danish friends that I'm writing about volunteering, they all tell me to 'talk to Diana'. I'm a little intimidated. Am I about to be *samfundssind*-shamed? (Clue: 'yes'.)

Diana Ringe Krogh is a vice-president of social responsibility at a major company. She's also parenting two children, has been on the board of the local gymnastics club, has organised annual gymnastics shows and fundraised for the gymnastics and football clubs. 'Then my husband – he's a teacher – coached football and gymnastics in his spare time.'

'Spare time?' *Wait one hot minute* . . . 'He was with children all day every day, then he came home to voluntarily help other people's children?'

'It's just what you do,' says Diana. 'Our grandparents volunteered, our parents volunteered – my dad still does and he's seventy-three.' Diana tells me how she grew up playing football, 'as well as coaching the younger kids and sitting on the board'.

'As a teenager?'

'Sure!'

This isn't unusual. Fellow twin mum Annika volunteers teaching swimming twice a week, runs 'movie club', organises gifts for the football coaches each year and is the class representative at school. 'If you want your children to go to an activity and you don't volunteer, then you don't have an activity,' is her rationale. Annika comes from a long line of volunteers and tells me that her parents ran the Scouts, gymnastics and the movie club – all while raising four children and working full time. 'You get a couple of places for free if you're the coach, so it meant that us kids could try out different things.' Annika tried handball, tennis, gymnastics, swimming, volleyball and karate before focusing on playing trumpet in a band. 'We practised three times a week and then played concerts for the community at the weekend.'

'All unpaid?'

'Of course!' She tells me her neighbour, aged seventy-five, organises board game nights at the nursing home and pushes wheelchairs, 'For the "old people" – she doesn't consider herself old. Helping out is just what you do.'

Studies show that having community-minded parents makes children more likely to volunteer. And research from Arizona State University found that parents who valued kindness and helpfulness above achievements and accomplishments had children with fewer symptoms of depression or low self-esteem.[3] The study concluded that being socially oriented makes for happier children – who, in turn, are more likely to be socially oriented.

Half of all Danish schools offer *legepatruljen* – or play patrol – where children volunteer to play with younger students during breaktimes. This has been proven to reduce bullying and foster friendships across classes. Children take it seriously, too, taking a training course before they can become 'play initiators' and arranging cover if they can't make their 'shift'. Which all sounds very noble.

'But there has been a change in recent years,' warns Diana. 'We are becoming more individually focused, just like elsewhere. Everyone pays high taxes in Denmark and there is sometimes the thought process of, "Isn't that enough?"'

It's not, I learn. A fellow international found this out the hard way when he tried throwing cash at the community-mindset conundrum, giving a generous donation to his son's sports club. 'I barely got a thank you!' he told me, confounded. Another parent took him aside and told him: 'They don't want your money – they want your time.' Because time is more precious.

'It's about care and involvement and effort,' says Diana, admitting that there's frustration when people from other cultures don't understand this. 'But it's never too late to start developing a community mindset – and it's never too early, either.' Diana's children joined her in fundraising for various charities as soon as they could walk. They also collect litter and help with a Christmas charity drive. 'Our kids are growing up in a society where they have everything, so we have to teach them about the importance of giving back. *Samfundssind* is a big part of being human.'

Family therapist and mother of three Sofie Münster chairs the education panel in Denmark's Ministry of Children and Social Affairs and recommends building *samfundssind* into daily discussions with children. Instead of just saying 'have a good day', she suggests: 'Remember to do something good for someone else today!' In the evenings, we should ask, 'Did you do something nice for someone else today?'

So the next morning, I try it. I tell the redhead: 'Remember to do something good for someone else today!'

'Is that the goal?' he asks. 'Not "no fighting"? Or "don't just eat raisins for lunch"?'

'Err . . .' Ideally, I'd like him to refrain from both hand-to-hand combat *and* an exclusively raisin diet, but beggars can't be choosers. 'Do you think you could maybe not fight *and* do something good?'

He thinks about this.

'I *might* be able to.' He nods seriously. 'But should I just relax about the raisins?'

'Sure . . .' *Mother of the Year Award, arriving yesterday.*

At pick-up, I ask: 'How was your day? Did you do something nice for someone else?'

To my delight, he nods.

'Daniel annoyed me, so I turned the other bum cheek,' he announces with pride.

'Sorry?' I fear my fleeting explanations of Bible idioms may have been inadequate.

'I didn't fight Daniel, okay?'

For a child uncompromising in his zeal for conflict, I acknowledge that this is a win of sorts. 'Okay! Great . . .'

'Anyway, what did you and Dad do for someone else today?' he asks, quite reasonably. I'm tempted to quip something about turning my own bum cheek but realise he's right: if we want to raise Vikings, we need to, in the words of the late, great Barry White, practise what we preach.

I used to volunteer before children and life took over, visiting elderly people in my local area for a charity called Age Concern. I played a lot of Scrabble, learned that 'tremendous character' was a euphemism for 'massive racist', and was once dumbfounded by a lovely lady called Ruby with a fierce competitive streak. In pursuit of a triple word score one Sunday, she began laying down tiles on an available 'c'. Next came 'u'. Then 'n'. I held my breath. *She wouldn't, would she?* She would. 'T' was carefully tapped into place before Ruby licked the end of her pencil and wrote: 'C, u, n, t. Eighteen points' – with all the satisfaction of a job well done. No modern-day volunteering is ever likely to live up to the highs of C-Bomb Ruby.

But we can try.

An opportunity presents itself that weekend at the five-year-olds' swimming lesson. This generally consists of one of us attempting not to be drowned (by Twin One, an aquaphobic limpet) and the other front crawling to keep up (with Twin Two, a dolphin). All while being shouted at in Danish by a teenage instructor and scowled at by his sidekick in tiny Speedos. For the past nine months of lessons, scowling sidekick has remained completely silent, spending thirty minutes every Sunday hanging on a pool noodle (*slange* in Danish or 'snake'). All he does is stare moodily into the middle distance, occasionally scratching a love bite. ('Shouty Instructor never has love bites,' Lego Man observes. 'Maybe that's why he's so shouty.')

Shouty Instructor tells us that he won't be here the following week as he's 'going to be ill'.

'Wait, what? He knows in advance?' Lego Man rasps, clamped at the neck by Twin One.

'I imagine it's the same way you're going to be "under the weather" after that stag do next month,' I wheeze, chasing Twin Two. There's a seal-like plunge as she breaks the surface of the water, reappearing at my side before I can take another stroke.

'So we need volunteers!' Shouty Instructor thunders.

'What's involved?' Lego Man bellows back on reflex.

I know what he's thinking: 'Will Love Bite step up? Could there be an opening for a daydreaming deputy dangling on a pool noodle?' Doubtless he'd enjoy that as a welcome break. But alas, they're after a bona fide instructor. A triangular-shaped swimming dad who brings his own nose clip to 'splash 'n' play' is selected as a replacement while my husband is thanked for his enthusiasm and put on 'another important job'. Namely: bin bags.

In Denmark, food waste goes into green bags, supplied by the municipality and delivered by various clubs or associations, paid by the council for taking the job off their hands. This means that new rolls of green bags can be delivered to your door by anyone from a preschooler to a CEO, helping to raise funds for their various clubs. It's a necessary if unglamorous job. But Lego Man isn't immediately sold.

'*Bin* bags? I'm on *refuse collection*? I've got a degree! I've got *two* degrees!'

I point out that I've also done my time on bin bags to raise money for my old choir and our son has done it for Scouts. 'None of us are too grand for bins in Denmark. Get on with it!'

With some grumbling, he does. That leaves me.

The news that preschoolers' ballet is cancelled due to lack of a teacher (early retirement, dodgy knee) is a blow. I loved ballet as a child and took classes as an adult before having children. My size-four satin shoes still dangle from their ribbon at the back of my wardrobe. *Could I . . . perhaps?*

'I can plié!' I write, fingers dancing over the keyboard. 'I remember most of the positions!' What could possibly go wrong? I mentally prepare for the fact that I may get 'green-bag duty' instead, but it feels good to offer.

All neurological research ever shows that we experience 'helpers' high' when we do something for someone else, and while it used to be believed that humans were innately selfish, scientists now agree that we are wired for empathy and built for community.[4] Teacher Louise tells me: 'We teach kids about *fællesskab* or "community" and its importance at school, too.' Teacher training has a curriculum around community, and lesson plans are expected to include it. And having a community mindset also means taking care of the natural environment.

Icelanders have a long tradition of activism, with 61 per cent taking part in some form of campaigning. In 1975, 90 per cent of Icelandic women went on strike to demand equal pay and rights, paving the way for the world's first democratically elected female president.[5] In 2019, Icelanders held a 'funeral' for a glacier lost to climate change with a Lorax-like plaque inscribed: 'A letter to the future'.[6] Swedish teenager Greta Thunberg sparked global protests about climate change because she saw that there was work to be done for the greater good. 'And becoming an activist gave me the feeling that I was not alone,' Greta told British diver Tom Daley on his podcast in 2023.[7] Danes stand up for their eco-rights, embracing wind power with a countryside stippled by wind turbines. There are disputes in the UK about these being a 'blot' on the landscape. But in Denmark they're accepted for the greater good. Wind power is now the country's number-one energy source. Okay, so the blustery weather makes me look as though I've emerged from a wind tunnel most days, but it's worth it.

Of course, Vikings aren't immune to the pressures of the modern world. There has been a growing movement towards individualisation, and Danish children have a hat-trick of near-unlimited freedom, an emphasis on autonomy and the influence of global culture.

'The decision on life choices has moved from the community to the family to the individual in Denmark,' says Rasmus Kjeldahl of Denmark's national association for children's rights, Børns Vilkår. 'We say, "My child has to decide for his or herself."' This is a challenge, since while some children may be ready, others may not: 'So we have to recognise that some children need more support, rather than more freedom.'

The Nordic countries aren't exempt from economic challenges, either. A Boston Consultancy Group report found that 73 per cent of people in the Nordic countries were worried about personal finances.[8] One in four households in Norway are now struggling to pay bills, while Swedish food prices are up 25 per cent.[9] 'People are more vulnerable than before,' says Diana, 'so some feel like they can't *also* give back to the community.'

'We have to be aware that we are living in an extraordinary time,' agrees Rasmus, 'but Denmark still offers the possibility of one of the best childhoods in the world. I'd still rather be a child in Denmark than anywhere else – because of *samfundssind* – because of the community.'

You're never totally alone as a parent in Denmark. Rather than just keeping an eye on your own children at any social gathering, Danes keep an eye on any children around them. There is a radius of care extending out and around each adult, so that all children are looked after. In a group with many circles, there is a Venn diagram of care.

'If there is a kid who needs help – changing, feeding, whatever – you help,' Veteran Viking explains. 'So you know that your kid is being looked after the same way, too.'

The overall direction of 'family' in the UK and the US has been to view it as a private unit and children as a private responsibility – encouraging families towards self-sufficiency with minimal state interference. But *samfundssind* means support for all.

'There is this sense of togetherness,' says psychologist Marie of the Danish approach, 'of having broader arms, beyond your own child, extending care and concern beyond the immediate circle. And just as you let others look after your children, there is an expectation that you will extend your umbrella to include others, too.'

This is something I've long been a beneficiary of. The time my toddler climbed into a toilet at a party? He was 'rescued' by another parent. When the redhead scaled a potato display at the supermarket? A fiercely tanned lady all in green hauled him down (older Danes still sunbathe like it's a sport). Then there was the time Lego Man ordered so much lumber during a particularly enthusiastic DIY phase that I couldn't get to the front door with newborn twins. The postman was my hero that bleak Monday. So now it's my turn to extend my umbrella.

The following week I do not panic (on the outside) when I find myself in loco parentis for eight children ranging from the ages of five to nine (one of whom I have never clapped eyes on before). I am at a popular 'Lego experience' with my three children when I spot a mum-friend in some distress. She has two children but each of them has a playdate and then she's taken pity on one of their classmates, who was feeling left out. Only a family emergency has arisen, and she needs to pick up an elderly relative from hospital (nothing life threatening: everyone's okay). I half offer, she half begs, then vanishes. And there I am. Knee-deep in children. I am only in charge of them for an hour or so. But it's a long hour or so, including snacks, toilet incidents and big questions . . .

'Is Santa real?' demands a flying child, plaits streaming behind her.

'What about God?' A serious-looking boy stares up at me.

'How do you make BABIES?!' a five-year-old yells.

I'm loosely prepared for these chats with my own children. *But with other people's?* What's the etiquette? Who's been told what? I trot out abstract answers along the lines of: 'Well, I've never seen him/her,' and, 'When two people share genetic material . . .' followed swiftly by: 'Who'd like a BANANA? SNACKS, anyone? NUTS? ANY ALLERGIES?'

Finally, a parent rocks up. Then another. I introduce myself, tell them their child is currently playing hide-and-seek somewhere . . . *and by the way, he now knows how to make babies,* I do not add. We find the missing child, the last parent arrives, and I leave, with just my three in tow. I feel – what is it? Capable? Competent? Relieved? All of the above?

I was trusted to look after other parents' precious offspring and we all survived and had a nice time. *I'm practically Kitta now!* I convince myself. Momentarily. Walking to the car, I check my phone. There's a message from my daughter's ballet.

This is it! I think, tapping the message with trembling fingers (though this could just be the excess adrenaline from the previous hour).

'Thank you so much for your offer . . .' I read, blah blah blah . . . 'won't be needing your services teaching . . . although we would appreciate help fundraising' and 'might you be available for green bags? ☺'

There it is . . .

'Sign me up,' I respond.

What I've learned about singing like a Viking and *samfundssind*

1. Singing is good for the soul. Singing together = better still. Being part of something bigger than ourselves is never more important than at the coalface of parenting. The world can feel small, all lunchboxes and laundry. It's good to remember that we're just one of eight billion human beings on a rock travelling around one of 100 billion stars. When we can't escape, or climb a mountain to get some perspective, we need to recalibrate another way. Instead of 'drinking to forget', let's all try 'singing to disappear' (cheaper and less chance of a hangover). Also: I need to 'make time' to join a choir again.

2. Building a circle of trust or making a pact to watch each other's children makes for a more relaxing time. Surrounded by other parents, collectively giving each other 'the look' that says 'we've got this', helps me to be a nicer person. Thinking 'we', not 'I', helps the community, children and caregivers, too.

3. If all I can do is hand out green bags, I should keep on handing out green bags (unless any sweary octogenarians fancy a game of Scrabble).

4. I have a long way to go before I'm Kitta. Or Annika. Or Diana. Or Peter Schmeichel. I still haven't got it sussed. At. All. As my neighbours are about to discover.

8

Show, Don't Tell: Discipline – Viking Style

I KNEW I'D hit an all-time low when I threw my children's bubble machine out of the window. In the morning rush in darkest January, my children were refusing to put their shoes on. Instead, the youngest retrieved a rainbow-maned unicorn to belch soapy spheres all over the kitchen. Blissfully unaware of any urgency, they cackled with glee and leapt about as bubbles grew into trembling balls, shimmering. I got dressed to leave the house in angry, irritated movements, jerking an arm into a jacket. After the third shoe-related request, with the clock ticking towards 'late', I snapped. Seizing this symbol of pure joy, I opened the kitchen window, and hurled it, overarm, into the inky blackness. Then I dropped everyone off and had a long, hard look at my life.

What is wrong with me?

On the street where I live, there are lots of families with young children. In summer, everyone has their doors and windows open. And I don't hear anyone else losing their mess and screaming into the void. But on an average morning, I go up and down the stairs so many times that my Fitbit thinks I've done a HIIT workout and by 7.30 a.m., I am a purée of despair.

Do Vikings just do things differently?

'Yes,' says Niki Brantmark in Sweden. Originally from London, Niki relocated to Skåne in 2004 with her Swedish husband. She now has two daughters, a stepson and an interiors empire (myscandinavianhome.com). 'Everyone is just so calm here! They rarely raise their voices!' She sounds baffled. 'Swedes often have this very soothing – pedagogical, almost – voice. I don't know how they do it. They always reason with children and try to be really fair. I've seen a child slap her father, and still no raised voice! Whereas when we grew up . . . well, I have memories of being chased up the stairs.'

I tell Niki about my morning and she tells me that her neighbour's daughter locked herself in the shed, making them late for work and school respectively.

'I asked my neighbour, "Did you lose your shit?" But no, she told me: "I just kept really *calm* – then I might bring it up the next day with something gentle like, 'It wasn't so nice, was it, when *this* happened – how did you feel?'" They always keep their cool.'

'And . . . what about shoes?' I ask. 'Don't you have shoe-wars in your house?'

'No: we use a horn.'

'Sorry?'

'Everyone does in Sweden – schools, daycares – you see them everywhere. It's much easier with a shoehorn. Try it!'

I tell her it's worth a go. 'But what about when you're trying to get children to do something they don't want to do?' I ask.

'They just . . . don't! I've witnessed a couple of instances where if a kid doesn't want to go to school, sometimes they *don't go.*' This isn't a daily occurrence 'and it's usually among younger kids'. But still. 'Giving kids a feeling that they are equals and that they get to make decisions is key.' Every Swede I ask about this concurs – and there's a similar approach in Denmark.

'The Danish way isn't to focus on *behaviour* – unlike in the UK and US,' says family therapist Sofie Münster, who studied in the US. 'In Denmark, we focus on what is behind that behaviour. I'd think, *What is the child trying to tell me?* So instead of a "time out", we would think, *This child is really angry*. And then say to the child, "I can see you're angry with me because I'm saying 'no' and that is really hard for you."' By saying this, we nourish the attachment bond rather than depleting it.

'Because what is the logical conclusion of the alternative? Does the child end up thinking, *I will only be loved when I'm behaving well*? Or that, *When I am annoying or difficult, I'm going to have to deal with it by myself*? *That I have to be alone with those hard feelings*? Over time,' says Sofie, 'this makes a child even more angry.'

'We also don't do ultimatums,' says my friend Rikke with the twinkly eyes, 'since with ultimatums there has to be a winner and a loser.'

'*No ultimatums?*'

'But there is always a cause and effect,' she adds.

'So if children won't put on shoes . . . just off the top of my head . . .?'

'I'll tell them, "If you don't put on your shoes, we'll be late for school" – because that's true. But I also know that when I go over, lay a hand on them and remind them gently, they may respond better. And if a child is too tired, or the fastenings on their shoes are too fiddly, then of course they're going to resist. Also, have you tried a shoehorn?'

Deep exhale

Nordic parenting fosters the notion that the child is essentially good and that there's always a reason for 'resistant' behaviour – from hunger, to tiredness, boredom or lack of a shoehorn.

'The Danish way is to reduce the friction for children,' says Rikke.

'Isn't that being a helicopter parent?' I ask.

'You mean "curling"?'

'Do I?'

'Don't you?'

I discover that what the rest of the world refers to as 'helicopter parenting', Danes call 'curling', likening the niche sixteenth-century Scottish broom sport with 'smoothing the way for a child'. Obviously.

'I don't see reducing friction as "curling",' says Rikke. 'I think much of kids' *lack* of self-sufficiency is actually because of us – overscheduling so they're tired; or putting the stuff they need out of reach; or clearing it away unduly. We know by age three that kindergarteners can do a lot themselves – Danish winter clothes are specifically designed so that the kids can put them on unaided.'

Another reason my stinky Paddington duffel coat fell at the first hurdle, I think: *too many toggles!*

'If kids aren't being self-sufficient,' says Rikke, 'we can look for the points of friction and try to be patient.' She tells me how, until recently, she poured the milk on her eight-year-old son's cereal. 'I did it because I couldn't face him doing it, spilling it, then trying to clean it up, not cleaning up right, leaving out a dirty cloth . . . you get the picture.'

I do.

'I would think, *I don't have a mental capacity for this today*.'

This sounds familiar.

'It became a habit that I would pour the milk for him. But I had to let go – to let him do it, make a mess, and learn. It's the same with many things.'

Rikke's husband comes from the UK and can occasionally be exasperated by the Danish way.

'He might say to our son: "By your age, you should be able to do X, Y and Z . . ." Because that's how it is in the UK. But how should kids know if we don't take the time to teach them? Or make sure they understand?'

'In the Danish way there is a focus on the process,' family therapist Sofie explains, 'so children have to learn to do certain things. But we acknowledge that it can be hard for them. And they may not "get there" as fast as we want or expect them to! So I'm very thorough, focused on going slow, and coaching children through things. You actually save time by giving time.'

'*Really?*' She can hear the scepticism in my voice.

'Well, I have a three-year-old, so let's talk about her. If you think about it, impatience and conflict actually take longer. So, for example, if I'm trying to get my daughter to put her shoes on in the morning—'

'Yes! THANK YOU!' I feel seen.

'Well, if I give her, say, thirty seconds to get used to the idea of putting her shoes on, I'm also investing in her learning this skill. I'm being with her in the here and now and helping her regulate a difficult emotion.'

The difficult emotion of 'I don't want to wear shoes'? *What is it with kids and shoes?*

'The grown-up is taking the lead, telling the child: "You have to learn it, but I'll be with you until you understand."'

There's an acceptance in Denmark that when children are preoccupied, they aren't going to listen. And this is okay, allegedly. We can't get mad at them, say my Danish friends, since when we do, they can't *actually* hear us.

How convenient, I think at first. But there's science here. Brain scans show that getting told off activates the more primitive parts of the brain, causing children to feel threatened and go into a defensive position. In this state, children have no capacity to relate to what parents are demanding.[1]

The late Danish family therapist Jesper Juul popularised Nordic ideas of non-authoritarian parenting in his 1995 book *Your Competent Child*.[2] He wrote that values like obedience and conformity governing traditional hierarchical families were now outdated, explaining how children parented 'the old way' might end up complying, but would lose far more in the long term. 'To defend punishment by claiming its efficacy is mistaken,' he writes, since, 'children willingly cooperate with any adults they love, trust and depend on. No matter how the adult behaves.'

Earlier theories of parenting were based on the idea that adults had to teach children how to cooperate, adapt and take others into consideration. But forty years of research into families shows that when children have to choose between preserving their own integrity and cooperating, children choose cooperation 90 per cent of the time, according to Jesper. In other words, most children *already* want to fit in and please their parents – what they need help with is learning to be themselves.

When toddlers begin to discover their autonomy in English-speaking countries, they're categorised as 'terrible twos' or 'threenagers'. In Danish, these terms don't exist. Instead, ages two to three are known as *trodsalder* or 'the boundary age'. Pushing boundaries is normal – not 'terrible'. This makes a difference in the way parents respond to toddler behaviour.

'We're always in dialogue with our children,' adds my friend Camilla (willowy artist, pee-your-pants-mothers'-group Camilla). 'A child's voice counts, so we listen to it.' And in Denmark, parents tend not to be ventriloquists for their children.

'We don't speak for them or "excuse" children with a "she's shy" – because the label can become self-fulfilling,' says Rikke.*

Instead, Danish children speak out.

'Kids are taught to question, "but why . . .?" and they're treated as equals,' says Rikke, explaining how her own parents treated her 'like one of them'.

'I grew up believing I had co-created our everyday life, from the food we ate to the clothes I wore,' says Rikke. 'For a long time I believed that I decided what kitchen we should have. I thought I made the decisions. But looking back, I didn't – how could I? I didn't buy the food. I didn't decide where to put the garden fence. But my parents were very good about autonomy.' This can present pitfalls later in life. 'It came as a bit of a shock

---

* Although this isn't a universal in the region. 'In Sweden, kids are not expected to speak to adults,' says Rikke: 'They're allowed to be shy and parents don't like to push them. So they may not look you in the eye or shake hands. They may not say "thanks for supper". They get there in the end. At around seventeen or eighteen, they're all polite. Somehow, they learn it. But it takes a while!'

to realise I didn't rule the world,' she grins. 'I only learned as an adult to be more conscious of my surroundings. But I really want to try and give my children that agency. I let them decide a lot.'

What about teaching respect?

'You don't have to "teach respect". The Danish way, it is assumed,' says Rikke.

This is a brain-twister for someone raised outside of the Nordics. *Respect for each other simply because we exist?* It's all very Mr Darcy telling Bridget Jones he likes her just the way she is. ('Not thinner? Not cleverer? Not with slightly bigger breasts or a slightly smaller nose?' as Bridget's friend Jude asks in the 2001 film.) Instead, Vikings show each other a basic level of respect, regardless.

'You don't criticise your kids or anyone else's,' says Camilla, 'so you can never be shitty about your kids' friends. If kids hear you criticising someone, they start thinking the same thing. They can't help it. It puts ideas in their heads.' Danes use their choice of language to teach empathy instead. 'We're always trying to find ways to get children to understand another child's behaviour without a negative label. So we might say, "Why do you think she said that?" or, "How does it make you feel when . . . ?" but we're not judging. We might say, "Maybe they were hungry? Or tired? You know how it feels to be hungry and tired, right?" Helping children understand the feelings *behind* behaviours leads them to be kinder and teaches empathy. And kids mirror us, so the language we use matters. If we are judgemental or critical or shaming, kids copy.'

I see this the very next day when a family elder speaks disparagingly about someone's weight in front of my son. Later that day, he tells me he doesn't want to eat too much as he 'doesn't want to get fat'. I'm mad at myself for not having spoken up to correct the family elder at the time. Instead, I'd changed the subject and turned on the radio.

Why wasn't I braver?

I tell Rikke about what happened and she nods, knowingly.

'I'm always struck by how much British parents worry about what other people think,' says Rikke. 'Because really, who cares?'

Family elders! That's who! But I know I need to woman-up.

'Parents also have to have empathy for themselves,' says Malene, another Danish mum and parenting psychologist: 'Parenting is hard – we don't always get it right and that's okay.' Thanks, Malene. 'Being understanding and forgiving of ourselves makes us better at forgiving our kids – and others.'

'I think one of the most important jobs for a parent is to show imperfection. To show failure, even – to teach your kids that it's okay,' says Camilla. And Danes are good on failure. Forget the idea that you get the drinks in after a hole-in-one on the golf course, or a successful business deal. In Denmark, if you've made a mistake, you treat the people who witnessed your failure to a pint. The tradition of *kvajebajer*, or 'failure beer', is a way of celebrating snafus and accepting that they're what make us human and help us learn (hopefully). Then there's the word *pyt*, which means a combination of 'oh well' and 'stuff happens'. Danes bear the slings and arrows of outrageous fortune with *pyt* – letting go of minor frustrations or mistakes. I now have letters spelling out PYT on a shelf above the desk where I work as a constant reminder (also: more great tattoo inspiration, not least because '*pyt*' is nice and short for minimal ouch factor).

Jesper encouraged parents to include their own wants, needs, feelings and failings in everyday exchanges. Instead of saying, 'What would you like for dinner?' he recommended something like: 'I'd like fish for dinner today. What would you like?' Rather than, 'What time should I pick you up?' he advocated saying: 'I'd like to pick you up at three o'clock. What do you think?'

According to JJ's manifesto, there's nothing wrong with expressing sadness, anger, even irritation as parents, since: 'Children learn that they cannot always get what they want, and that individuals exist within the context of family life.'

Head explodes

But wait, there's more: Vikings don't over-praise either. While many cultures adopt the idea that constant praise enhances the development of self-esteem ('Who's my CLEVER BOY! That's the BEST poo I've ever seen!'), Danes just . . . don't.

'In the UK or the US you're almost rude if you're not effusive,' says Rikke, 'but it's not in our culture or language to praise all the time – it's too easy and it doesn't mean anything if you do it all the time.'

Friends tell tales of non-competitive school sports days in the UK, where 'everyone wins and all must have prizes' so no children feel left out. But in Denmark, no one wins and none get prizes. There are no sports days as we know them. Every October, there's a 'sporty day' where Danish schoolchildren run around as much as they can, for fun. But no one's getting medals for that. Gutted though I am to be deprived of the opportunity to aggressively heckle my children to victory or take home a rosette for 'participation', there is method in this madness. Team sports in Denmark are open to all, regardless of ability, so that all children remain active. But they don't expect a medal for it. Which might be a kinder way to prepare children for adult life, where relatively few of us are ever likely to have trophies flung at us for our efforts. The reward is in the doing, not in the praise of others.

Jesper Juul believed that over-praise led to inflated egos and a poor sense of self. And Danes have long lived by the tenets of Jante's Law – the fictional Scandinavian set of beliefs immortalised by the Danish-Norwegian author Aksel Sandemose in his 1933 satirical novel *A Fugitive Crosses His Tracks*.[3] These are:

1. *You're not to think you're anything special.*
2. *You're not to think you're as good as us.*
3. *You're not to think you're smarter than us.*
4. *You're not to convince yourself that you're better than us.*
5. *You're not to think you know more than us.*
6. *You're not to think you're more important than us.*
7. *You're not to think you're good at anything.*
8. *You're not to laugh at us.*
9. *You're not to think anyone cares about you.*
10. *You're not to think you can teach us anything.*

Intended in jest, the Law of Jante became shorthand for the egalitarian nature of the Nordic countries. A harsh-but-fair belief system that persists today.

I gathered early on that Danes didn't go in for 'gushing'. During my first trip to a Danish clothing shop, I emerged from the fitting room only to be told by the sales assistant: 'No. That doesn't suit you at all.'

'But I'm wearing my own clothes . . .?'

Far from creating a culture of downtrodden dolts, it contributes to a sense that everyone is worthy, just *because*.

'When kids say, "Look at this!" it's their way of requesting our attention,' says family therapist Sofie. 'They're not actually asking for praise. So it's better to teach them to evaluate things for themselves, otherwise they'll spend their lives looking for external validation. We want to raise kids to have a strong inner voice and sense of self.' And this is something Danish parents do well.

'You feel like, *I am all right; I am of value just because I exist*,' says Camilla. Rikke agrees: 'I would never know if my parents thought something I'd done was good, but also, it wasn't *important*. I assumed they loved me. It was taken for granted, not based on achievement.'

This feels like a game-changer: to be loved 'just because'? Isn't that what all children want?

Danes replace praise with interest. I hear a lot of 'how did you do that?' or 'tell me more . . .' or 'I can see that you have . . .'

'This shows kids that it is *them* and not their "results" that we are concerned with,' says Rikke. 'Plus, when you're honest, it helps kids learn the importance of telling the truth, and right from wrong.'

Sometimes . . . I think.

Before my mother's first visit to her grandchildren's Danish kindergarten, I tried to warn her that my newly adopted countryfolk were a tad lax on swearing. But she was so busy admiring the daffodils outside that I wasn't sure she'd heard. We walked in to walls decorated with 'artwork' and 'about me' presentations by the new intake of three-year-olds, transcribed by teachers (it'll be a long time before a Viking is writing). The display was all in Danish with a few notable exceptions. I browsed a couple, as did my mother, until I heard her exclamation of: 'Good gracious!'

Her hand fluttered to her heart like a Victorian gentlewoman and she stood stock-still. I followed her eyeline to one particular three-year-old's 'about me' presentation and scanned swiftly:

Favourite food: pancakes
Favourite sport: football . . .

Unable to see anything amiss, I read on, hurriedly.

Funniest word I know . . .

Oh . . .

While others had cited 'buttocks' and 'fart' (*numser* and *prut* respectively – both pretty funny, to be fair), this child had chosen:

FUCK!

. . . a word that is, helpfully, the same in Danish and English and so the only word my mother could read. Transcribed by the teacher. Of a three-year-old.

'It's everywhere!' says the headteacher at my eldest's school. 'Even the milk commercial uses the F-word here. At some schools, teachers say: "Get the eff over here!" to kids in the playground! It just doesn't have the same power.'

'It does to my mother,' I tell her.

'I think we're just a lot freer here,' she says. 'Kids know the "bad words" and they have the responsibility to know when to use them.'

What, like in kindergarten presentations? I think.

'Freedom with responsibility' is a guiding principle for parenting throughout the Nordic countries. Only trying to be okay with the idea of 'freedom' means letting go of many of the assumptions about parenting that I picked up as a child or from the rhetoric of motherhood (most of us start with a manual under our arm nowadays, 'Only babies don't read them,' as Veteran Viking likes to remind me). Take bedtime. I have been doggedly clinging to my children's 7 p.m. bedtime, since it's only after that when I feel I can have some 'evening' to myself. But according to Jesper Juul, if a child complains about bedtime and asks: 'Why do I have to go to bed so early?' parents should categorically *not* say: 'Because you're tired and have to get up in the morning.' Apparently, we should just say: 'I want you to go to bed now because I want time to myself.'

That's it? That's the big idea? Telling the truth? What's the world coming to? Also: how will they ever get up in the morning? *How will I get the RUDDY SHOES ON THE RUDDY CHILDREN AND GET OUT OF THE RUDDY DOOR?*

Jesper has thought of that: he recommends alarm clocks, since 'children older than five can wake themselves'.

Ambitious, I think. But also: *tempting.*

JJ advises sitting the child down and telling them explicitly why an alarm clock is coming their way and even suggests a script for this delicate encounter (buckle up . . .): 'Now listen, when you were young, we thought it was nice to wake you up in the morning, so we took the responsibility of making sure that you got up. But we don't think so any more. In fact, we feel irritated almost every day. So now we've decided to give the responsibility for this back to you. If now and again you go to bed late and worry you won't hear the alarm clock, then you just have to tell us and we will help you. But other-wise, you'll have to make sure you get up every morning from now on.'[4]

Blimey! And this is love? I ask the dog, who rolls over for a tummy rub.

'Yes' is the resounding response from the Danes I poll: it's direct and it's true.

Okay then, I think, *bring on Operation Alarm Clock!*

That night, I break it to the redhead, then brace myself for a fight.

'So I'm getting an alarm clock?'

I nod.

'Cool,' he nods and turns off his light.

A Viking parenting win.

* * *

I know already about the importance of family meals and food in Danish culture, so I'm surprised to hear about a much more relaxed perspective on dinner times than anticipated from the Danes I survey. Like celebrated Danish chef and food writer Trine Hahnemann, who tells me that her policy is: 'When children are hungry, you feed them.'

That's it? No 'eat your broccoli first or you don't get pudding'? No bribery? No blackmail?

'No, nothing.'

What? So snacks on demand?

But this is another hallowed Jesper Juul-ism. Children, he says, may have an idiosyncratic biological clock, so may not be hungry when we are, but might develop an appetite half an hour later. The refusal of food at mealtimes can also be a signal that all is not well. Children may lose their appetite when they sit down to eat with the rest of the family if the atmosphere at the table is tense or destructive. When a child can't put this into words, they choose not to eat.

'Because when you're five, you don't have too many other choices,' as my dad-of-two friend Peter Schmeichel says. 'You make your power moves where you can.'

This makes more sense to me. I'm very aware of the impulse for control around food, having grown up a kid of 1980s and '90s diet culture and working in women's magazines in my twenties. I don't want to pass on any of my own issues here (I'll just mess my kids up in other ways . . .). So a liberal approach to meals I can live with, even if our extended relations remain unconvinced.

But the next Viking parenting policy seems batshit.

According to Jesper's law, we should let children 'intuitively eat' as many sweets – *slik* in Danish – as they want. And, since the custom is to let Danish children pick-a-mix themselves a bag every Friday, there's often *slik* knocking around.

Sweets on demand? This seems like staggeringly bad parenting. I cast around for an actual grownup to consult but, finding none, opt for my usual resort: *What would Mary Poppins do?* I'm pretty sure 'unlimited sweets' isn't a hallowed Poppin-ism. Julie Andrews doesn't sing songs about bottomless bonbon bags. Are Vikings QUITE mad?

'No,' is the response I get from all Nordic parents ever. The 'logic'? If a child is given a bag of candy ('Well, there's your first mistake!' I hear my mother's voice ringing out at this point) and then we take it away or tell them to stop eating, we ruin the child's 'sensible sense of naturally learning how many sweets to eat on their own', as Jesper phrases it.

At which point I, along with every other non-Viking in the vicinity, roll my eyes in the manner of Dorothy from *The Golden Girls*. It feels like very bad parenting indeed to let a child run off with a vat of glucose syrup. Also, I'm not sure I do have an 'off' switch.

'Maybe you would if you'd been raised the Danish way,' Veteran Viking tells me.

Touché. Although what about the boundaries that Pia and Kitta talked about?

Veteran Viking sees no contradiction here: 'We bring up kids to make their own choices. We don't teach them to place all their trust in external authority – political, religious or philosophical. It all goes back to our occupation in the Second World War.'

Are we equating my M&M habit with Nazism? This feels harsh. But I take her point: how will they learn if we don't let them?

Jesper believed there were three areas of life that children must be allowed to assume personal responsibility over in order to stay healthy: their senses (what tastes good, what doesn't; what feels hot or cold); their feelings (like happiness, friendship, anger, frustration, sorrow, pain); and their needs (so hunger, thirst, sleep, nearness, distance).

I ask my Danish parent friends and learn that, for the most part, they agree with Jesper Juul's philosophy and somehow manage to live by it, too. Many enjoyed similar freedoms when they were growing up.

'My mum raised me with three rules,' says Rikke with the twinkly eyes:

'One: Treat others like you would want them to treat you.

'Two: Speak nicely to me, I'm your mother.

'Three: You need warm feet and ears. Always.'

I tell her I like the sound of her mum and reflect that as well as giving children responsibility, this gives freedom back to parents, too.

So could it work?

That night, I tell my son: 'I'm going to say goodnight now because I want to go to bed soon, too.' This isn't much of an exaggeration: I am a husk by 9 p.m.

'Okay.' He flicks through *Dog Man* for half an hour, then turns his light off and gets into bed. No fuss. And he's up with the alarm in the morning.

'Does he make his own bed now, too?' asks my mother, always eager for the next step.

'Sadly not,' I tell her.

'Oh, that's a pity – you do look *very* tired . . .'

I don't know how to tell her that this is just my face now. Or how I can't force my children to make their own beds, according to Viking rules.

'We don't "make" children do chores,' Veteran Viking tells me. 'We "encourage help" so children feel like valuable members of the "team".'

So mini-Vikings won't be obliged to help around the house, I just have to hope that they 'want to'? Come off it!

This feels far-fetched. I can, however, talk on the phone. When I have to make a call and children are inevitably running wild (see *ramasjang* or 'hullabaloo' in Chapter 4 – actively encouraged in Denmark), I should just *say* so. Rather than a polite appeal of: 'Mummy would really like to just hear what this person is saying on the phone,' JJ has us rephrase our request in an active voice to become: 'I want you to keep it down while I'm talking to the dentist/my friend Kate.'

When I hear this coming out of my mouth, I feel selfish – not at all the saintly mother figure most of the parenting 'advice' from back home suggests I aim for. But my children? They get it. This is how their brains work and it makes sense to them. Plus I'm showing them that I have needs, too. Needs for a hygienist's appointment or a chat with Kate. I'm not asking for things that appear arbitrary and just 'because' I say so: I'm modelling autonomy. And getting clean teeth. And chats. And early nights.

'No, you can't watch more TV,' I can legitimately tell my children in Denmark, 'because it's finished now.'

'Finished? Television is never finished, *is it*?' asks Lego Man when he hears this. He didn't have a television growing up and so can never be quite sure (he once watched the clown and the girl with the chalkboard at a friend's house for ten whole minutes, enrapt). But children's TV on Denmark's equivalent of the BBC really does 'go off' at 8 p.m. After that, instead of playing reruns or going dark, DRTV shows a continuous loop of its most popular characters – pirates, puppets, artisanal cheesemaker types (just wait until Chapter 12) – fast asleep in bed.

'It's easier to get kids to bed when you show them the rest of the world – including TV – has shut down, too,' Veteran Viking tells me. In other markets, children's programming transitions into youth or adult shows at night, but DR chose not to. Which was kind of them. *And smart*, I can't help thinking, remembering the time I let my kids watch *Winnie-the-Pooh* – the wholly innocent 100-minute film that I allowed to roll on a fraction too long. They ended up watching the next film alphabetically in our TV's film library: *Withnail & I*. The drink-and-drug-fuelled comedy that elevated swearing to an art form wasn't quite what anyone was ready for ('Mummy, is Christopher Robin just really angry now he's all grown up?'). So Viking TV scheduling, I can handle.

But the final obstacle in the show-don't-tell parenting training course is the hardest yet.

'You have to let kids fight sometimes,' says my son's teacher. This isn't what I was expecting. 'You have to let them have conflict,' she tells me. 'So my kids will be fist-fighting and I'll have to let them. I don't always manage this; in the supermarket, for example, I might say, "Okay, stop." But at home or in a safe environment, with friends or family, we always see if they can solve it themselves. If they can get themselves to the peace table.'* I like the idea of a peace table. 'The most important experience the child gets when he experiences a clash is that we can disagree, but still agree.'

Or as my friend Rikke says: 'There is still love, no matter what.'

Studies show that playfighting is an important part of a child's development, teaching cooperation, building confidence and appropriate judgement. Rats deprived of the opportunity to playfight with their peers (but given socialisation and care by older, female rats) don't learn when it's appropriate to fight.[5] This means they tend to be a bit lairy as adults and lash out when it's not needed. They haven't learned 'the rules' of society. Experts have extrapolated that play fighting helps us learn to socialise. Playfighting is the most common play type across all mammals, but it's also the type of play that parents and teachers are most likely to discourage – in some US institutions there's even a zero-tolerance policy. But not for Vikings. Throughout the Nordic countries, adults let children handle their own conflicts. 'We jump in only when they really start hurting each other,' one Icelandic mum tells me.

'Like choking,' my son's teacher tells me. 'We draw the line at choking.'

How comforting.

---

* FYI, her children are now nice, well-adjusted teenagers. So she may be on to something . . .

But 'it's about self-governance', says Professor Ning de Coninck-Smith, an expert in the history of play and childhood at Aarhus University. And in this self-governing culture for children, they learn about the limits of themselves and other people.

I give this a shot the following day on a dog walk, when there is a dispute over who gets to hold the lead (this is standard). The redhead, sensing the exhilaration of battle, insists it's his turn. His brother and sister disagree. They're all needling each other, but instead of intervening as usual, I say . . . nothing. I do nothing. I slow my pace, even – the locomotive equivalent of 'sitting on my hands' as pedagogue Lise, the Viking from Valhalla, taught me. Soon I hear shrieks of frustration from my daughter (also standard). It takes every ounce of self-control I have not to go to her. I stand still. Knowing if I move, I will run to her. I love her. I will not leave her. But I also need to let her win. On her own. There is some jostling. Light shoving, even. But she is more evenly matched with her brothers than I have given her credit for.

Good on her . . .

After what feels like an eternity, there is another sound: '*NO!*' My daughter roars at her brothers: '*MIN!*', or 'mine' in Danish. I'm interested that she reverts to Danish when asserting herself. After some negotiations I can't quite make out, the lead is hers and she holds it aloft above her head, victorious. Ponytail swishing, arms swinging, she strides home, the dog prancing with projected pride a few paces ahead. I may be imagining it, but I could swear she looks a good inch taller than she did when we set out on this walk.

My daughter arrives home before the rest of us to a package on the doorstep.

'Can I open it?' she calls back to me.

'To the victor, the spoils!'
She tears apart a brown paper package to reveal . . .
'A shoehorn?'
All hail Viking parenting.

What I've learned about discipline, Viking style

1. Respect is a given. It doesn't need to be earned (I know! Madness!). Just imagine how different the world could be had we all been raised this way. In the spirit of self-parenting, I am savouring this gem: we are all worthy. We are enough. Simply because we exist.

2. Don't 'curl', but reduce friction where possible. They'll reach the top drawer when they're big enough to reach the top drawer. Until then, I'm putting all the kid-stuff in drawers they can actually reach. And I'm trying to be more patient, too. Allowing them time, coaching them if needed, and making sure they get enough sleep (mine turn into Gremlins on fewer than ten hours a night).

3. Be nice about other people's children and don't over-praise your own – not every picture needs to go on the fridge (or we'll run out of 'fridge'). This feels revolutionary, since half of us were raised in the 'how wonderful' mode while the other half were dragged up with the old-school idea of 'never praise, never apologise'. Neither approach works if parents are still making critical comments about other children. Because small people internalise this. I did. Vikings play it cool about their children – as well as everyone else's.

4. Let them fight it out and see if they can come to the

'peace table' by themselves. This way self-governance lies, apparently. I didn't have brothers or sisters growing up. I went to an all-girls' Catholic school intended to turn out 'young ladies'. There was no fighting. How different would I be now, I wonder, had I *grappled* a little more? Roughhoused, even? Before having children, I'd never had non-romantic physical contact beyond hugging friends. Then I had babies. Then toddlers. And parenting toddlers is 50 per cent running and 50 per cent WWE wrestling. And I loved it! My children taught me that. They're raising me just as much as I'm raising them, for which I'm eternally grateful.

9

Play (Well)

BIRDS DO IT. Bumblebees do it. Even bison run onto frozen lakes and slide on all fours to do it. Throughout the animal kingdom, there is play. Macaques make snowballs. Otters prank each other. Hippos do backflips and my children play with Lego. At every opportunity. At the doctor's. At the dentist's. At 7 a.m. while I'm ~~yelling/telling~~ *coaching* them to: 'Put shoes on!' At the craft fair they begged me to attend (my daughter is such a prolific crafter that glue-gun access is now rationed at kindergarten), they look around for precisely eight minutes before gravitating towards the 'Lego table' (there's always a 'Lego table').

Why are we here?! How is this still fun?! I wonder, looking longingly at a nearby display of arty knick-knacks. But all my children want to do when they're not wrestling me/each other is play. In an assortment of imaginary worlds (dragons, pirates, cafés, police procedurals, you name it). I know how much people love Lego. I love people who love Lego. But, in truth, I'm agnostic *sings 'Everything Is Awesome!!!' lest I be struck down by a yellow minifigure with u-shaped hands*. I appreciate that I am in the minority, since the clickety-plastic bricks are regularly voted the most popular toy in the world. The plastic part may seem surprising in our eco-aware age.* But Lego bricks are reusable – often passed down through generations. They're also insanely durable, as anyone who's ever heard alarming clackety noises from the washing machine can testify. It's not advised, but if you *do* end up putting Lego on a spin cycle after a child has forgotten to empty their pockets, you can still click the bricks together afterwards, I hear . . .

The name 'Lego' is an abbreviation of the two Danish words *leg godt*, meaning 'play well'. The company began in 1932 when Ole Kirk Kristiansen – a widowed carpenter struggling to feed his four children – made toys to survive. He started off with yoyos, until yoyos weren't cool (who knew?), so he used the ones he couldn't shift as wheels on toy trucks. He made more wooden toys and just about got by until his wood-heavy work-shop burned down. Determined to catch a break, he turned to plastic bricks post-war, inspired by the colours of Dutch artist Piet Mondrian and a department-store buyer he met on a boat. The Lego minifigure debuted in 1978, designed by Jens Nygaard Knudsen – and it was a hit. When Jens died in 2020, one epitaph read: 'He leaves a loving wife, three children, two grandchildren and over eight billion little plastic people infused with life by children's imaginations.'

The Lego company passed from Ole Kirk Kristiansen to his son, Godtfred, who drew up a set of guidelines, 'The Lego Constitution', in 1963 to decree that Lego should offer unlim-ited play possibilities for girls and for boys, inspire enthusiasm in all ages, foster imagination, creativity and development, and

---

* Although they now make some bricks from sugarcane.

encourage play all year round. And 'play' is still at the centre of it all today, signposted in six-foot-high letters in clicky-bricks in the entrance of Lego's Billund HQ. The word 'play' is in English – but it's the Nordic versions I'm interested in.

Remember how Lego is made up of the words 'play' and 'well'? In Danish, 'play' is *leg*. But 'play' is also *spille*. *Spille* is used when referring to play as in sports, music, or a game – something structured, or with rules attached. Whereas *leg* is just for fun. And in fact, all of the Nordic languages double up on play. Just as Hawaiians have 200 words for rain, signalling the importance of water in Hawaiian culture, Vikings love to play. The verb forms of 'play' in Finnish, Swedish, Icelandic and Norwegian refer specifically to unstructured, imaginative, enjoyable and intrinsically motivated activities – so personally rewarding, rather than done for an external goal.* But if you're playing sport, a board game or a musical instrument, you use *spille* in Danish and Norwegian, *spela* in Swedish and *spila* in Icelandic. Finns go off piste with *pelata*, but the fact remains: play is so big, they named it twice.

So why does play *matter* so much?

To find out, I visit Marc Malmdorf Andersen, a cognitive scientist and play researcher from Aarhus University in Denmark. 'Play is a sign of well-being,' he tells me. 'Among animals who play, it only occurs in the absence of illness, hunger and stress. After our basic needs are met, we play. So if we're not playing, it can sometimes be a sign that something is wrong.'

Dr Stuart Brown from the US National Institute for Play calls play 'probably the most important factor in being a fulfilled human being' and says that 'when we stop playing, we start

---

* *Leikkiä*, *leka*, *leika* and *leka* respectively.

dying'.[1] This seems a bit much. But Marc agrees that play is intrinsic from birth.

I scroll back through my parenting ride, remembering six-week-old babies delightedly scrunching up paper or making faces in a mirror. Toddlers occupying themselves for hours with a cardboard box. Children are nothing if not resourceful, 'And they will readily manufacture their own toys and invent their own play,' says Marc. Like the two-year-old at my children's daycare who gnaws his rye bread into the shape of a gun to shoot with ('pow pow!').

Studies suggest that play makes us happier and healthier, and can aid learning, improve problem-solving, and even help with social mobility and reducing inequality.[2] 'Some types of play also seem to be able to make us braver and help us learn to deal with adverse emotions,' says Marc. In a game, we can 'become' someone else – but there's less at stake if things don't go as we'd hoped. 'And kids learn a lot from "just" playing,' says Marc, 'like taking turns, conflict management, social interaction, negotiation, motor skills and problem-solving.' Only play is under threat.

Many US children are now so overscheduled with school and extracurricular activities that they have no time to play, according to a report from the American Academy of Pediatrics.[3] Research conducted by Lego found that the toy company's main 'threat' isn't a competitor toy – it's time. Or rather, children's lack of it. Playtime for UK and US children has decreased by 25 per cent in recent years – and unstructured outdoor activity has declined by 50 per cent.[4] Some schools in the US are doing away with breaktimes altogether in a rush to 'catch up' with academic work post-lockdowns. And yet the enforced isolation without peers to play with has made playtime more important than ever, with children's social and emotional learning 'stalled', says Professor Paul Ramchandani from Cambridge University. 'Children are increasingly under pressure to "succeed" and rushed through times when they should be playing,' says Paul. 'Even the best universities are now admitting that "smart students" aren't necessarily those with astounding academic grades – they're the ones who can think outside the box; solve problems; try and fail' - i.e. 'play'. In this respect, play is the supreme competitive edge.

Studies show that a play deficit is like a sleep deficit. Animals deprived of play will engage in extra play when it's safe to do so again. So experts want parents to protect and promote children's playtime.

'But some adults fail to see the value of play,' says Marc, 'and then it can be harder to prioritise as a parent. This is largely because adults become narrow-minded and cognitively inflexible with age.' *Speak for yourself* . . . But Marc explains how: 'long ago, before we became boring adults, we already thoroughly explored and experimented with how the world works, and the more knowledge we amass, the more certain we become that the world works in certain ways'. Which means that we rely on our *assumptions* of how everything works, rather than testing things out and experimenting, as children do.

This makes sense, but it's a problem, since adults who don't (or won't, or *can't*) play become anhedonic – incapable of feeling sustained pleasure. I remember how animals who are stressed won't play.

Is the same true of humans? Are stressed-out parents less likely to play?

'Undoubtedly,' says Marc. 'So we see in countries like Denmark, where there is a shorter working week, parents should, in theory, be able to play more.' Danes do 'play' more as adults than I had been used to back home, getting together 'just for fun' as part of a hobby club or association. Veteran Viking does CrossFit. Peter Schmeichel plays basketball. American Mom is part of an 'improv choir' she keeps asking me to join. Everyone is a part of something in Denmark. The average Dane is a member of 2.8 clubs (fun fact), so everyone gets to 'play' at something outside of their day job. This time spent playing doesn't detract from work, either – it enhances it, increasing feelings of well-being, belonging, identity and creativity. Vikings punch above their weight on creativity and innovation, with global companies like IKEA, H&M, Spotify, Volvo, Ericsson, Bang & Olufsen, Electrolux, Pandora, Tetra Pak, Minecraft, Lego, Skype and Nokia all coming out of a tiny clump of countries.

Could a Viking-style shorter working week help the rest of us play more? As well as keeping our mental health on track and allowing for more time with family?

Alex Soojung-Kim Pang thinks so. He's a rest researcher and director of 4 Day Week Global, an organisation aiming to reshape the way we work. Because outside of the Nordic countries, he tells me, 'People are reaching the physical limits of their ability to work.' Particularly parents. 'We all overestimate the degree to which we can handle a heavy workload, especially as our lives change and especially as we become parents. Society dangerously underestimates the importance and difficulty of parenthood.' The answer, he believes, is a four-day week. 'This has been proven to improve our personal life, by giving us more free time.' He wants employers to offer 100 per cent pay for a four-day week, promising 100 per cent productivity. Because, spoiler alert, it's possible. Microsoft Japan found that staff productivity increased by 40 per cent after a trial of the four-day work week.[5] New Zealand finance company Perpetual Guardian cut the working week to four days and saw a 20 per cent rise in productivity.[6] Pilot schemes are now springing up worldwide, with devotees claiming that the four-day week can boost productivity, improve employee mental health and restore a sense of play.

Throughout the Nordic countries, there is play. All Vikings play for longer before starting school, and research from Stanford in the US and Aarhus University in Denmark have found huge benefits to starting later. By delaying kindergarten for a year, they noted a reduction in attention problems and hyperactivity by 73 per cent.[7] Some experts now believe a sharp decline in play over the last few decades may be a contributing factor to the overdiagnosis of ADHD. Researchers from Michigan State University claim 20 per cent of US children receiving treatment for ADHD are likely to have been misdiagnosed.[8] And a Harvard study of 407,000 children found that the youngest in a class are 35 per cent more likely to be diagnosed than their peers, despite the fact that any fidgety behaviour is probably down to their relative immaturity.[9] As Finnish educator Pasi Sahlberg put it after a long day explaining to an American psychologist why five-year-olds struggle to sit still: 'In Finland, we have ADHD, too, but we have a different name for it: we call it "childhood".'[10]

There's another important way that Danes embrace play. 'Playgrounds are a barometer of development in society's view of childhood,' says Professor Ning de Coninck-Smith, 'and in Denmark, we take playgrounds very seriously indeed.' Ning has studied the cultural history of Danish playgrounds over the past 150 years since Copenhagen philanthropists decided to set aside land in densely populated urban areas for play. These merchants and businessmen could have capitalised on prized land and made a quick buck. But instead, they thought about the future of children growing up there. 'It was decided that the areas should not be built on,' says Ning. 'That was quite unusual, investing in children in this way. The original playgrounds had a focus on physical development, but in time, playgrounds with swings and slides, etc. were joined by "junk playgrounds" with a focus on construction.'

'Junk' and 'playgrounds' aren't words that normally go together, but Ning explains how junk playgrounds came about during Denmark's occupation in the Second World War. Nazi defences were built across the country and there were no resources for playgrounds, so kids got used to playing with whatever building materials were lying around. 'They built huts and constructions in trees,' says Ning, 'and also played with ammunition, dropped by British aeroplanes to the resistance movement.' Children played with the residual 'junk' of war. In 1943, the first official junk playground, or *skrammellegeplads* in Danish, opened in Emdrup, outside Copenhagen. It had no swings, climbing frames or sandpits – just old wheelbarrows, planks of wood and, well, junk. 'The idea was that children thrive when they have opportunities to unfold creatively,' says Ning. Within hours, children transformed the 'junk' into caves, houses and towers. And the concept spread countrywide. 'Junk playgrounds were – and still are – the exception, but they made Denmark famous,' says Ning, who wrote the 2022 book *Skrammellegepladsen – The History of Danish Playgrounds* (including a photo of former First Lady Eleanor Roosevelt visiting one). 'There are still a few of these around,' says Ning as I watch my children build a den from forklift-truck pallets that Lego Man left lying around (our garden is a lot like a junk playground). 'But there's been an increasing focus on the aesthetics and quality of playgrounds,' says Ning (unlike our garden). Today, the playground industry is worth billions and Denmark is home to the biggest playground maker in the world, Kompan. Founder Tom Lindhardt started out as a sculptor in the 1970s but, seeing how much children loved to play on his art, he decided to make play spaces just for them. Now, the company design, manufacture and install 1,000 playgrounds a month across ninety countries – that's one every forty-four minutes. Denmark is also home to the globally renowned Monstrum playground makers. I spend a lot of time with my children at their eponymously named 'whale playground' near me, as well as the helicopter, rocket, shark and camel constructions in Billund.

A common criticism levelled at custom-made play spaces is that they are 'too easy', 'too sanitised', and that 'nature is always better'. But play historian Ning isn't buying this: 'Some constructions are really challenging.' Lego Man still remembers the time he got wedged, Winnie-the-Pooh style, in a twenty-foot-high metal tube rescuing our daughter from a sheer drop at one such 'adventure' play park. 'I think our playgrounds reflect a growing creativity when thinking about the needs of children and families living in cities,' says Ning. 'And play is something Denmark gets really "right".'

Play is so important that Denmark is home to a global play experiment at a test centre for Harvard University's Project Zero, a research organisation founded in 1967 with a focus on creative learning.[11] A test school in Jutland is now exploring the pedagogy of play – with every aspect of the school filtered through the prism of play.

So mini-Vikings play all day, every day before they start school in the world's best playgrounds, with the world's biggest toy, Lego. Then, once they get to school, they play there, too?

I'm feeling pretty good about all this. Surely my parenting work is done?

'No,' says Veteran Viking, along with every Nordic parent and researcher ever, *'you* have to play, too.'

'What?' I deflate, realising I have some spadework ahead. I love my children. But there are THREE of them. And often three different games on the go. I find myself setting a timer for five minutes – 'then I'll play with your brother . . . then I'll play with your sister . . .' – until I feel like I'm letting everyone down ('Is ANYONE having fun?' I ask despairingly as five-year-olds sob and an eight-year-old wrestles me for the sand timer).

Is this really necessary? Wasn't there something in the wedding vows about putting away childish things?

I grew up in the 1980s and '90s. Parents didn't play with children. Children played and parents worked. Or had dinner parties. Or watched *Dallas.* Right?

Wrong, apparently.

'Parents have to play with their kids, it's really important,' says Professor Paul from Cambridge University. All of the experts I speak to echo his view – verified by a barrage of news articles and 'shocking new survey results'. In one day, I read how one in five parents haven't played with their children in two days and that 54 per cent spend 'less than four hours a week playing with their children'.

I don't mean to be a Grinch, but four hours a week sounds a lot. I don't have four hours a week to do anything else – like exercise or read or see friends.

Or go to the bathroom alone. Or shower in peace . . .

Another article tells me that 53 per cent of parents struggle to find time or energy to play with their children but still manage to spend 1,300 hours – the equivalent of fifty-four full days – playing before a child turns five.[12] And in the first five years of a child's life, parents play peekaboo for an average of ninety-five hours.

Ninety-five hours?

The dog yawns in sympathy.

On peekaboo?!

But peekaboo, it turns out, isn't 'just peekaboo'. It's psychological tennis. When a 'player' serves, they know their opponent is ready to return the ball and that's what children expect, too. If a child hides behind their hands, they want us to search for them. If we do the hiding, they 'search'. Researchers from Harvard University found that 'predictable' serves and returns lead to better physical and mental health, empathy and language in children.[13] Brains change as we learn, and when children do things over and over, this creates new pathways in the brain. So if children 'serve' too often without a return, they miss opportunities to create and reinforce valuable connections in their brains.

But ninety-five hours!

That's twelve working days. I could have done a diving course. Or learned to drive an HGV. *And I spent it playing PEEKABOO?* Plus I had small babies twice, with the redhead and twins. I must be nearing 200 hours of peekaboo by now. I could officially have become a commercial pilot in that time, had I not been so exhausted. I feel weary at the thought that even though I've spent 200 hours on peekaboo, I *still* may not have played enough. I speak to numerous experts on this, often older and male, but get the sense that someone else is doing a lot of the parenting. I want advice from a parent still in the trenches. So I ask Sabilah Eboo Alwani from the Faculty of Education at the University of Cambridge, the woman leading a project on play today while parenting young daughters.

How are parents supposed to do it all?

'I get it,' she tells me. 'It's a lot.'

Does it only work if one parent stays home? Is she a secret John Bowlby attachment-theory sleeper cell?

Sabilah smiles and tells me: 'The ideas around attachment theory are almost a luxury for many parents these days because the decision about whether one parent can or should stay home longer has become more about economic viability than what's best for child development.'

So everyone's working now but we're *still* playing peekaboo for ninety-five hours? I mention how no one my age had parents who consistently played with them, 'And we turned out all right . . . ish . . .'

'Ye-es,' she hesitates, diplomatically, 'but today, the research has moved on, so surely we could and should act on this?'

I mumble a 's'pose so', then ask why it's so important for parents to play with children.

'Today, we know that the early-years period of birth to five is a golden window for a child's development. And the biggest influence on a child at this age is usually their parents. That's why parents have a key role as their child's first teachers and playmates. A parent knows their child more than a teacher or daycare worker ever can,' says Sabilah. Also: times have changed. 'A generation ago, children ran outside to play and came home by dinner; they'd ride off on their bikes and have adventures.'

'Like *Stranger Things* but less supernatural?'

'Exactly.'

Especially in Denmark, an agricultural nation until recently, where children were left to their own devices. Farmers began work early, then napped at midday, while kids roamed free. Older Danes recall these 'wild times' as among the best of their lives.

'But now we know kids are not doing all this,' says Sabilah, 'and think about what they are doing instead. Big slices of "the pie" of their time are now spent on devices.' Consoles, tablets and smartphones have replaced the 'wild times'. Were the film *ET* to be set in the 2020s, there'd be no gangs of feral ten-year-olds rampaging on BMXs without helmets or adult supervision. Elliott wouldn't be outside throwing a ball at a toolshed – he'd be in on an iPad.

And so, Sabilah explains, we can't just expect children to play in a way that they did historically. They need someone to play *with*.

'Aha! But mine have siblings . . .'

Surely siblings are a 'get out of jail free' card!

I didn't have siblings growing up: I had Swingball. A game of 'hit a ball on a string' that I'd play for hours, until callouses formed on my palms from crudely moulded plastic paddles. Then came the arrival of Screwball Scramble in 1988, aka The Christmas That Changed Everything.* *Good times,* I think back fondly. But actual playmates on tap? Ready and willing and contractually obliged to be linked their whole lives long? That must get me off the hook, surely?

'Sibling play is hugely valuable,' Sabilah agrees. 'It's customised one-to-one peer play, ticking many of the boxes. But playing with a parent is still important.'

Urgh. 'Why?'

'Bonding.'

'Oh.'

According to a Lego 'Play Well' study, 84 per cent of children wish they could play more with their parents.[14]

The guilt of parenting never ends.

---

* A much-loved game that you could play solo.

'I'm not saying it's easy,' says Sabilah. 'I get my kids home by maybe 4.15 p.m.; I have to get dinner on the table by 5 p.m. They're exhausted, it's nobody's best time of day . . .' She tails off and we both take a moment to wish we were on a silent retreat in Tuscany (then again, I could just be projecting).

'So, when are parents supposed to find this mythical rainbow playtime?' I ask.

'Well, these days I try and do something in the morning, like read a story or two at breakfast. Or I pick and choose my moments throughout the week so that by the end of the week, hand on heart I can think: *Did I actually sit on the floor with them and play? Did I host that teddy bears' tea party? Did we do that puzzle together? Were they happy? In their eyes, how was I this week?* Did they feel Mum and Dad were there for them? Because they don't care about chores – they don't care how dirty the house is, or whether the laundry gets done. They want you.'

But it's not just about putting in the hours, either. The type of play parents engage in matters, too. *Jesus wept* . . . There are different ways of playing – all important and all essential to help children learn different life skills (I know: it's a lot. Make tea/have a power nap, then come back if you can't take this next part right now).

Ready?

Okay.

There's a lot of research on play. I've read it and it's frankly tough going (unfortunate for play research). So, to explain it in ways that won't make anyone's eyes bleed, there are four different types of play that I now think of in terms of decorating a cake.[15] First up, there's free play – giving a child bowls of icing, sprinkles and other toppings and leaving them to create whatever they fancy. Then there's guided play – saying, 'Hey!

Who can decorate the most colourful cake?' or, 'Can you make your cake look like a narwhal?' Then there's gamification – racing a child to see who can decorate their cake the fastest. And last but not least, instruction – so sitting down with step-by-step directions for decorating the cake and encouraging small people to follow them (good luck with this one . . . best attempted after a *really* good night's sleep).

Et voilà! Cake.

'But now you just need to do it,' says Sabilah.

So I do.

The next time all three children are about to pulverise each other, I declare that I am *all in*: ready and willing to be part of whatever play they choose for the rest of the afternoon. *Sylvanian Family-Hot Wheels mash-up here I come!*

There follows the most surreal hour of my life.

'Emergency, emergency! There's been a car crash! IN THE RABBIT'S FACE!' my son announces, somewhat disturbingly, as we begin our 'free play'.

Wait, what? Okay, play along . . . 'Oh no! What shall we do?'

'Quick: biscuits!' My daughter's recommendation.

Biscuits?

'NOW!' youngest son chimes in.

Okay . . . how about guided play? 'Does the rabbit need any medical attention?'

Youngest son: 'Yes! Susan needs a sleepover!'

'Susan'? *No one has been christened Susan since approximately 1983 . . .*

'Her name is Susan?'

Daughter: '*Their* name!'

'Susan uses *they*?'

Daughter: 'Yes!'

I apologise to Susan for making such binary presumptions and decide to bring on the gamification: 'Who can help Susan the fastest?'

'Me! Susan needs a sleepover and biscuits, stat!' youngest son announces.

'Okay. Right. Well. Err . . . here's a biscuit!'

Daughter goes for the jugular: 'Susan doesn't like your biscuits.'

What the @$%&? Say that to MY FACE, Susan!

The redhead changes tack and takes on 'instruction mode': 'I'm directing a movie, out of my way. This is a raid!'

A raid? Do their brains work faster than mine? Why can't I keep up?!

Daughter: 'You better say sorry, or you're not coming to my birthday party!'

What? Why? What am I sorry for?

Youngest son, shaking his head: 'Susan is REALLY mad now!'

No arguments there . . . Susan appears completely bananas . . .

Daughter: 'It's the village party and rabbit's birthday.'

Redhead: 'And they've won the World Cup.'

'Who? Susan?'

Shouts in unison 'Yes!'

Then the raid gets underway, youngest son announces he's changed *his* name to 'Frank the Tank', and the Hot Wheels cars do stunts over the Sylvanian Family village party as my daughter shouts at the world: 'SUSAN HATES YOUR BISCUITS!'

Ahh, the magic of child's play . . .

What I've learned about how to play like a Viking

1. We all need to play to stay happy and healthy, regardless of our age. Or whether or not we grew up a bookish only child in the 1980s.
2. Playmates matter. Friends and siblings are good. But parents need to step up, too.
3. We should make space for games (*spille*) and just-for-the-heck-of-it play (*leg*). I find this hard, on both counts. As an adult, I barely remember what it feels like to have free time. I'm not always sure I can remember what 'fun' is, let alone how to do it, guilt-free. And this isn't because I'm any sort of martyr-like domestic goddess – it's because I'm knackered. But if it's going to make me a better parent and human, I'll prioritise fun (and let my domestic standards slip still further . . . oh well #selfparenting).
4. Remember the cake analogy? Embrace free play ('you know where Mummy keeps the Friday *slik*? Go wild . . .'), guided play ('who can decorate the most colourful cake?'), games ('who can eat their cake first? Mummy can!') and instruction ('here's a recipe – make Mummy a cake'). Then eat the cake.
5. Parenting is officially insane. But at least Susan and the Sylvanian crew are relatively low stakes. The next aspect of Danish play is likely to result in far more grey hairs, if not plaster casts. *Strap in . . .*

10

Risk (aka Viking Health and Safety)

IN EIGHT HOURS' time, I'll be in hospital. I don't know this as I begin the day shovelling snow. Not unusual in Denmark in December, where it's your civic duty to clear the pavement outside your home before 8 a.m. so that passers-by don't do a Bambi. It's -5°C, snowing hard, and the world is muffled in a thick white blanket. Driving carefully, I drop the twins at daycare and the redhead at school, where I gather that today's 'gym' class is 'sledging'. It's breathtakingly cold and barely light, but I presume the teachers know what they're doing. With a few minutes to spare before work, I stand and watch in an attempt to 'be more present' and savour the 'magical moments' of childhood people are always telling me about.

Snow glistens in the dawn and I wave to my son as he reaches the top of the hill, adjacent to the school. He waves back a gloved hand, while the other clutches a bum sledge. Various children I vaguely recognise are already bombing downhill (it's tough to tell who's who when everyone's wearing a balaclava and the same navy blue, maroon or green snowsuit). I pull my collar a little higher around my neck as I follow the figure I'm assuming is my child.

There must be a knack to sledging, I think. I'm not a huge fan of a cold bottom, so I can't be sure he's doing it right. *But he's with school; they wouldn't let him do anything daft, would they?*

I notice he's going quite fast.

He'll definitely slow down at some point. Or turn. Won't he? He'll probably turn . . . I tell myself. He does not.

I notice he is going *very* fast now.

Aren't you supposed to throw yourself off the sledge? Abort mission if it feels out of control? I make waving motions to indicate 'abandon ship'.

He does not.

And then I notice that he's running out of 'hill'.

There's a rudimentary 'fence' made up of two wires at the bottom, but we're in farmer country here and I'm not entirely sure if it's electric or not.

If he doesn't get electrocuted, I calculate, *he will almost certainly be garrotted . . .*

A sickening feeling spreads in my stomach and I begin a run towards the careering figure. But moving in Moon Boots (see -5°C) is akin to a treacle-trudge. The sledge is hurtling at an alarming velocity. I'm running/trudging. Other people are shouting. The child is leaning back, screaming.

Or is it more of a 'whoop' . . .?

The figure reclines flat against the snow. The fence looms closer and the child . . . passes underneath the lowest wire.

He hasn't been electrocuted or garrotted! Hallelujah!

But still the sledge does not stop.

It keeps going, leaving the field and skidding into the adjacent *road*.

Oh God . . .

Treacle-Moon-Boots and I move in slow motion as the sledge sails across the first lane of traffic, coming to a stop at the centre line in the middle of the road. Time stands still as cars screech. The figure on the bum sledge slowly scrambles up, pulls off the balaclava to reveal a beaming smile and . . . a shock of red hair. The driver of a blue Volvo (welcome to Scandinavia) gets out and I wonder whether he's going to give my son a telling-off. But instead, he crouches, puts a hand on his shoulder, then gives him a high five before leaving with a wave of '*god tur!*' ('good trip!').

My son, seeing my stricken face approaching, asks: 'Are you okay?'

To which I respond: '*?!?!?!?!*$?*'

I'm relieved when his teacher appears and announces it's time to go inside. But nothing more is said. There is no 'bump report'. No apology. No drama – except from me, it seems. And then my phone rings. With a sinking feeling I see that it's daycare calling. This never means good news.

'Your daughter hit her head,' the pedagogue tells me calmly. *Sweet Jesus.*

'She was playing and tripped over—'

'I'm on my way.'

My daughter has not simply 'hit her head'. She has, it emerges, gashed her face from eyebrow to eyebrow.

'On an IKEA table,' the pedagogue adds.

'An *IKEA* table?' What are Scandinavians DOING to me today?

'It was a *Lack* . . .' the teacher nods, as though the Swedish furniture-maker's most basic design has let us all down today and is wholly responsible.

We see a doctor, who confirms that the cut is 'pretty bad'

and needs stitches. Immediately. We're sent to A&E to wait but my daughter is, understandably, distraught. Eventually we're told she needs to go under general anaesthetic to be sewn up again and, 'Has she eaten in the last four hours?'

I check with daycare.

'Oh yes, I gave her carrots as soon as she fell . . .'

Carrots?! Is this an approved Viking cure? Root vegetables?

We sit and wait until she has an empty stomach for the general anaesthetic. Several hours and twelve stitches later, I'm watching my daughter's oxygen monitor go up and down like a helter-skelter. This is the third time I've seen one of my children go under general anaesthetic and it doesn't get any easier. My thumping heart feels too big for my chest.

Am I a terrible mother? Am I doing this parenting thing all wrong?

'No!' fellow daycare dad Peter Schmeichel tells me. He drops by to pick up house keys and let the dog out for a wee in my hour of need. 'This is why we pay taxes!' Peter Schmeichel insists: 'We have healthcare so you can live how you like. You can take risks.'

'I'm not sure I want to take risks. At least, not with my children.'

'You have to,' he says, suddenly serious, 'otherwise you really are doing it wrong.'

Wait, what?

He shrugs: 'That's how I was raised.'

Our daughter is allowed home later that night. I put her to bed and stroke her hair, spread out like a fan on the pillow. Everyone else in the house is asleep, but the adrenaline is still surging through my veins. So I do exactly what the experts warn against: I google. By the blue light of my phone at my daughter's bedside, I begin investigating the Danish attitude to risk – and learn that it isn't just Denmark where there's a relaxed slant on health and safety.

Norwegian professor and former rector of the Norwegian Sports Academy Gunnar Breivik believes that children 'have the right to freeze from time to time'. He says we have 'failed as parents' if our children haven't broken any bones by the time they turn eighteen.[1] He also thinks we should let them 'be hungry once in a while, to get scratches . . . and to bleed a little'.[2] *So I'm . . . winning?* I watch minutes flick by on the clock. *Because this really doesn't feel like winning . . .*

Once it's a decent enough hour, I call Marc, the play researcher. He's been exploring the importance of fear and risk in play to help with growth and resilience. I tell him *my* fear and he tells me: 'Sure: in the short term, risk could in principle increase your chance of dying.'

Not the pep talk I'd been hoping for, Marc.

'But in the long term it increases your chance of survival!'

Okay, tell me more . . .

'Think about it: children are curious because curiosity helps them learn effectively,' says Marc. 'It's crucial. Compared to adults, children have a low certainty of the consequences of their actions. They wonder, "What does this grill do?" "Is fire hot?" "If I jump off this table, what will happen?" The brain wants to increase certainty in its predictions by seeking out uncertainty.'

My brow furrows as I try to follow: 'So children are programmed to seek risk?'

'In a way, yes! For a child, risky play can be very rewarding and "fun" because it allows the child to transform the uncertainty of a situation into something more certain and predictable, which in turn feels good,' he says.

Not for parents, it doesn't. I reflect on recent brushes with electrocution, garrotting and IKEA tables.

Marc tells me how many modern parents discourage children from activities like tree climbing and unsupervised outdoor play: 'They're afraid kids will get hurt. And due to urbanisation and heavier traffic, they also keep kids indoors more.'

And this is . . . *a Bad Thing?*

Marc understands the reluctance of some parents to embrace so-called risky play: 'It's actually undergoing something of a rebrand, with many preferring to refer to it as "adventurous play". Partly to stop parents getting scared by it and partly because often it isn't really risky at all – yet the child might perceive it to be, and that's the point! For children, "risky" or adventurous play is an important way of gathering information about the world and about themselves.'

Professor Ellen Beate Hansen Sandseter explores risky play, well-being and outdoor education in early childhood at Queen Maud University College in Trondheim, Norway. As well as Marc's information-gathering theory, Ellen believes our desire for danger is a necessary part of our psychological development.

'The way children approach risky play is a way of getting rid of some innate fear they may have when they're born,' she tells me. 'From birth, children will have these instinctive fears – like fear of separation from caregivers or fear of heights.' These make sense in evolutionary terms: staying close to our caregivers was more likely to keep us alive. Dangling from a tall tree? Less so. 'During play, children test this – climbing a tree branch by branch, working on their motor and physical skills until they can handle it, then building up courage until they can get all the way up.' This is what psychologists call 'exposure therapy' – exposing us to the things we may be afraid of in incremental steps. 'We learn that this is something we can manage, and we develop mastery,' says Ellen. Studies following kids from birth show that it's not the ones who climb a tree, fall and break a leg who have a fear of heights – it's the ones who never climbed a tree. Play in this way has an anti-phobic affect.' Ellen supports Gunnar's theory that we fail as caregivers if we *don't* provide opportunities for risky play.

But I find this hard. Really hard.

Losing my sister at an early age, years of infertility, then finally having babies who all spent time in special care with tubes up their tiny noses, my natural inclination is to cocoon them in bubble-wrap AT ALL TIMES. I assume the risk researchers I'm speaking to are natural thrill-seekers, so I'm surprised to learn that Marc has a similar story to my own. His sister died when he was young and his parents were understandably vigilant from then on: 'They wrapped me in cotton wool – so I get it.' He tells me how risky play is regularly repressed for those who grow up as only children. 'My colleagues tell me this is something they see a lot in China, following years of the one-child policy – if you only have one child, you tend to shield them even more from any type of potential danger, big or small.'

I wonder how he copes now, as a father.

'How do you manage not to be a helicopter parent? Or rather, in Denmark, a "curling" one?'

'I don't!' he tells me. 'Luckily, I married someone who reminds me to let my kids experience risk: to let them climb a tree, to let them run off on their own. I find it hard. But I'm really happy my wife is different to me on this, because I definitely need it.'

This is something else we have in common. My children are saved from my own cotton-wool tendencies by a father who is far more outdoorsy, gung-ho and a power-tool devotee (this isn't a euphemism: our local DIY outlet sent him a 'loyalty dagger' for his generous patronage. Peter Schmeichel was livid: 'I've been going there for years and nothing!').

So are some people just naturally more comfortable with risk?

Ellen researches into risk-seeking personalities and has found that these can be loosely divided into two categories: 'There's negative risk-seeking, like criminal behaviour or drug abuse, behaviour that doesn't quite follow the law or is not socially acceptable. And then there are positive risk-taking tendencies, towards things like extreme sports.' But here's the thing: there's only a paper-thin gap between the two. Risk-seeking person-alities deprived of peril in childhood can often face difficulties in adolescence and adulthood. 'High-sensation-seeking person-alities who *don't* have the chance in school or family life to get their thrills through positive experiences are more inclined to seek them out via negative experiences in later life.'

This seems self-evident – but it's something I've never consid-ered before. Is it just me? Am I a total idiot? (Probably.) Why don't more of us know about this?

'Ethically, it's challenging to get hard data,' Ellen says: 'By now, we have a lot of literature indicating that risk in childhood has a positive effect later on. But you can't just throw kids into something risky. And if you have a hunch that experiencing physical risk is good for children, you can't then ethically deprive children of risky play!'

Fortunately, these ideas are spreading organically. In Germany, insurers recently demanded that playgrounds build in risk to make children more resilient.[3] Swedish children in the Sollentuna municipality take part in *isvaksovning* – a hole-in-the-ice exercise where they jump into a frozen lake to test their mettle and make sure they know what to do if they fall in by accident. In the UK, David Ball at Middlesex University and Tim Gill, former director of the Children's Play Council (now Play England), are working to turn around the British approach to health and safety. Instead of just doing a risk assessment or a risk analysis for all potentially thrilling play, they are demanding a 'risk and benefit' assessment.[4]

'Of course, having a tax-funded healthcare system helps,' says Ellen. 'No family is going to be bankrupt if a child breaks a leg, whereas in the US this could be a catastrophe. If there is no safety net, this will impact children's play.' It's easier to have a Viking attitude to risk when you know you'll be taken care of and a broken leg is 'just' (just!) a broken leg, rather than medical bankruptcy. 'In some countries, litigation is a real problem,' adds Ellen, as we talk about parents suing local authorities in the US.[5] 'This isn't the case in the Nordic countries, but we still have to work at it.' She tells me how, even in Norway, 'parents who aren't as familiar with being outside and challenging environments are more cautious. Plus, media is all around us now, with rolling news and smartphones. People get the idea that there are more accidents. No one wants to be on the front page of a newspaper if something terrible happens,' says Ellen.

Or at the top of Google, I think, *or trending on Twitter* . . .

'There is often a different approach to risk generationally, too,' says Ellen. Bente Liers from Norway's *friluftsliv* association tells me how the fifty-plus generation 'consider taking risks to be a cultural competence': 'We grew up believing children should learn to feel their own limits, to make sound decisions, and be responsible.' But this belief is under threat. 'We see in schools that younger teachers in their forties don't feel so comfortable taking risks in the outdoors.'

While delighted to hear forty-somethings described as 'younger', I'm sorry to hear that my generation is less confident.

'There is an increasing tendency among younger teachers to want professional guides on school trips to avoid accidents,' Bente adds, 'but this is not how we've done things historically. You can't blame others if something goes wrong: you have to take risks and take responsibility. So it's something we're working on now. We can make a change: but *now* is the moment.'

Finns seem to have their risk-o-meter in a good place, with an emphasis on *sisu* (or 'grit'), meaning that things can be hard – even scary at times – but you keep going, says *Everyday Sisu* author Katja. Icelandic children are all allowed to roam free until their state-sanctioned 'curfew'. During school termtime, children under the age of twelve can be outside until 8 p.m., while thirteen- to sixteen-year-olds have to be home by 10 p.m. 'It's quite useful as a parent,' says psychologist Hrund Þrándardóttir from Reykjavík, 'because you can defer on any curfew negotiations and say to kids, "Sorry: it's the law!"' In the summer holidays, when Iceland enjoys twenty-four-hour sun, thirteen- to sixteen-year-olds are allowed to run wild until midnight, while children up to the age of twelve have to be home by 10 p.m.

'Wait, so children as young as six or seven are actually out till 10 p.m. in the summer?'

'Yes!' she tells me.

'What helps is that it's pretty safe and we have a small population,' says Hrund. In fact, Iceland is ranked the safest country in the world (for the fourteenth year in a row, according to the Global Peace Index).[6] The rest of the Nordic countries don't do too badly either, with the region considered the safest in the world. Whereas the UK comes in at thirty-four, while the United States ranks 129th.

So is it really fair to expect the rest of the world to embrace risk in countries where healthcare isn't so accessible and streets may not be so safe?

Marc and Ellen recognise the challenges here. 'But we still owe it to parents to share research about what risky play seems to do,' says Marc. 'And we see the evidence that encouraging children to use their bodies is beneficial, wherever they are,' says Ellen, 'so that's what we have to aim for.'

* * *

Just up the road from where I live is a treetop wonderland bringing risky play to those who may not be so comfortable with the concept. Like me. Walking through a forest of 7,000 trees, I meet Jacob Hindhede, ostensibly to chat 'risk' but in reality to foster a blossoming bromance between our two dogs (mine: a lamb who thinks he's a lion. Jacob's: an enormous woolly creature who thinks he's a kitten). Jacob is a tall, tanned, rangy Viking who screams 'health' and exudes 'hearty outdoor living' from every pore. He and his brother grew up the children of tenth-generation farmers. 'It was a tough life. My parents would be up at 4 a.m., working,' Jacob tells me. 'Then, in common with much of that generation of farmers, they would sleep at midday, working more later on. As kids, we were on our own a lot. I spent hours a day out in the forest, building treehouses, rigging rope swings, digging tunnels and building campfires.' Growing up, his brother continued in the family business while Jacob left to train as a physiotherapist. But, becoming parents, both brothers wanted to give their children a taste of the wild magic they'd enjoyed growing up ('and keep them off screens for as long as possible'). So they bought a patch of woodland the size of forty football pitches and lashed together suspension bridges, giant Tarzan swings and treehouses. Wow Park Billund opened in 2020 with a rough-and-ready, hand-whittled feel. There are no harnesses (unlike at Go Ape in the UK) and accidents happen. 'There are some sprains,' Jacob admits, 'some twists. Some breaks . . .'

Isn't that terrifying?

Jacob is thoughtful: 'It's more that bodily risk is so important – if you don't take risks, it's not only that you're not as good at using your body, but you're not as *confident*, either. By using your body in the natural environment, you develop yourself. You can transfer what you learn to other areas,' he says. 'If a kid develops mastery of something? That's a really good feeling.'

We pass cloud-scraping A-frame rope swings. Jacob tells me how his eight-year-old daughter can hang on them with one arm.

One arm? I can't manage with two!

'She's lighter than adults, but she's also strong. And she takes the risk that she will fall. I think that's something we're really good at in Denmark – getting kids into risk and physical activity.'

I bring my children to the park, and the redhead, who's harboured a fear of heights since toddlerdom, takes precisely ten minutes to acclimatise before heading 14 metres up a tree and down a zipline. Whooping all the way. The twins take to it like monkeys, scrambling to the top of conifers and down again for an hour, then announcing 'low blood sugar'. The park has fire pits and plenty of wood. So we build a fire, sharpen sticks with the eight-year-old's dagger, and toast the marsh-mallows I just happen to have in my backpack (see 'food bribery' in Chapter 5). And just like that, we have an outdoor feast. As well as every conceivable danger you could probably cram into one of those 'What's wrong with this picture?' hazard-identification exercises where you have to circle all the risks.

This is all good preparation for the ultimate Viking challenge: Scouts. Yes, as well as *samfundssind*, Danish Scouts are grandmasters of risk.

'Scouts here is about fun but also about *bøvl*,' says Andreas, the Scout leader with the kindest face in Denmark. *Bøvl* is a Danish word that basically means 'trouble'. And rather than telling children to 'keep out of trouble', Vikings lean in to it.

'*Bøvl* builds you up as a person,' says Andreas. His Finnish wife and fellow Scout leader Emilia, a petite brunette with big blue eyes, puts it in a more pragmatic way, in line with the Finnish idea of *sisu*: 'We are raising their tolerance for discomfort. When they have managed to do a hard thing, they feel good. They feel mastery.'

There it is again, I think, *mastery*. That singular sensation that makes you feel as though you can take on the world.

Emilia tells me about an early Scouting trip where she got lost, aged seven. 'It was raining, it was late, we were miserable. But looking back on it now, it was a really great experience.'

'You didn't panic?' I ask.

'No: I just got lost.'

I get lost in the town where I've lived for eight years. And I panic. How do I not panic?

'It's about perspective,' she says.

'Of course, we are *aware* of safety,' adds Andreas, 'but not too much. You get lost? You get lost. You break your arm? Then you broke your arm. That's not our aim. But children have to get experiences on their own. For us as Scout leaders and parents, it is important to find out – and discuss – how much and what kind of risk you are willing to take.'

Andreas and his fellow Scout leaders aim to give children two things: 'responsibility for what seems appropriate at that time and the competencies to handle this responsibility'. Take the knife badge: 'Once they've been introduced thoroughly to how to use a knife, if they try hard, they should be able to succeed. Some things can go wrong. But it's important to give children the possibility to explore their physical limits.'

So now, every Wednesday, the redhead goes marauding with his knife (as I murmur: 'You'd get four years for that in London . . .'). His siblings go to 'family Scouts' for under-sixes. It's pretty much the same, but their blade use is supervised by adults, since they haven't yet earned their knife skills badge.

'Scouts earn badges for knife skills, sewing, axe skills,' Andreas tells me, as though these are all on a par, 'but badges can also be taken away if they're not safe. It doesn't happen very often, but it can. It's important for children to learn that sometimes there are hard outcomes and sometimes it hurts.'

It hurts all right: I used to sit between the twins at family Scouts to prevent bickering. I'd help hold sticks as they whittled with borrowed blades to make kindling. Until one day, a twin muddled up the direction of attack and confused 'stick' with 'my hand'. As I turned to assess the damage of the cut on my right hand, the other twin sliced into my left.

'*Fuuuc-goodness' sake!* Daddy's turn to take you next time . . .' I managed to wince.

This year, the redhead has his first 'jamboree' where 40,000 Scouts descend on Roskilde, near Copenhagen, for the largest camp in the Nordics. I was already apprehensive when I received the letter home that read:

Dear Scouts, pack light: no one is changing their underwear every day ;)

The instructions were to let children pack for themselves, with assistance if absolutely necessary. So obviously, I ignored this and laid out everything I thought he might need. *Pyjamas, t-shirts, toothbrush and charger, socks, shorts* . . . Somehow, I managed to fit all this in his backpack and off he went into the unknown. Free from all the trappings of modern life and his mother for five whole days.

I miss him terribly while he's away but try to keep it together.

The day before pick-up, I mention to Peter Schmeichel that I'll be getting off the train at Roskilde in the morning. His face contorts and he snorts slightly.

'What?'

'Roskilde is the penultimate stop on the train from Jutland to Copenhagen. So if you're getting off just before the big attraction, you're . . . you know!'

I stare blankly. He raises an eyebrow.

I continue to stare blankly, until he explains that 'getting off at Roskilde' is a euphemism for the withdrawal method, or coitus interruptus, in Denmark.

'Aren't you Catholic? I'd have thought you'd know that!'

'I'm lapsed,' I tell him, and decide to drive instead to avoid lugging an enormous rucksack on the train. That way, Lego Man can come for the ride to relive his Scouting youth and we can show the twins what they've got to look forward to next year.

As it happens, the extra manpower proves advantageous. The camp is immense and I feel instantly overwhelmed. A red alert above my head projects a BUBBLE WRAP! bat light that I am sure must be visible for miles around.

Lego Man and I take a twin each and head in opposite directions, looking for a feral child among 40,000 other feral children. It's as though they've escaped the twenty-first century to live as their Viking ancestors did. We pass a few leathery-looking grown-ups in shorts, legs like knotted rope, but none of the Scout leaders seem to know the whereabouts of my son's 'patrol'.

'*No sign yet,*' I message Lego Man. '*How's it going your end?*'

'*Like Glastonbury but with more woggles!*' is all he responds.

My daughter points out a strong smell of burning in the air but also . . . could it be . . . pizza? I spot flatbread cooking in pans and see someone kneading in wild garlic. Another opens a tin of tomatoes while a third grates a gnarled hunk of cheese for an ad hoc margherita. I'm impressed.

We're still sidetracked by pizza when, grinning from ear to ear with approximately 10,000 new freckles, the redhead rambles into view. He has grown at least a foot and has a swagger of independence I haven't seen before. But still, he runs and flings his arms around me. I squeeze and don't let go.

'It's so good to see you! How did it go? Are you okay?'

'Y-es,' he says, a slight wobble in his voice.

'What is it?'

'I haven't exactly brushed my teeth like you said.'

'Oh, okay. Um, why?'

'My Scout leader said he wasn't quite sure where to charge the electric toothbrush . . . '

Oh crap . . .

' . . . everyone else had a normal one.'

'Sorry!'

'Maybe I should pack next time?'

'I think that might be a good idea.' I ruffle his hair and inhale woodsmoke. 'Wait, so there's going to be a next time? You want to come again next year?'

'Definitely!'

What I've learned about risky play

1. Let them climb; let them fall; let them maraud. I'm learning to turn off the BUBBLE WRAP! bat light (or rather ignore it. Occasionally). I'll never stop worrying. But I'm trying to let my children grow and face challenges on their own, taking incremental steps so that they build up Viking-style 'mastery'.

2. I'm attempting this in my own life, too. As a self-parenting experiment, I'm approaching daunting tasks with an uncharacteristically can-do attitude, safe in the knowledge that if I do something – anything – I'll have made a start. I'll be moving in the right direction. In the words of Anna from *Frozen II*: I'll do 'The Next Right Thing'.

3. If the world around us doesn't allow for risky play, we're going to have to seek it out. Or make like Jacob and create it from scratch. What scary thing should we all do this month?

4. With fresh air in my lungs, no children in hospital for at least a week, and something approaching muscle definition on my upper arms, I feel like a bona fide, North Face 'n' Patagonia-clad outdoorsy type. A Viking, even! Then hubris deals me a massive blow. Because it turns out that there's a third way Danes play. A mighty game on a vast web to threaten the very foundation of our Danish-style parenting efforts to date. *Cracks knuckles* Shoulders back, head up, let's go . . .

11

Digital Blind Spot

I N A D A R K E N E D room, blinds drawn, a dozen bodies lie, lit only by the glow of iPads. Slim fluorescent cans of a particularly pungent energy drink are dotted about. There's a stack of pizza boxes in one corner, next to a mound of sleeping bags. Because this is a 'sleepover'. For nine-year-olds.

'It was meant to be a "party",' says my American Mom friend with the Whitestrips smile and great hair, 'but no one was talking to each other, and the parents told me the kids normally "played" online – until around 2 a.m.'

I tell her that's crazy.

She tells me that's nothing: her son's friends play *Minecraft* for seven hours at the weekend. 'And I mean seven hours a *day*.'

'Is that . . . normal?' I can't help asking. 'Is that even fun?'

'It is for boys,' says science journalist and technology researcher Søren Hebsgaard, who works with Danish schools. I call him up to find out more on a day when the air is filled with a hopeless damp and I am filled with a horrible head cold. Between honks on Kleenex and sips of honey and hot lemon

(Danes don't do Lemsip), Søren brings me up to speed on Denmark's digital climate. He explains that a gender divide begins to emerge 'around age ten', with girls becoming interested in the social side and boys getting more into gaming. Half of all Danish children are now 'daily gamers', according to Denmark's Media Council for Children and Young People.[1] For Danish parents, this is 'the new normal', I learn, as somewhere in the distance a dog howls dismally. Danes may 'play' more and take risks, but they're just as suspectable to the lure of screens as the rest of us. And digital gaming is huge.

Full confession: I never so much as played Pac-Man growing up. Friends at university spent hours with a boxy Pierce Brosnan playing *GoldenEye* as I looked on, nonplussed. Lego Man is no help here, either. Deprived of even a TV growing up, he took to 'improvising' the plot of *The A-Team* to keep up with his peers ('it never ended well'). He's grateful for many aspects of his ye-olden-days upbringing, but still swears that missing out on 'all cultural references ever' put him at a social disadvantage. So as the redhead begins to express an interest in *Minecraft* – the modern gaming gateway drug – I realise we may have to visit this Brave New World.

Although aren't we supposed to spend less time on screens, not more? Aren't grown-ups always in trouble for being on their phones too much? How is giving a child a screen going to help?

A British study of 1,000 parents back in 2018 found that by the age of seven, most children have spent a year, alone, in front of screens – more than double the amount of time they've spent playing outside with others.[2] Ofcom data shows that the majority of children in the UK own a smartphone by the age of eleven.[3] But in Denmark, it's *nine*. At a school near me, six-year-olds have 'game day' every Wednesday where they're asked to bring in 'either a phone, a Switch or a tablet' to play with. All day.

I watch my eight-year-old 'play' on the family iPad, hunched over, legs tucked under him. After thirty minutes I tell him his time is up (what can I say? I'm mean). He attempts to move, legs rubbery from having sat still for so long. I think of something former physio Jacob from Wow Park told me recently: 'It's not just that spending time in front of a screen leaves less time for physical activity – it's that being stationary for so long may be actively harming their bodies.'

Researchers from the University of Copenhagen found that the more time children spend in front of a screen, the greater their risk of developing neck or back pain – as early as eleven years old.[4] And a US study found that when children spend more than two hours a day in front of the screen, it damages their concentration, language skills, memory and sleep.[5]

The redhead starts 'dreaming in *Minecraft*'. He complains of headaches and has trouble concentrating. This could just be 'being an eight-year-old', but Lego Man is a lifelong glasses wearer and in recent years, I've succumbed.

So, could screentime be damaging his eyes, too?

I take him for an eye test, and he gets drops to make his pupils dilate until he looks as though he's on mind-altering substances. He has to wear my outsized sunglasses for the next five hours like a 1970s Elton John. The redhead's eyes are deemed 'fine for now' but I'm told to have him checked annually. The typical age for a child to develop myopia was between eight and twelve years old. But there's growing concern for the eyesight of children as young as four, since excess screentime can increase the risk of short-sightedness by up to 80 per cent, according to a study published in *The*

Lancet.[6] And Danish children spend among the most time playing digital games *globally*, according to research conducted by Lego. A 2022 survey of 55,000 parents and children worldwide found that Danish children came fifth in terms of 'most screentime'.[7] Children in the UK and the US came in at third and second respectively. And Brazil tops the charts in terms of digital play. But the findings still come as a surprise after the Enid Blyton-style upbringing my children have experienced so far. The idea that digital devices are about to encroach on the outdoorsy idyll, thrusting my mini-Vikings into the twenty-first century, is unsettling.

So why is it happening?

'In Denmark there is a social codex to give kids freedom,' says Jacob, physiotherapist turned outdoor living evangelist. This is thought to be because of the legacy of trust and freedom after the Second World War. Remember the farmers' children running wild? Well, today's young Danes are being allowed to do the same, *online*.

'But screens are addictive. The mechanisms have been carefully designed to override what might feel "right" to a child – or any of us,' says Jacob. He rubs his forehead at the mere thought. 'No matter how much we try, this is something we can never beat. The best minds in the world, the best psychologists, have all thought, *How can we fuck up as many minds as possible?* And it's working.'

I'm a grown-up and I struggle to stop scrolling on Instagram. *What hope does a child have?*

I think about this as I stand under the shower for far too long the next morning, like someone waiting for a bus in the rain. I think about it in the night when I wake and check my phone on autopilot. I think about it when I get up the next morning to surly weather and a melancholic mood, no clearer on what to do.

'It's addictive,' Søren commiserates. 'Even as an adult whose job it is to know all the research, all the dangers, it can still "get you".'

After trying and failing to become a parent for so long, when it finally happened, I had lofty goals that my children would never see my face lit up by a screen. Then came 2020, when lockdowns thrust all of us into the digital space, whether we wanted it or not.

'Parents allowed children to be at home and on their devices for the first time,' says Bente Lier from Norway's *friuftsliv* association. 'Norway has always had such an active culture, but in the pandemic, people took to their sofas. Now it's a challenge to get them off again.' The number of Norwegian children who played outside after school daily has dropped from 41 per cent in 2015 to 18 per cent in 2022.[8] 'We're seeing now that the consequences for mental health are very negative.' And in countries with particularly pronounced outdoor lifestyles, like Norway, a dramatic increase in myopia rates is expected thanks to screentime during lockdowns.[9]

Many now believe that the benefits of technology in education have been grossly overstated. Naomi Schaefer Riley, visiting fellow at the American Enterprise Institute, told the *New York Times* that: 'The real digital divide . . . is not between children who have access to the internet and those who don't. It's between children whose parents know that they have to restrict screentime and those whose parents have been sold a bill of goods by schools and politicians that more screens are key to success.'[10]

So how much screentime is too much?

The World Health Organization (WHO) published screen-time recommendations for under-fives in 2019. For children under the age of three, it's zero, while those aged three and four should not have more than an hour a day. The American Academy of Pediatrics, Canadian Paediatric Society, Norwegian Health Authorities and Icelandic parents' associations all followed suit with similar guidelines. China went further, clamping down on 'spiritual opium' and limiting video gaming for under-eighteens to an hour on Fridays, weekends and holidays. The UK keeps things vague, with the Royal College of Paediatrics and Child Health suggesting families 'negotiate' with their children based on the individual child (thanks for that . . .). But for parents in Sweden, Finland and Denmark, there has been no advice, historically.

In 2023, a digital taskforce for the Danish government recommended a time limit for children's use of social media and raising the age of consent for the processing of personal data from thirteen to sixteen years.[11] At the time of writing, the government has agreed to raise the age limit for consent to share data with companies like Meta and Snapchat.[12] But in terms of social media use and screentime? Nothing. Denmark's Minister for Children and Education, Mattias Tesfaye, called for a change to the legislation so that children up to the age of six use screens as little as possible 'to protect children from potential negative consequences'. But so far? The law has not changed.

'I'm determined to wait for hard evidence,' says Stine Liv Johansen from the Centre for Children's Literature and Media at Aarhus University. Stine helped advise the Danish health authorities on their current legislation. We meet in her plant-filled office at the university, and she wears an olive-green jumpsuit that I instantly covet. The overall effect is one of pastoral bliss rather than advocate for a digital age. But Stine insists that the threat of screens has been overplayed: 'Many of the studies WHO have taken into account are based on data from Asia, where there is a very different culture.' Stine is currently taking part in a Danish research project exploring the use of digital media by children up to the age of eight in everyday life and says: 'If all the basics are in place for a child – good sleep, a good experience at school, good parents, etc. – then the time a child spends with digital devices shouldn't make much difference. The screentime itself is not the problem.'

Isn't this a bit 'guns don't kill people, bullets do'?

'It's more about the idea of a one-size-fits-all rule,' says Stine, who said of the global screentime restrictions in one interview on Denmark's TV 2: 'It's like saying that all children must wear rubber boots in October.'

Not a bad idea, I think, *it does rain most days . . .*

'The WHO data is just so black and white,' says Stine. 'They say a one-year-old can never see a screen – but imagine you're waiting at a doctor's surgery with a ten-month-old screaming its head off. Why not show them a video on your phone? Instead of focusing on "x number of minutes on screen", the conversation should be about the three Cs: content, context and connections.' She points out that it's not the first time 'older generations' (*thanks . . .*) have been suspicious of new technology. 'Before we were afraid of the iPad and the internet, we were afraid of cartoons, considered "lowbrow", "killing books" and "stunting children's development". Then came VHS. There's always been something people liked to worry about.'

Video killed the radio star back in 1979. Are screens really so different? *Am I just a dinosaur? Or worse, a snob?*

Stine has a novel argument in *praise* of screentime, too. 'The digital world is a bit like a schoolyard,' she tells me, 'You meet risks – and children should experience risk, learn coping skills and so grow. In this way, the risks of a digital life for a child have some benefit,' she believes – to survive in the modern world.

So how can we keep children safe? Allowing them to take 'risks' without going too far?

'By being with them,' is Stine's answer. Denmark's National Board of Health officially encourages parents to get gaming and 'take an interest in your child's online life'.[13] 'Just as we take our children to football and school events, we should help our children with digital media,' says Stine.

I struggle with a value judgement here: isn't football fractionally more improving? And I say this as someone who gives no hoots about balls.

But Stine calls me out: 'Parents need to stop condemning – stop standing with raised eyebrows and expressing that you think what young people are preoccupied with is stupid or a waste of time. Then you definitely shut down the dialogue.'

That's me told.

'If you don't understand what they're doing, ask – and listen!' Stine reads my mind as she continues: 'Many parents feel like they don't have the time, the energy or the will. But think of it like football again. I don't have to learn the rules of football to be able to talk to my son about football – about the team, how he feels when he wins, when he loses – to bake for the team, wash the kit, be a taxi to games, etc.'

Well, this sounds exhausting . . .

'The point *is*, I'm supporting him and inviting him to tell me about the experience,' says Stine, 'even though I don't personally care about football.'

So now I have to pretend I care about football AND Minecraft? I experience a wave of weariness. But Lego Man is coming around to the idea.

'You know what they say—'

'No? What do "they" say?'

'It's better to be inside the tent pissing *out* than on the outside pissing in.'

'Sorry?'

'We're all "sorry". I'm just saying that with this *gaming* stuff, we may as well be in it to see what's going on.'

I'm not sure who's the tent, who's the urinator, or who's the urine in this analogy, but I catch his drift.

'Children will come into contact with gaming or social media with or without parental permission,' says Stine. 'And if they use it without their parents, they'll be alone if they get into trouble.' She wants parents to roll their sleeves up and get involved. 'If your child expresses an interest in YouTube or other social media, see it as an opportunity to start researching the media yourself and get involved together with the child. Like the Münster family.'

Naja Münster is a thirteen-year-old Danish YouTuber with 232,000 subscribers, who's been online from the age of three ('And she and her family are all still very nice and normal!' Stine assures me).

I get in touch with Naja who does, indeed, come across as fairly grounded.

'I make one video a week for my channel, and that can take between one and three hours,' she tells me, 'so I use my phone a lot, but not more than my friends. And it doesn't take up any more of my time than my friends' sport clubs do. I go to YouTube while others go to gymnastics. Being on social media is also entertainment for me – like watching something funny on TV,' says Naja. 'Plus you're creative when you make videos for YouTube. There are some parents who think it's "dangerous" to be on social media. I think it's because they haven't familiarised themselves with what social media contains. You don't have to sit still for hours behind a screen because you are active on social media. You can actually be creative and active at the same time.'

This is a drum that Stine in the olive jumpsuit likes to bang, too. 'Screens aren't in opposition to an outdoorsy life, they're "as well as" – because kids can bring the iPads outdoors, filming nature and being creative.'

But who are these mini-Vikings making nature documentaries? Mine have never once done this. It's an expensive piece of kit, for starters. On the odd day when it's not raining or snowing in Denmark, the sun may deign to shine, in which case, one word: glare. And yet the chair of Denmark's teachers' union, BUPL, is another champion of 'screens in nature'. Elisa Rimpler recently told public service broadcaster DR that when children 'meet an animal and want to find out more about it . . . today, it is natural to use an app and not look up a book'.[14]

Orders books on animals and bug identification. Immediately.

As well as 'pro digital' Stine and her supporters, there's also the 'we've got it so may as well like it' gang. This includes the historian of play, Professor Ning, who takes a more pragmatic position: 'A lot of people say everything is worse these days. But, actually, combining gaming with physical play is a smart move, and a good answer to the constant complaining.' Because Luddites like me may be fighting a losing battle.

The Danish government has made a commitment to be 'digital by default', with paper used only as a last resort, so if you need to pay taxes or make an appointment with the doctor, you do it from a screen. The government's vision is that Denmark should be a digital frontrunner, globally, and many schools are now predominantly digital. 'My kids went to school in Odder,' says Stine, 'the first municipality in Denmark to give iPads to all children in schools in 2010.'

In Sweden, Malmö Council gave every child a laptop to bring home and work on. Most children get their own phones by the age of eight or nine, when they go to school by themselves, and Sweden has long been a cashless society. 'So kids need their phones for everything from their bus pass to their Swish – the app-based payment method in Sweden,' says Niki Brantmark, mother of daughters in Malmö. 'It's not like it was when we grew up!'

And perhaps this is it.

'The challenge must be to be able to keep up and accept the developments,' says YouTuber Naja's mum, Hanne. 'Denmark is a very open country. And we are also very open when it comes to raising our children. Another positive about social media is that it creates contacts and friendships. Back then, the child who had no friends at school went home and was alone. Today, the same child goes home and is with his online friends.' Because online, everyone can find a community somewhere.

But don't we all have to learn to respect and work with all sorts of people? Isn't the Nordic way about getting on with everyone? Even when we might not agree with them?

Research from the University of Michigan found that

empathy levels have decreased by 40 per cent in recent years.[15] Authors of the study fear we have become desensitised because of the technological world. Having online friends is easy, as we can tune out when things feel hard – but this approach is trickling down into real life. According to the Danish neuro-scientist Albert Gjedde, 'being on the iPad, computer or PlayStation a lot prevents children from meeting in reality and using all their senses. We can find it difficult to be together socially if our brain is not trained for it while we are children' (although I checked, and he plays a lot of Wordle, then posts about it on Twitter. So none of us are immune).[16] Adults are often sub-par digital role models – taking emails from work on their phone around the house or scrolling Facebook, Instagram – even Tinder. A third of Danish children told Nordic parenting group NOPA that their parents spend more time on the screen than on them.[17] Rasmus from Denmark's children's rights association hears this a lot. 'Now when kids are seven or eight, they realise that their parents are less inter-ested in them than they are in their iPhones.'

'Which is just so sad!' I try telling Veteran Viking, but she's playing chess on her smartphone.

'Which is just so sad!' I try again to American Mom, who puts down her iPad and lays her hands on my shoulders.

'Listen, grasshopper' – she's using her no-nonsense voice – 'we *all* wish it was the good old days when kids played with Rubik's Cubes, but we live in the *real* world. Your kids are still small. But mine are older: I've seen the future. And all of this . . .' – she lets go of me to gesture all around her at the iPad, iPhone, Apple TV and three children, all engaged in different screen-based pursuits – ' . . . isn't going anywhere. This generation will never use a watch to tell the time unless they get rich and buy a Rolex. They'll never order pizza from a big book. They'll never go to Blockbuster, even! Times change. We move on. Suck it up.'

I sniff slightly and blow my nose. *No Rubik's Cubes? She'll tell me kids don't play conkers next* . . .

'Anyway, I'd rather my kids were gaming than watching conspiracy theorists on TikTok.'

Oh God, I hadn't thought about this . . .

'And so – and I say this with love – stop being a BIG BABY!'

'You say this "with love"?!'

'I do.' She nods. 'Now let it go.'

I know I need to live in the real world. But as I scroll through my phone in bed that night (like I said: hypocrite), I see a post from the psychologist Adam Grant saying that the earlier kids get smartphones, the worse their mental health as adults.[18] He references a Sapien Labs study of more than 27,000 volunteers showing that owning a smartphone at a younger age predicts lower self-worth, motivation and resilience. It's also associated with an increase in sadness, anxiety and aggression, especially for girls.[19] The take-home? Smartphones should wait until children are thirteen.[20]

'There should be regulation and a real age limit on social media,' agrees technology researcher Søren. 'Parents often feel very alone in their decisions, but we know enough now that the health department and schools could all say to parents, "This is our advice." It would be easy for schools to tell all the parents of first graders, age six, not to give them a smartphone until they are, say, ten. And not to be on social media until at least thirteen. Because at present, social media is actually rewiring the whole idea of friendship, and kids' brains aren't ready for it.'

Silicon Valley leaders typically shield their own children from digital devices until they're in their teens. Bill Gates didn't let his kids have a phone until they turned fourteen. 'The people who work with this stuff don't want their kids to be around it,' Søren points out. His own daughter asked if she could go on Snapchat, aged twelve. 'And my answer was no,' he tells me, 'because there is an obvious business model for Snapchat and I don't feel my daughter should be helping them to profit from this.'

Rasmus goes further: 'I would compare it to the tobacco industry. The tech industry has spent billions lobbying for their "market" – which, by the way, is kids' attention. It has been disseminating information along the lines of "is it really so bad?" But it is. It really is. And we have the balance completely wrong at present.'

At this, the neighbourhood dogs start up again, setting each other off in a chorus of elegiac yowls as though sensing my growing despair. I hang up the call and stare at my laptop. If we decide to push back against screentime for our own children, it's unlikely they'll thank us. Or even like us. Being among the holdout parents won't be easy.

Isn't it the duty of the state to regulate technology that's harmful to its population? What happened to Denmark being a rules-based society? *Where are the boundaries? I need boundaries!*

My laptop doesn't respond, so I seek out the Vicks VapoRub and hide from the world under a tea towel and over a basin of hot water to inhale steam and attempt to shift my cold. The radio is on and I hear something that lift my spirits. A UCLA study of eleven- to thirteen-year-olds found that after just five days at an outdoor camp with no devices, children were able to read facial expressions and emotion significantly better.

After just five days!

So can I perhaps match my son's lust for gaming or balance it out with other things? Keep him busy? With improving, outdoorsy hobbies? In the spirit of *samfundssind*?! I stand at the window doomscrolling (#hypocrite) as an invitation arrives for a 10-kilometre hike with the Scouts. It's on Sunday – the day the redhead is normally allowed to play *Minecraft*. I ask him whether or not he'd like to go. He thinks about this, weighing it up.

'If I go, will there be snacks?' the redhead asks slowly.

'Loads,' I tell him.

'I'm in.'

Lego Man exhales.

One day at a time. Just take things one day at a time. Filling up his days with enough 'other stuff' that screentime is mini-mised – for now.

Full of ardent, if vague and snotty, purpose, I sally forth and sign him up.

What I've learned about Denmark's digital blind spot

1. Fucked. We're all fucked. No, but really, I need rules. Ideally from the government. Or the health authorities. Or schools (or prison-guard-turned-pedagogue Kitta . . .?!). Otherwise, it's on parents, and many of us are addicted, too. The evidence is clear: even if children under fourteen need phones for communication, they don't need smartphones or social media. I would love for parents to align on waiting so there aren't just a few children who feel left out of the phone arms race.

2. I've realised how much I rely on parents of older children for wisdom on what's to come. Self-parenting 101:
   find good role models who can offer advice and inter-
   ventions where necessary.
3. The redhead now has his 'hiker' badge and insists on
   telling everyone, just casually: 'Oh hey, just done a
   10km hike, no biggie . . .' Keeping kids busy with other
   things helps 'balance out' the digital/analogue diet.
4. I've fallen a little out of love with the Nordic dream. So
   I do what I always do when I'm sad: I read. Buried in
   a book and weighed down by a ten-tog duvet, things
   start to feel better. And after three chapters and two
   cups of tea, I get one marvellous idea to lift the spirits:
   an adventure.

12

The New Norse Sagas

THERE'S A SCENT of honeysuckle in the air and the rolling hills look a lot like home, were it not for the fact that they're dotted with pink-and-white . . . marshmallows?

'Why are there Flumps in the fields?' the youngest (by two minutes) asks.

'For the horses,' Lego Man tells him.

A firework display goes off in his tiny head: 'They feed horses Flumps here?'

'Yes, son. Yes, they do,' I very much want to reply, but the eldest butts in (age eight, he *knows* stuff and wants you to *know* he knows stuff).

'No: they wrap hay in pink-and-white plastic here,' the redhead informs him with a world-weary sigh. 'I know because my teacher told me.'

We're driving to Sweden in pursuit of another redhead – the ultimate Nordic hero. No, not Erik the Red or even Thor, but a nine-year-old girl.

Pippi Longstocking is the red-haired, freckled, super-humanly strong rebel girl who lives alone with her trusty horse and a monkey named Mr Nielsen. Leader of the 'plucky redhead' troop that includes orphan Annie and Anne of Green Gables, Pippi is the GOAT.* She befriends Tommy and Annika, the more conventional children next door, and all manner of scrapes ensue. Written in 1944 by the grandmother of Swedish literature, Astrid Lindgren, *Pippi Longstocking* became a best-seller. Five more Pippi books followed, and Astrid Lindgren sold 165 million copies worldwide, translated into 107 different languages. A TV show based on Pippi ran for just thirteen episodes in 1969 but is still one of the most popular programmes on TV in the Nordics today. 'It's always in the top five,' says Kajsa Peters, executive producer at Swedish national public television broadcaster SVT. Morten Skov, head of the children's division at Danish public-service broadcaster DR, agrees: 'Pippi has a huge influence.' So to understand modern Vikings, I must get to grips with Pippi.

Old Norse literature emphasised self-reliance, loyalty, modesty, hospitality, compassion, courage and wisdom through experience – the modern equivalents encourage similar qualities. The original sagas of the ninth century were oral histories of heroes, passed down from fathers to sons and mothers to daughters in Iceland, only written down in the thirteenth century. Then there were the Eddas, very much the soap operas of Viking times. Together, they inspired generations of writers (oh hi, Tolkien). And the *new* Norse sagas continue to influence mini-Vikings today.

School refusenik Pippi is the OG *Home Alone*, who holds no truck with societal norms. When told that children should be seen and not heard, Pippi retorts: 'People have got both eyes

---

* Greatest Of All Time.

and ears, I would hope. And even though I'm an absolute treat to look at, I definitely think ears benefit from a little exercise.'

As well as one-handed horse-lifting and besting strongmen, Pippi stops local boys beating up a smaller child and is a fierce defender of the underdog, since: 'If you are very strong, you must also be very kind.'

Astrid Lindgren's books – and *Pippi* in particular – are so influential in Europe that they were used after the Second World War to help 'de-Nazify' German youth, according to Astrid's great-grandson Johan Palmberg. Johan told the BBC that her rebellious, free-thinking approach to life combined with an inherent kindness and generosity was deemed 'the perfect thing' for children growing up in a war-ravaged Germany. And her books were an easy sell, since: 'She had this understanding of what a child might be interested in,' said Johan. 'She would be the first one to climb the trees and have the children follow her up.'[1]

So now I'm following her up the metaphorical tree. And I'm taking my children with me. We're making a pilgrimage to Astrid Lindgren's World in her hometown of Vimmerby, Sweden, a seven-hour drive from home through fields of Flumps to learn more about the gospel according to Pippi. While most theme parks are heavy on plastic tat and marketing opportunities, Astrid Lindgren's World is built on a 1:3 scale from predominantly natural materials and is mesmeric in its attention to detail. It's raining (because: Scandinavia) but this doesn't stop flocks of fans from scaling Pippi's house, clambering on her roof, meeting her horse and trying their hand at sailing her boat. The universe of Astrid's imagination is brought to life at the park, and we learn that Pippi isn't the only role model Vikings can thank Astrid Lindgren for. In her *Emil* stories, the eponymous hero runs away from home, steals a horse and tries to join the army, aged five. In *Nothing But Fun in Noisy Village*, the perpetually fidgeting Lasse is sent home from school by his remarkably farsighted teacher until the following year because, she senses, 'he had more playing to do' first. In Astrid's *Lotta* books, a kindergartener decides to move in with her elderly neighbour. Lotta is only four, but she's already an independent thinker. And this was important to her creator.

Born in 1907, Astrid Lindgren was a rebel from the start. She was the first girl in her town to cut her hair short, causing quite a stir (passers-by would ask her to remove her hat for a look). Aged eighteen, she became pregnant after a relationship with a married man who already had seven children. The scandal forced Astrid to leave Vimmerby. Her son, Lars, was born at Rigshospitalet in Copenhagen, where women were allowed to give birth without having to reveal the father's name. She left Lars in the care of a foster mother for three years to work in Stockholm. Astrid worked as a typist and stenographer, saving whatever she could to travel and be with Lars. Eventually, she could afford to raise him herself. But Astrid's early struggles had a huge impact on her work. She was a lifelong activist and helped ban corporal punishment of children in Sweden – the first country to do so in 1979. Throughout her books, strength of body and spirit is matched by kindness, generosity and independent thinking. Her creations continue to move Vikings today (Pippi Longstocking is still a popular fancy-dress outfit for adults and children alike).

'Pippi taught us never to underestimate children,' says Kim Fupz Aakeson, an award-winning contemporary children's writer in Denmark. 'She taught us that everyone should be valued as individuals, and we all get to find our way in the world.' This is a red thread in Astrid's books. 'Kids can do more than we believe as grown-ups,' says Kim, 'so nothing should be off-limits. And I think there's more fluidity in Denmark about what is appropriate for kids.' As well as children's books, Kim writes for adults, including gritty Nordic Noir and even a Dogme film, following the principles of the decidedly un-child-friendly Lars von Trier. But changing his audience doesn't mean as much of a gear shift as it might elsewhere. 'I deal with big themes in all my work: death, alcoholism – you name it. If we talk about life's highs and lows and normalise them from an early age, children will be more resilient in the long run. And books are a great way to teach empathy.'

Researchers from Oxford Brookes University have found that books let children 'try on' situations and feelings for themselves and help promote empathy for those who are different from us.[2] 'So why wouldn't we write about everything?' Kim asks. 'We also go further in Denmark. We feel we can write about more, and we write about the kind of kids you'd meet on the street.'

More so than in the other Nordic countries?

'Oh yes! In Sweden and Norway there's a shitshow if I use the language I hear on the street here. My approach is that if I hear it in the schoolyard, I can use it in my books. I don't want to *teach* kids "bad" words, but we have to be realistic. We have to dare to tell them the truth. I don't "clean things up".'

Kim is currently working on a prison drama, followed by a retelling of Norse mythology. 'The Norse gods feel very human,' he observes. 'They're good at fucking each other up!' Last year, he wrote a children's Bible. 'It's striking the difference in approach between the two – it says a lot about our cultures.'

How so?

'Shame and guilt are not so much of an issue in Norse mythology as they are in Christianity. You just have to be strong and brave in the Nordic tradition.'

Rather than a hierarchical deity who can smite you for eating the wrong type of fruit . . .?

Kim laughs. 'There's a darkness to the Nordic approach, too. But then, life can be dark.' So can the weather.

'I think there's a link between the two,' says Morten from DRTV, and most Vikings agree that the climate encourages Nordics to develop a strong interior life.

'When it's dark all the time, you're driven to tell stories,' says my Icelandic friend Birna in Reykjavik. 'It engages the imagination.'

Books have a special place in Icelanders' hearts and Iceland has more writers, more books published, and more books read per head than anywhere else in the world. Birna's husband Siggi tells me that there's a running joke that one day they'll erect a statue in Reykjavik 'to honour the only Icelander who never wrote a book'. Because stories matter.

Denmark's most famous storyteller, Hans Christian Andersen, was a master of darkness. The original Little Mermaid doesn't get the guy: instead, her tongue is cut out and her new legs feel like knives, slicing her with every step. The prince makes her sleep on a cushion outside his door like a dog, marries someone else, and our heroine turns to sea foam in a 'fairytale ending'. Then there's the Tin Soldier, who only has one leg, ends up in a drain, then a fish, then a fire. Your typical romcom. In *The Red Shoes*, a girl called Karen gets her feet chopped off. In *The Storks*, a boy who teases birds is given a dead baby brother as punishment. Weirdly, this hasn't been snatched up by Disney yet.

My youngest is still having flashbacks after our last visit to the Hans Christian Andersen Museum in Odense, the story-teller's hometown, where all of his tales are 'brought to life'. *The Tinder Box* had already driven him to the brink when *The Little Match Girl's* audio narration ended abruptly with: 'I am dead. The story is over. Do you want to see me die again?'

Bottom lip quivering, my son pointed nervously at the next exhibit: 'Mummy? Is that another one where they all die?'

'Um . . . it *might* be . . . '

It was.

'We do "darkness" well,' agrees Morten from DR, 'but it's how kids feel. They have big feelings, even from very young, and we should respect that. Nordic storytelling is good at helping children feel less alone.'

In the classic Finnish Moomin tales by Tove Jansson, the presence of deeper philosophical thoughts is normalised. Finland's most successful writer and illustrator introduced the world to the Moomin family in 1945 with the release of *The Moomins and the Great Flood*. Seven decades later, her white hippo-like animals with long, rounded snouts are more popular than ever. They go on adventures, meeting new friends and mysterious strangers, from the Groke, who freezes everything she encounters, to the small but fierce Little My and the harmonica-playing Snufkin. They confront obstacles in the natural world (comets, floods) as well as personal hurdles. In one of her most loved tales, *Moominpappa at Sea* (1965), Tove maps out midlife malaise in one of the most poignant descriptions of what it feels like to experience an episode of depression I've ever encountered. From grey-sky thinking ('the sea's just a weak character you can't rely on . . . ') to despair ('it takes a long time sometimes . . . a terrible long time before things sort themselves out') to a day when the sun finally comes out again and he allows himself to 'live and lead a wonderful life, full of troubles'.

Tove Jansson's niece, Sophia Jansson, believes the secret behind her aunt's success is that 'people find themselves in what she writes – it's personal but also universal'. And Tove was always interested in other people and the world around her. Sophia remembers that her aunt never treated her as a child growing up, but 'as interesting as anyone else in the room – it didn't matter who you were, she fixed her eyes on you and was interested'. Tove started writing seriously after the Second World War, a period she described as 'utterly hellish'. She felt a strong wish to write about a better world – and chose strange hippo creatures as the vehicle to do so.

'Moomins are very "human", but they're *not* human, so Tove had that extra freedom,' says Sophia. 'There is room for imagination that things might be different, and hence better. This has always been a solace for readers.'

In her 1960 book *Who Will Comfort Toffle?* the hero 'doesn't notice quite how lonely he has grown'. Tove notes: 'If all you do is hide away, you'll never find a friend.' Toffle eventually finds a purpose when a smaller creature needs his help: 'Both had seen the end of fear and fright and long, dark night, now each has found a friend.' (No: YOU'RE crying . . .)

In the warmth of the Moomin House, all are welcome and safe. Tove always believed in equality regardless of sex, gender, race. 'The soul behind the outer shell was what was important to her,' says Sophia, who has fond memories of summers spent with Tove and her partner, the artist Tuulikki Pietilä. As a high-profile lesbian, Tove has long been an icon in the LGBTQ+ community 'And many of her characters in the Moomin books are non-binary or non-gender specific,' Sophia tells me.

I think about this. Okay, so the Hemulen 'always wore a dress he inherited from his aunt'. But aren't the core family of Moominmamma, Moominpappa, Moomintroll and the Snork Maiden fairly . . . traditional?

'Yes and no,' says Sophia. 'They are gifted with personality traits that are not necessarily stereotypical.'

What about Moominmamma's apron?

'Oh, that was for syndication,' she tells me. 'They felt they needed to distinguish characters. That was why Pappa got a cane and Mamma got an apron. But that came later – her original stories were much less stereotypical. These gender stereotypes were not Tove's intentions; it was society putting constraints on the Moomins.'

Society, messing things up for everyone . . .

Changes like this may seem small, but they have an impact on receptive young minds. Global headlines roared that it was 'political correctness gone mad' in 2015 when Sweden added the gender-neutral pronoun *hen* into the official dictionary. There was predictable outrage in some quarters, but as my Swedish friend and mum of two Maria tells me, '*Hen* is very useful if it's unclear who's involved or it doesn't matter what gender someone is. I think it's smart. In children's books, when it doesn't matter if they are male or female animal characters, they'll use *hen*.' A Florida State University sociologist led a comprehensive study of twentieth-century children's books and found that heroes were more than twice as likely to be male.[3] Books featuring animals have even more of a gender bias, with heroic male animals outnumbering females three to one. So it might be high time we all embraced *hen*. 'It's fairer and it's important for children to see that girls and boys can be the key player in a story,' agrees Maria. I am forever editing children's books as I read them aloud. I don't want my small people getting the idea that only boys go on adventures and that girls are always the sensible ones (or 'fun-killers' as Lego Man puts it).

'We've got all these history books filled with men and written by men, so it's a helpful way of redressing this, and understanding that when you're writing about a character, it doesn't always matter whether they're a boy or a girl,' says Maria. 'It's not that Swedish children don't say "he" or "she" in kindergarten, it's just that we use *hen* when it doesn't matter.'

My children have known and understood when to use they/them pronouns since starting kindergarten in Denmark. A fuss-free, open-hearted approach of inclusivity has meant that by the time they're talking, it's second nature for mini-Vikings. Two children in the year above my son at school are non-binary. Some parents and teachers are still getting their heads around this. But the kids are all right: their classmates are just their classmates.

Sophia describes the Nordic perspective in children's literature as 'very humanistic', adding: 'Tove always recognised that everyone should have a voice and everyone should be seen.' Like in 'The Invisible Child' story (*Tales from Moominvalley*, 1962) where a small, scared girl called Ninny has been so neglected, she disappears. Ninny is welcomed into the Moomin family and treated with care and respect. As she gets her confidence back, she becomes visible, bit by bit. Tove knew how much a child could be damaged by not being loved. And unqualified love is fundamental in the new Norse sagas.

You don't have to 'win' or 'be the best' or even behave well to be loved as a child. 'It's unconditional,' says Morten. 'We're not afraid of kids being unfair, or hurting themselves, or losing, because that's part of life. They are still loved.' Pippi

Longstocking is a prolific liar, but Tommy's and Annika's friendship is given freely with no strings attached. Another of Astrid's protagonists, Emil, is described as 'a dreadful little boy' who 'got up to more mischief than there were days in the year'. He annoys the people of his town so much that they collect money to send him away to America. His mother, horrified, announces that they will do no such thing: 'We love him just as he is.' (To which the housemaid adds: 'We ought to think about those Americans, too. They haven't done us any harm, so why should we dump Emil on them?')

'I like this approach, because it's real,' says the chef Trine Hahnemann, who raised her children in the US and the UK. 'In some countries it can all get so sickly sweet in books and TV for children.' She tells me how when her children were small, they would watch things like Barney, the big purple dinosaur. 'I just remember thinking it was so fake! One character would hold the door open for the other and they would say "thank you" and I just thought: *No child is like that!* Children can annoy each other and they can be selfish. That's what kids do. And that's okay.' It's even expected in the Nordic countries.

Take Bamse, the big yellow teddy bear who has been the star of Denmark's most popular children's series *Bamses Billedbog* (*Teddy Bear's Picture Book*) for the past forty years. And he's a little shit.

'It comes naturally to Bamse to believe that he is the centre of the world, and he can be a little despotic now and then,' reads the official character breakdown for Denmark's most famous bear. But he is still loved. 'Children identify with him because he is spontaneous and selfish,' says Morten from DRTV, home to Bamse's show. 'He's a universal character in whom children can recognise themselves.' Bamse lives in the woods, bossing around his friend Kylling – or 'Chicken' – who plays a younger sibling role. 'This mirrors kids' reality,' says Morten. 'They get used to being in relationships that are difficult and where there is conflict, but you can still be friends. That's a powerful message.'

So the fluffy tyrant is actually teaching us all a valuable lesson? I'm not sure it's one I ever learned during a childhood where eyebrows were often raised but never voices. Conflict, I summised, was 'bad' and to be avoided at all costs. But that's not life. And it's not how Vikings are raised. 'There is huge value in not only talking about the "good" and "easy" things – we should train our kids in talking about and accepting more complex emotions, too,' says Morten, because 'there are no "wrong" feelings'. Bamse's show is so big in Denmark that when the man who plays Chicken had his fiftieth birthday party and guests travelled from all over, Danish border guards happily waved one merrymaker through, despite the fact that she'd forgotten her passport. Apparently, any friend of Chicken was a friend of Denmark.

*   *   *

Since the original Norse sagas were told, rather than read, I'm interested in what the modern 'talkies' – aka kids' TV – can teach me about raising Vikings. Danish anthropologist Christian Groes describes watching Danish children's television as a lot like taking LSD (and he's Danish). So in the name of research and the pursuit of a natural high, I tune in. On day one of this experiment, my children and I are greeted with an animated series aimed at four- to eight-year-olds about John Dillermand, a man who overcomes hardships with his record-breaking genitals. Danish slang for penis is *diller,* while *mand* means 'man'. So 'Dillermand' directly translates as 'penis-man'. He wears a woollen hat and a knee-length red-and-white striped bathing suit. Like an X-rated Wally in *Where's Wally?* (*Where's Willy?*). There's also Onkel Reje – or Uncle Prawn. A sweary Satanist in a heavy metal band, who we first encounter wearing a black-leather thong and a studded bra, scratching his bare behind before doing a fart – as my children hoot with laughter.

Do my children have terrible taste? Or do all children have terrible taste? I wonder. Out loud. To Morten at DRTV, who programmes these shows.

'These stories work because in all of us there is rebellion,' says Morten. 'Parents don't always like this, but then it's not important that parents love it. They show kids it's okay to be different.' Uncle Prawn and John Dillermand are anarchists in the Pippi Longstocking mould. But there's also an attempt to represent other outlooks in Nordic children's culture, too.

'We can't all lift a horse, is the way I look at it,' says Hr. Skæg or Mr Beard – a six-foot-five-inch giant of a man with a floor-skimming beard who looks like he makes artisanal cheese but is basically Beyoncé in Denmark. Real name Mikkel Lomborg, he fronts a TV show about letters and numbers and is swamped by fans wherever he goes. Curious to find out more, I arrange to meet him, and he tells me how he too is inspired by the Pippi Longstocking stories: 'But Hr. Skæg isn't a rebel, he represents Tommy and Annika – because they are the iden-tification figures for many. Hr. Skæg normalises failure and the underdog. He teaches kids that this is okay.'

Interesting, I think. And then: *You wouldn't get that back home . . .*

We have a photo together in the hope that it might give me

some street cred with my own children, but when I get home, they have other plans. My daughter is staggering around with a puzzled dog while my son is dressed as a monkey. It's hard to know where to start.

'What are you doing with the dog?' I try.

'It's not a dog: it's a horse and I'm Pippi – so strong I can lift a horse. That's Tommy and he's Mr Nielsen, the monkey.' She points at her brothers. Apparently, there weren't any takers for Annika. 'We're making a new book, so if you don't mind . . .?' She proceeds to dictate a fanciful array of dark twists involving pancakes, pirates and several secondary characters, all called Susan.

Anarchy: check.

Empowered female leads: check.

Love and tolerance no matter what? Pending . . .

'Come on!' my daughter continues from behind armfuls of dog: 'We haven't got all day! We're trying to find hidden treasure. Or *leverpostej* sandwiches. Whichever we find first. Ready? Let's go . . .'

The redhead and his brother follow along as best they can, and a new Norse saga begins.

What I've learned about the new Norse Sagas

1. Never underestimate. Even very young children can surprise us in their abilities and understanding. The fact that my smalls have been able to talk about life, the universe and everything in age-appropriate language since toddlerhood has astounded me (and their grandparents). Life can get gritty, but honesty might actually be a pretty good policy. I once interviewed a child

psychotherapist who told me that if we don't tell children the truth, they make it up. They invent their own version of what's happened. And often, what children imagine is worse than the reality. So from a really young age, Vikings are told the truth.

2. We shouldn't shy away from the dark side. We don't have to go full-on *Little Mermaid*, but life isn't a series of Disney dance-to-credits endings. Life won't always be fair. We don't always win, and that's okay. Children can handle this. A few smaller 'practice hurts' in childhood means they'll cope better with the bigger hurts that can blindside us in adulthood.

3. All are worthy, no matter what. And everyone deserves love (even if they're behaving like a little shit. I'm looking at you, Bamse). Being around these stories and TV shows as an adult has helped me shake off decades of social conditioning and realise that I am enough. Even on days when my parenting is sub-optimal (hi, unicorn bubble-machine day!). Even on days when my children are feral (hi, every day!), I have hope. That we'll be okay. Probably.

13

Schooltime (Barely)

I T CAME WITHOUT warning. With no heads-up. No disclaimer to sign ('Tick here if you're happy for your child to turn temporarily vegan!'). In the spring of the year my eldest started school, he emerged one afternoon white as a sheet. Which is saying something when you already have red hair, pale skin and live in Mordor.

'Are you okay?'

'Mmm . . .' is all he would mumble.

On the way home, past tractors trundling manure and carpets of yellow rapeseed flowers, he barely spoke. Turning off onto side streets lined with trees, heavy with pink blossom, he asked what was for dinner.

'Pasta,' I told him, and his shoulders lowered slightly. Back home, I FaceTimed my fellow fish-out-of-water friend, American Mom, to ask if she had any intel, and she informed me that it had been 'spontaneous dissection day' for some classes. Teachers invited a parent who also happens to be an emergency-room doctor to come in with a cow's heart and a pig's liver for the most visceral biology lesson ever.

WTF? I did biology GCSE without so much as holding a scalpel. But in Denmark they let six-year-olds loose with a surgeon's knife? He'd only just started school. *Shouldn't reading, writing and the number stuff come first? What's with the Tarantino scenes?*

American Mom shook her blow-dry and said that was nothing: her eldest dissected an eyeball last year. 'And you still have the school trip to look forward to!'

Oh God . . .

I learned about these 'educational' excursions when I first arrived in Denmark. Peter Sandøe, professor of bioethics at the University of Copenhagen, explained how dissections were an old Danish tradition going back 400 years. He assured me that taking a trip to see a dissection was 'a typical thing to do' in Denmark to 'open children's eyes to the world of science'. Dissections are carried out countrywide, on creatures from snakes to seals, whales to wolves, lions to lizards. Every Dane remembers their first 'dissection trip', and animal autopsies are so popular in Denmark that there are often two a day in school holidays to meet demand.

'Danes just aren't squeamish about animals,' local teacher Louise Lingaard told me. 'We were an agricultural nation for so long that we're still pretty used to the circle of life and all that. Take horses.'

Okay . . .

'We're huge horse lovers in our family, but sometimes a horse has to be put down and fed to the lions,' she says, just casually. 'I think my daughter was around the same age as your son when we watched a horse autopsy together.'

Ahh, mother–daughter bonding.

'At one point, the intestine sprung out at her, and I was

worried she would freak out.' Horse guts are huge, I'm told. 'But she was fine! There's an understanding that you can be a horse lover *and* be interested in the way an animal's body works. That you can be a meat eater and you can know that animals are part of the food chain. It's all part of a child's education.'

'And don't worry: the veganism doesn't last long!' American Mom messaged with a thumbs-up emoji.

Two days later, my son made himself a liver-pâté sandwich and I overheard him telling his then three-year-old siblings, with some authority, how the left ventricle of the heart was 'the powerhouse of the whole body'.

Is it? I was amazed. *He knows things! He can't read but he already knows things! Beyond his parents' knowledge pay-grade! How did that happen?*

'School,' said Veteran Viking, who has a tendency to take things literally.

'Yes, thank you.'

'I mean *Danish* school. We do things differently.' She can say that again.

All children in Denmark have access to tuition-free government *folkeskole* from the age of six until they turn sixteen. There's no scramble to secure a place or move house to a good 'catchment zone'.

'You just go to the local school,' says my willowy artist friend Camilla, whose daughters go to the same school as she did ('with many of the same teachers!').

Some parents choose a private school or *friskole* because they're smaller or have a particular educational stance or specialism. 'But in Denmark a private school is not very private,' says Veteran Viking. Three-quarters of the fees are paid by the government, so private schools in Denmark often cost no more than daycare.

'It's very different from the situation in the UK,' says Professor Ning. Parents might pay around DKK 3,000 a month (£350) for private-school education, from breakfast club at 6.30 a.m. to after-school club until 5 p.m. 'So if you have that money accounted for in your budget from daycare, it's quite normal for parents to send their children to a *friskole*,' says Ning. 'In Copenhagen and other big cities, I'd say around 50 per cent of parents do this.' As one *friskole* dad says: 'The Danish government are prepared to subsidise a very good education – it's an investment in our children.' Because for every DKK 3,000 a parent pays for a private school education each month, the government contributes DKK 9,000 (£1,040) from the communal pot, replenished via taxes.

Either way, a child will rock up at school aged six in Denmark, Sweden, Iceland and Norway, or aged seven in Finland.

'And once they start, I imagine they get down to work, right?' every friend and relation from back home asks (regularly). 'I suppose they really knuckle down, catch up on all they've missed by starting school so late?'

'Err, not so much.'

Because it's still pretty relaxed, compared to other cultures. The current Danish system can be traced back to our old friend and founder of Denmark's group-singing tradition, N. F. S. Grundtvig. The nineteenth-century clergyman, politician and poet advocated a new outlook on education: teaching according to children's interests and inspiring them to learn, rather than forcing them to. More carrot, less stick.

After the Second World War, Danes added another layer to

their promise for future generations: prioritising free-thinking above all else. There was a movement to emphasise democracy in schools, to catch children early, in the hope that something like a Nazi occupation could never happen again. And free-thinking plus an anti-authoritarian streak have been championed ever since. Teachers are addressed by their first name, there is no uniform, and schools remain unlocked, because 'there is trust that students won't run off!' says Mette Bay Velling, a teacher from Mariager in Jutland, who I meet at a Schools Democracy Festival (Danes love democracy).

'There's still respect for teachers, but the relationship between child and teacher is equal,' says Mette. 'A teacher may have a lot of knowledge, but children should also be respected as individuals.'

This way of thinking has been widespread in Denmark for generations. 'I would always argue with my teachers and my parents,' says teacher Louise. 'If I could argue that something was reasonable, that it was important, then I would be heard. It's healthy when kids are so secure that they dare to tell us what they'd do differently.' Vikings are encouraged to be free-thinkers. 'We ask kids their opinion and encourage them to consider: what do I like? What do I want to do? How do I feel? How can I solve this problem? They're taught to think – not just pass exams.'

From the start of school in Denmark, children learn to question, debate and stand up for what they believe in. Literally. 'Kids do show and tell, or sing a song – anything, really – we normalise standing up and opening our mouths very early,' says Louise.

I wonder how this fits with Jante's Law, where no one is to think they're special and showing off is frowned upon.

'Ah, but they're not showing off – they're speaking out.

There's a difference,' says Louise. 'You have to stand up for what you want, or argue your case in Denmark.' Whether you like it or not. 'Many aren't so confident, but they know that there's no way out!'

The redhead hated speaking out at school when he started. Two years on and he still doesn't love it, but he knows that it's important to have a voice. He's accepted public speaking as part of school life and his nervousness has lessened. Primary-school assembly has become another form of exposure therapy and his confidence is growing.

I love this, since public speaking is seldom taught at state schools in the UK. The Oracy campaign is fighting to change this, with speaking now part of the curriculum in Scotland and Wales. But few places elsewhere prioritise public speaking. Denmark is an outlier among the Nordic countries in oracy skills. 'We don't do that so much in Finland,' says Emilia, the Finnish Scout leader with the big blue eyes, married to my Danish friend Andreas. 'I always see how comfortable Andreas is when he has to speak at an event or give a toast at a family gathering or anything like that – and I think it's a great skill to teach children. I definitely missed out on that in Finland. I'm glad our boys are going to school in Denmark, where they'll learn public speaking as part of their education. Eventually.'

'Eventually' is the word.

'Oh, but I love the fact there's not a lot of pressure on kids here,' says Niki in Sweden: 'I remember visiting the UK when my kids were in kindergarten and all the other kids that age could write. Parents would say to their children, "Why don't you read this out loud to us?" Showing off. And I'd think, *Oh God! I'm failing them!* But back in Sweden this was no problem. I asked the pedagogues, "Should I be helping them learn to read?" And they told me: "No! You be the parent; we'll be the teacher. When they're ready, they'll do it." And they did.' Niki has seen first-hand how all of her children 'got the hang of reading' when they were ready, 'in a way that was less stressful for kids and for parents'. She's grateful now that Swedes take things more slowly. 'Friends in the UK have kids who spend hours each night doing homework – so they do, too. And then everyone's miserable!'

Homework in the Nordic countries is minimal. Sabilah Eboo Alwani from the Faculty of Education at the University of Cambridge thinks that this is a good thing, since 'the early onset of lots of homework erodes quality time from a developmental point of view'. I'll just let that sink in, for any policymakers reading.

'Until you reach the age of ten, there is no homework at all where we are,' says Niki. 'Even after that, they're not allowed homework on Fridays for the weekend or over the holidays – because they don't want to stress kids out.' Niki tells me how her twelve-year-old has only just started getting grades. 'And there's no competition at school, either – I'm really pleased and protective of this. It means children are much more creative, as they have opportunity to just *play*.'

Photographer and father of three Johannes in Helsinki says that there isn't a culture of pushing children to 'excel' in Finland, either. He explains how his eleven-year-old and thirteen-year-old sons have been deemed 'high achievers' at school, 'So we're actually encouraging them to do less. We don't want them to push themselves too hard. We keep telling them, "It's okay! It's enough! You are enough."'

Astonishing, I think. But also: *smart*, since confidence, motivation, resilience and communication have been found to be 'as or more important than academic qualifications', according to the education charity Sutton Trust.[1]

The Danish school system largely avoids class rankings and formal tests until the end of *gymnasium* school, aged eighteen or nineteen (more in Chapter 16). This is the equivalent of A-levels in the UK and high school in the US. In Denmark, graduating teens get a score from -3 all the way up to 12. Local teacher Louise tells me that when her daughter graduated, she thought she'd get a double zero: 'We call this the "glasses grade",' she tells me, making two circle shapes with her fingers and holding them up to her eyes to make spectacles. 'So I sat her down and I told her: "You know what? It doesn't matter. I didn't get high grades at school, neither did your dad, and we turned out just fine. We have great jobs and we have a great life!" Most kids born today will live for 100 years. Your life is not over as a teenager if you don't get top grades.'

She's right, I know. But still. We're all thinking it: *How did her daughter do?*

Louise makes the glasses sign: 'She got a double zero. But that's okay! She's gone on to get a good job as a police officer, she has a great life. I'm incredibly proud of her!'

This attitude sounds outlandish to many of us. I was drilled to 'succeed' at school, encouraged to grasp for exceptionalism. Yet I'm now parenting an eight-year-old who's only just learning to read. A sentence that still makes me a little queasy.

'But, darling, you were on *Point Horror* books by the time you were eight!' my mother tells me.

'Well, that's not how they do things here,' I tell her.

'Oh dear.' She shakes her head. 'You do look tired. Hollow eyes.'

'Thank you.'

'Dark circles.'

'This is actually quite confronting . . .' I don't know if I mean the unspoken criticism of my son's reading ability or my increasingly ragged complexion. Both, probably. The truth is, my eight-year-old is still sounding out sentences one at a time. But he *is* sounding out Richard Dawkins (the YA one, but still). Mini-Vikings may not be able to read by the time their UK and US peers can, but they're taking in the world around them at an astounding pace. This means that by the time they can read, they can tackle far more interesting books than early readers elsewhere. There is no *Roger Red Hat* in the land of Nord. I'm trying hard to be okay with this (rather than a dirty bomb of cynicism) because: science.

Research now shows that pressuring children to read too early can cause stress and anxiety. A study from the University of Regensburg in Germany found that later readers easily catch up with and even surpass early readers.[2] Learning later allows children to match their knowledge of the world to the word's they learn, as 'they've got to unlock the ideas,' says Professor Sebastian Suggate, who led the study. He also found that learning to read early has 'no discernible benefits' by the time a child turns fifteen.[3]

The latest Programme for International Student Assessment (PISA) data on students' proficiency in reading ranks all the Nordic countries above the OECD average in terms of students' proficiency in reading, with Denmark and Finland ahead of both the UK and the US.[4] By age fifteen, Danish students are also ahead of the OECD average in mathematics and science.[5] UNICEF's latest global league table of children's overall academic and social skills ranks Norway at number one.

Denmark comes seventh, Finland, ninth, and Sweden four-teenth. The UK and the US? Numbers twenty-six and thirty-two respectively.[6] The *Cambridge Primary Review* concluded: 'There is no evidence that a child who spends more time learning through lessons – as opposed to learning through play – will "do better" in the long run.'[7] So children in the Nordic countries play for longer, learn later, but still do better than children in the US and the UK – and they're happier, too.[8] I look out at the smalls currently gambolling in the garden at a time when their contemporaries in the UK and US would be knuckling down to homework and think perhaps my Viking neighbours are on to something.

I still worry that children learning to read so late will miss out on the full canon of children's literature. 'How can they possibly cram it all in?' I ask my son's teacher, who assures me that mini-Vikings don't miss out.

'We recommend parents read to children, for twenty to thirty minutes a day, until they reach around the age of twelve. Even when they *can* read, it's a *hyggelig* bonding activity between parent and child.' Reading bedtime stories is one of the lovelier parts of parenting and I remember how play researcher Sabilah told me that reading to children 'counted' as play, too.

Two birds with one book . . . But still: until they're twelve?

Reading aloud for thirty minutes a day, every day, for twelve years clocks in at 2,190 hours. That's 292 working days. More than a year's work.

I could do an MBA in that time! Train to be a phlebotomist!

'Yes, but would your children be happier?' says Veteran Viking.

'Err . . .'

She looks around her before divulging: 'You can cheat a little.

We do half reading, half audiobooks.' Veteran Viking plugs her youngest into an iPhone and I thank her for her honesty.

But that doesn't mean parents get to kick back until their children turn fifteen. Since the 1970s in Denmark, parents have been mandated by law to be 'collaborators' with their children's education. 'It doesn't matter whether you're a CEO or a stay-at-home parent [rare in Denmark]; you will be expected to be involved in school life,' says Professor Ning.

'It's a lot, but it's understood by employers that you just take the time off for your kids,' says Nadine, the Dane who spent ten years in Silicon Valley. 'In the US I was a "reading mom", reading two hours a week to kids because teachers didn't have time. It felt like a civic duty and I wanted to be supportive, but it was optional. In Denmark, it's expected to a far greater extent – that you'll just take the morning off to be at your kids' craft day or leave work early to help with a class event.'

I get daily updates from my son's school via not one, not two, but three different forms of intranet (why?), informing me of parent-participation days, annual meetings and events. Then there are the in-theory-optional-but-in-practice-obligatory committees and social groups. I currently see my children's classmates' more than I see my closest friends. As Nadine said, this isn't exclusive to Denmark. But parents in Denmark are expected to do all of this on top of a full-time job.

Which is fine if your Danish employers are on board. But for friends who work remotely for British or US employers, it's not so easy. As a freelancer, I can usually be flexible. But there are times of the year when it all gets too much and I wonder whether the sheer organisation required to parent a child in Denmark – let alone three – is beyond me.

'How do I do this?' I wail. To anyone who will listen.

American Mom flashes me a Whitestrips-bright smile and tells me she manages it with 'a whiteboard and caffeine'.

I tell her I might need something stronger. Especially since schools also encourage 'playgroups' outside of school. Class representatives organise a rota so that once a month, parents invite five or six children over for *spise og lege* (or 'eat and play') after school. 'It's a different mix of children at a different house every time, so everyone participates. It's really *hyggeligt*,' says Lise, the Viking from Valhalla, 'and it fosters trust and community.'

'There's a lot of focus on making all kids feel welcome,' agrees my friend Camilla, 'with open doors between classrooms and *hygge* hour every Friday. Children take it in turns to bake, then they have an hour a week where it's more relaxed.'

'More' relaxed? As in 'horizontal'?!

'They can just socialise – something Danish schools do very well and helps a child learn to be a good person,' says Camilla. In fact, tolerance and social skills appear to be major parts of the curriculum.

This feels important, since many schools around my way aren't exactly diverse. We've been lucky where my children have ended up. But I've been to events at friends' schools where there's a sea of flaxen-haired children, so similar-looking that often no one's quite sure whose offspring is whose. I don't want my children growing up thinking this is 'normal'.

'We absolutely teach kids that you have to get along with different people from different backgrounds who experience life differently,' teacher Mette tells me. Although because Denmark is still more homogenous than the US or the UK, this is often focused on different age groups in lieu of any *actual* diversity in class. 'We have a special bonding session each week where seventh graders [age twelve to thirteen in Denmark] have "friendship class" with second graders [seven- to eight-year-olds], for example. The little ones learn a lot from the big kids and the bigger kids remember what it was like to be small and so develop their empathy. There's a team coordinator there if needed, but mostly we see that kids manage themselves in friendship class. It has a really positive impact.'

This is like Lise's 'sit on your hands' tactic in *vuggestue* or even the 'alloparent' idea in *børnehave* (see Chapter 4). 'We get a child to where we want them, but at their own pace,' agrees teacher and head of Denmark's 'Playful Learning' programme Tobias Heiberg. 'It's a deliberate tactic to just lean back. Shut your mouth. *Wait.* Raising Vikings has a lot to do with ninja skills . . .'

Isn't this disingenuous? Aren't we all supposed to be equal? Or, in the words of George Orwell (almost), are some Vikings more equal than others?

'I think we have to remember that we are the grown-ups,' is how Tobias justifies it. 'We can think ahead. We can be flexible. And tactical. And sensitive. The Nordic countries are all pretty similar in this respect. And it's an approach that we see works.'

Even though it's sneaky?

'It's "tactical",' Tobias corrects me.

Mette agrees: 'In Denmark we always believe in the good of the kids, that they always want to do the "right thing". If kids are acting out of the ordinary, it's a sign that something is out of whack. And *then* we help. If they can't fulfil what we want them to do, it's not on them,' says Mette. 'Teachers here never talk about kids being "bad" – instead, it's the adults' responsibility to change their behaviour and meet the child where they are.'

Blimey, I think: *this sounds like hard work.* I'm very glad home-schooling days are over. Teachers are a special kind of saint.

In Denmark, there's been a policy of including all students in mainstream public schooling where possible – whether they have ADHD or dyslexia or other challenges that may impact learning. 'But more and more have a diagnosis of one kind or another nowadays,' says my friend Anne, a teacher of sixteen years' standing, who I met at choir in my childfree days. Anne puts the hike in diagnosis in Danish classrooms down to better detection, but also fears that with greater awareness may have come overdiagnosis ('we talk about it so much now'). Either way, it makes teaching trickier. 'There may be a few in each class taking up all of the teacher's attention.' And class sizes have stretched. 'We're supposed to have twenty-four to twenty-eight students per class, but many classes exceed this,' says Anne.

Just like at home, I think, disheartened.

Denmark's school system is far from perfect. In 2022 a TV 2 documentary exposed accusations of abuse, bullying and violence at an elite Danish boarding school attended by royalty. Crown Prince Frederik of Denmark and Princess Mary immediately pulled their son from Herlufsholm school, saying they were 'deeply shaken by the reports'. But the exposé showed that within the walls of Europe's exclusive boarding schools, things look much the same as elsewhere: with social privilege outweighing cultural norms.

There's a common misconception that private schools don't exist in Finland, although around 2 per cent of schools are private, according to the Finnish Ministry of Education and Culture. But *profiting* from education is prohibited, and the goal of the public education system since the 1970s has been to equalise Finnish society. There's no school selection and because everyone attends the same state schools, even the wealthiest and most educated members of society are invested in making these great. And they are great. Since the 2000s, Finland has been a global leader in education. To understand why, I get a quick history recap from Finnish friends.

When Finland emerged from years of war against the Soviet Union in the late 1940s, it was poor, with few natural resources. Finns felt that educating children was the best way for the next generation to get ahead. But Finns also value childhood. So school doesn't start until children turn seven and schooldays are short – 8 a.m. until noon or 2 p.m., depending on the day and group. Lessons last forty-five minutes with a fifteen-minute break after each one, for play. After-school provision is usually offered until 4 p.m., when parents leave work to pick children up. So in Finland, students spend only 600 hours in school. While in the US, the average time spent at school is 1,100 hours – almost double that of Finnish children.*

Finns see the goal of education as not to prepare children for tests, but for life. Finns of both sexes study carpentry, sewing and cooking. Oh, and 'teaching to test' is an alien concept – Finland spends ten times more on teacher training and career development than it does on testing. Teachers are trusted as professionals and enjoy significant leeway in classrooms – sensible, since research suggests that teacher autonomy is linked with happier classrooms. Teachers working with seven-to-thirteen-year-olds must have a master's in education, while

---

* The UK doesn't currently collect OECD data on this. So who knows how long British schoolchildren are slogging away for?

those working with older children have a master's degree in their subject.

'I've been very impressed and pleased with the school system,' says Katja in Helsinki. 'The Finnish approach is inclusive and they'll work with the students – so they'll vote on what they're going to be eating, what activity to do. Schools work with a child to find out what they need and their specialist interests. My son is into coding, so gets a free after-school coding programme. The teachers have said, "He knows more than we do!" but they still do all they can to help him. In North America, when I was growing up, you'd get less encouragement for individual skills. You had to fit a mould, and you'd only get extra help in something if the school knew how to manage it. In Finland, you get help and support regardless. And we all work better when we're able to use our strengths.'

'We always feel supported as parents, too,' says Johannes in Helsinki. His daughter is non-verbal and attends a school for children with special needs. 'The headteacher told us on day one: "Your role is to be parents. Nothing else." And this was so refreshing. Because when you have a child with special needs, it feels like the list of things that you *could* or *should* be doing is endless. But all that her teachers want us to do is love her. I'm really satisfied with the system here.'

I think perhaps I might be, too – eyeing my eight-year-old who has just built a fighter jet out of Lego, freestyle, and is now explaining life cycles to one twin and the D-Day landings to the other. *Extraordinary* . . .

Trine Hahnemann schooled her children in the UK and US as well as in Denmark and reflects on how the education systems compare. 'We pay high taxes in Denmark, but I think we get a lot back.' As Denmark's most beloved baker, who has been running her own businesses for years, it's safe to say Trine contributes a lot in Danish tax – more than she would do in the UK or US. 'But a friend from the UK who sent her kids to private school and I sat down and looked at everything from the amount of tax we've both paid over the course of our children's education, to uniform and school fees. And honestly? When it all adds up? We both "paid" about the same. But I said to her: "You only put your kids through school with that amount. I put other people's kids through school, too. Those who didn't have high-earning parents got a better education as a result. So I got better value for money, as I helped other children, too." I feel proud of that.'

She should feel proud. All Vikings should. Remember the tax-maths my US friend and I did after we left hospital, post-birth? How Danes pay high taxes but actually end up with more disposable income than the average American or Brit? How they're happier? And less stressed? Well, most of the Vikings I speak to take this for granted. It's only internationals who see this as oddly eccentric. And it's only Nordic nationals who've spent time overseas and experienced the alternative – like Trine – who are quite so grateful to have been born Viking. Getting children through school in a way that doesn't break their spirit or put them under undue pressure feels like a goal worth fighting for. Rather than viewing the school years as hurried, intense preparation for adulthood, what if we saw them as an opportunity to encourage a love of learning?

What I've learned about schooling Vikings

1. Nordics take their time. As the alumna of a school where pushy parents were the norm,* this has been hard to swallow. But I'm trying to have *tillid* – trust and faith – that my children will get there in the end.
2. Danes teach children *how* to think, not *what* to think. Which, in our fast-paced digital world, where AI is likely to make much of what we currently 'know' redundant, might be a good move.
3. Vikings don't test, they don't do homework and they let teachers do their job of inspiring the next generation. Teacher autonomy makes for happier classrooms, so everyone benefits.
4. Children are encouraged to find their voice and use it. I love this. Especially for girls, who are often told to be quiet. To live small. Well, not me. Not my kids. Public-speaking skills shouldn't be the preserve of the privately educated, as is often the case back home. Oracy is for everyone.
5. It feels really good to finally get at least one of my mini-Vikings something approaching an education. I share my sunny outlook with Veteran Viking, who promptly sits on it: 'Not for much longer.' 'Sorry?' 'Nearly vacation time. They'll be home again before you know it.' She's right. They will.

---

* Half were ageing rock stars or light entertainers who somehow swerved Operation Yewtree; the other half were 'stage parents' shuttling offspring to perform in the West End several nights a week. It was A Lot #jazzhands.

14

God Ferie! Holidaying Like a Viking

Dust motes dance in sunbeams as the dog dozes. It's a lazy Saturday and all is momentarily peaceful before my daughter flops dramatically back in her chair and announces: 'I need a holiday!'

'You're five!'

'Yes?'

'So what do you need a holiday from?' I ask.

She gestures with a glue gun at the mountain of craft she's already made this morning. 'Everything! I'm exhausted!'

'It's not the worst idea,' says Lego Man, already on his third coffee. He's recently gone Viking on caffeine, even ordering a post-dinner espresso (like a LUNATIC).

We're approaching July or 'Tumbleweed Time', when schools and offices shut, the streets empty, and traffic lights turn from green to red and back again – without any cars coming near. The air is close, heavy with jasmine. And the country powers down as the entire nation takes their summer holiday en masse. Try contacting a Viking any time in July and you'll be lucky to get a response. In the UK, we were always encouraged to 'stagger' holiday with colleagues so that work could carry on as normal – and I never took more than two weeks off at a time. But Danes have a whole month off to *hav en god ferie* or 'have a good holiday'.

Studies from Sweden show that this 'collective restoration', as it's called, increases levels of well-being and contentment because everyone's off at the same time, doing the same thing – so there's none of the pressure of feeling like you should be working, or that you must just check your email. Everyone's off together, so you're guaranteed quality time with friends and family. Then when everyone comes back, they are rested and restored.

For Nordics, holiday time is a treasured opportunity to switch off from work, digital devices and whirring brains. To be with family (even more), celebrating simple pleasures. And what Vikings love best is doing all this in a hut somewhere. Norwegians call it a *hytte*, Icelandics have *sumarbústaður* or *sumarhús*. Finns favour a *kesämökki*, while Swedes love a traditional red-and-white hut or *sommarstuga*. In Sweden there are around 610,000 of these countrywide, and 51 per cent of Swedes have access to a summer cabin through extended family or friends.[1]

Danish *sommerhuse* or summer houses are a core part of Danish culture, going back 400 years. The government began offering plots to industrial workers to give them a place to grow fresh produce and a smog-free getaway (the olden days were grubby in Denmark, too).

Today, there are more than 180,000 summer houses in Denmark, but many are pretty basic. We're talking ancient plumbing, mismatched crockery and no Wi-Fi, so you have to talk, like it's the nineties. I know this because around 40 per cent of Danish summer houses are rented out on Airbnb for those of us not fortunate enough to have been born Viking. By July, the archipelago waters are a bearable temperature for swimming, so smart Vikings take a holiday within the country – when the weather's in with a chance of being decent.

The forecast may be unpredictable and facilities may be minimal, but the point of a summer house is not to replicate home comforts – it's to strip everything back, slacken the pace of 'normal life' and find serenity.

'We eat pretty simply when at the summer house,' says Esben from Copenhagen, who still takes his three children to the cabin his grandfather built in the 1950s. 'We might pick up some salad leaves, new potatoes or fruit from the produce stands with honesty boxes along the roads. And there's a small fishing hut where a fisherman and his son smoke fish and sell great seafood.' Esben's summer house is on the Helgenæs peninsula – known locally as the 'snot drip' of Jutland (there's a bump on the east coast that looks a little like a nose). The house was built with two tiny bedrooms, a kitchen, a living room and a toilet. 'There was no bath – you just washed in the sea, a hundred metres away,' says Esben. He spent three weeks there every summer growing up. 'We swam, ate straw-berries and the sun was always shining – at least that's how I remember it.' Now he takes his wife and children there every summer to spend time with extended family. 'My dad built another small house on the same plot to fit everyone in, but there's usually still someone sleeping on the sofa or the floor.' Not a lot goes on – but that's part of the attraction. 'To get to the house you have to go down an overgrown track, and there's hardly any phone signal. We spend our time swimming, talking, walking and barbecuing. If we're ever in need of fancier attractions, we go to Ebeltoft, an old port town thirty minutes' drive away.'

What can you do there?

'Um.' He thinks. 'Well . . . there's a glass museum?'

It's not exactly Ibiza.

'Or there's a brewery. They do a nice IPA. And really, what more do you need?' The place isn't anything posh ('although we did install an indoor shower in the 1990s'), but Esben loves it. 'My wife and I even got married there.'

Swedish summer houses take simplicity to a whole other level. Most have rudimentary cooking facilities and perhaps running water in the kitchen, but that's it. Showers are considered an unnecessary extravagance, so most Swedish families will walk from their summer house to a nearby lake or the sea for a morning bathe. Lack of plumbing is a running theme, and many Swedish cabins have a dry outdoor toilet, or *utedass*, in a separate wooden hut a stone's throw from the house.

'What is *that*?' the redhead asked, mystified, when we first encountered a plank of wood and a bucket in lieu of an *actual* loo.

'That, son, is our toilet,' Lego Man assured him with all the confidence of a seasoned camper used to even more primitive facilities (cut him and he bleeds canvas).

In case you're unfamiliar with the delights of a Swedish summer-house loo, you perch over a hole and then throw a handful of dry earth or sawdust over your 'output'. This is intended to aid rapid composting and prevent odours. Although, in a hot July, 'odours' triumph. Composting loos may be eco-friendly but they still smell. Bad. When waste buckets are full, they're emptied into a composting area ('bagsy not by me!'). But what Swedish summer-house loos lack in water, they make up for in vistas. With a traditional heart-shaped hole in the door, there's nothing like a smallest room with a view. 'And if you haven't seen a shooting star while taking a midnight dump, have you really lived?' as my friend Peter Schmeichel says.

'No . . .?' appears to be the answer.

The low-key *lagom* living of Swedish summer houses attracts an array of luminaries, from ABBA's Björn and Benny, who wrote floor-filler 'Dancing Queen' from their cottage on the island of Viggsö, to Will Ferrell and his Swedish wife, the actor Viveca Paulin, in Gnesta, south of Stockholm. And then there's Ingmar Bergman, who had a cottage on the islet of Fårö, off Gotland. Writing about Sweden's Vikings for a UK newspaper, I met Lars Kruthof of Gotland's Museum, who grew up on Fårö. He told me how the filmmaker would teach local children photography, even letting them be in his movies. 'We looked out for him in return,' Lars remembers. 'When American tourists would flood in every summer asking, "Where's Ingmar Bergman's house?" we'd send them in the wrong direction . . .'

Forget the Hamptons or a Nordic Lake Como. Here, simplicity is the measure of happiness.

'You get to a summer house and your daily life and habits are totally different,' says Veteran Viking, stepping over a cat and removing an iPad from her youngest. 'Instead of looking at screens, you look at each other.'

After all I've learned about Denmark's digital blind spot, this appeals.

'Then when you get sick of each other,' she adds, ever the pragmatist, 'you look at the view. Or trees. You slow down.'

She looks at me and we try not to laugh: both of us are bad at this and we know it. *But I'm working on it*, I think. And so is she.

'As soon as I turn down the dirt track where we go, I feel

the stress leaving my shoulders.' She rotates them to illustrate. 'I become 20 per cent more relaxed.'

'Twenty per cent?'

'I know: "have some ambition". I'm trying for 30 per cent this year.'

I'm not sure relaxation works like that. *But then, what do I know?*

'The great thing is you can just throw a few things in the car and drive there,' she adds. Considering the hassle of holidaying abroad post-Brexit, I'm surprised more of my countryfolk don't do this.

'It sounds lovely,' I tell her.

But just packing up the car won't suffice for Lego Man this time.

'I want to feel like I'm going somewhere,' he tells me.

'You are going somewhere: to a summer house. Via road.'

'I don't want roads . . .'

'What do you want?'

'. . . Sea!'

Denmark is made up of 406 islands (more, even, than Greece) and 5,437 miles of coastline – so you're never more than thirty miles from the sea. Aside from Jutland's 42-mile boundary with Germany, Denmark is entirely surrounded by water. A lot like the UK. Only Vikings seem to have a special affinity with the sea – the great unknown that's always there but never the same. On the west coast of Jutland, waves roar as the North Sea brings an icy slap to the air and sand blasts old bunkers from the Second World War. Of the 8,000 bunkers in Denmark built by Germans during the occupation, 7,000 of them are on the West Coast.

Further north, Klitmøller is known as 'Cold Hawaii', thanks

to seven foot-high waves and a wicked wind from the west. Camper vans stacked high with surfboards rumble along coastal roads where everything that might get blown away has to be lashed down. 'There's a strong history of fear around the water here – and respect for it, too,' says Casper Steinfath, Klitmøller local and world champion stand-up paddle surfer, who I interview for a magazine. He tells me about a tradition of going swimming with a rope tied around your waist, for fear of being pulled under. I shudder. Lego Man dislocated his shoulder swimming on the west coast and very nearly didn't make it back. Casper nods. 'We have a west-coast saying that we're "born against the wind" – but it makes us stronger.'

At the northernmost tip of Jutland is Skagen, where the Baltic Sea meets the North Sea, and you can stand in the shallows to feel currents converge. Skagen used to be a fishing hub but now it's famed for otherworldly sand dunes and a luminous light that's inspired everyone from the Skagen Painters in the nineteenth century to artists today. 'Salt crystals found in the air from the sea are reflected in the sand, so we have a special light,' local artist Niels Poplens tells me. 'In Skagen even the shadows are bright.' He's right, they are. I visited while pregnant with the redhead, waddling the beach at dusk, or 'blue hour', when sea and sky appear to merge. It was a transcendent experience, in spite of the fact that I was completely sober and wearing compression socks for varicose veins. It was THAT good.

All this water was perfect in Viking times, when sailing was the best way to get around. But today, water means leisure for most Danes: 'We take it for granted – it's a way of life,' says Rikke Johansen, curator at Denmark's Viking Ship Museum. 'For many, looking out at water every day is key.'

But Lego Man doesn't just want to look at water: he wants to be in it. Surrounded by it. He wants an island.

We've already ticked off a fair few of these in our *Ø Pas* or 'island passport' – from Samsø, to Strynø and Fanø (Ø means 'island'). Every island ferry has a brass plate that you can take a rubbing of in your 'passport' to mark off those you've visited (a solid five minutes of 'entertainment' for the smalls on each boat trip). A few favourites include Bornholm, where you can walk barefoot in sand so fine it was used in sand timers until recently. Or Anholt, the bird-shaped island a three-hour ferry ride from both Jutland and Sweden. Or Møn's Klint, the dramatic chalk cliff on the island of Møn, famed for its dark skies and lack of light pollution, where you're supposed to be able to see the Milky Way (I didn't). And then there's Ærø, the island off the south-east coast of Denmark famed for its beer and beach huts, including the yellow beach hut from the cover of my first book. Also: it's beautiful, all low-timbered houses on cobbled streets, flanked by hollyhocks. It's one of the leading renewable-energy islands in the world, on track to be carbon-neutral and self-sufficient by 2025, with an electric ferry and free buses with bicycle racks, so you can go there car-free. So we have. Twice.

And yet he wants more islands? Jeez . . .

'What do you actually do on these "holidays"?' Deep V bachelor friend asks, making air quotes around the word 'holiday'. He's just back from two weeks in Barbados and has the tan lines to show it.

'Um . . . chat?' I suggest. He looks sceptical. 'Eat? Play cards? Uno . . . ?'

He recoils with a look that says: 'You do *you*.'

It's fair to say that when it comes to island life, there's not much going on. Perhaps a seasonal café or a *kro* – the closest thing Danes have to pubs. Then every second street has an honesty box selling salad leaves, potatoes or honey. You'll never run short of honey on a Danish island. And for everything else, there's usually a Co-op.

Aware that my children are getting older and the delights of 'ooh, look! More artisanal honey!' may be wearing thin, I ask Veteran Viking for further inspiration. She's making coffee while messaging her daughter to empty the cats' litter tray, but manages to share: 'If kids start complaining, send them out to collect rocks.'

Rocks? Did she say 'rocks?' Rocks aren't fun, are they?

'Yes, they are,' says Veteran Viking and every other Dane I meet. On the west coast, lucky beachcombers can come across fist-sized pieces of amber, just there for the taking. And all over Denmark there are *hulsten* or 'hole stones', formed on beaches where currents collide. Small pebbles come crashing down on larger stones, eventually wearing them through. 'It's tradition to collect the stones for good luck, hanging them from twine in your doorway back home or just keeping them,' says Veteran Viking. She hands me one from a tastefully arranged jar of pebbles on her otherwise minimalist shelf. It's surprisingly soothing to feel the smooth, sun-warmed stone. 'And if they get tired of stone collecting,' she tells me, 'send them out on the water.'

Denmark has 1,300 beaches and a population of just 5.8 million. So, often, we have a beach to ourselves. I learn that there are all manner of sea-based leisure activities available to the intrepid Viking in summer, with its long, light days – from paddleboarding, to sailing, rowing, kayaking and wild swimming. 'Though there isn't much water-skiing or wakeboarding,' I mention to Veteran Viking, 'and you don't see a jet-ski in Jutland.'

She winces at such ostentation: 'Jante's Law and jet-skis don't mix. Anything that needs an engine is a little . . . showy.' Her nose wrinkles. 'Plus we're all meant to be "relaxing". Remember?'

'I remember'.

Being around a large expanse of water has been shown to help with relaxation.[2] Experiencing nature on holiday has been found to improve our well-being and spending time by the water may even help us sleep better.[3] Researchers from Northwestern University found that those who fell asleep listening to water slept more deeply, and a National Trust study found that participants slept forty-seven minutes longer, on average, after a seaside hike.[4] I point out to Lego Man that we live just ten minutes from the sea by car. But apparently a 'seaside hike' near home won't cut it. And so, despite the extra admin of adding 'ferry' to an otherwise relatively easy summer-house break, we're going.

A week later, we set off for an hour's drive followed by a ferry to Avernakø, an island south of Funen that's just 2km by 1km with a population of 106 (if you think that's small, neighbouring Hjortø has a population of just seven. *SEVEN!*). An expanse of open water separates 'real life' from pancakes-for-breakfast holiday mode, offering mental and physical distance from all that has gone before. The water's choppy and the air has a chill to it, so we head inside to nosy around, and spot cupboards marked 'toys for the ferry children', 'books for the ferry children' and 'craft supplies'. I'm wondering whether my smalls count as 'ferry children', so ask the steward, who tells me 'No'. She explains that there's no kindergarten or school on the island of Avernakø, so children going to *børnehave* must travel to the mainland. That meant a half-hour ferry ride there and back for parents, twice a day. Which was, you know, a *faff*. So the local council put their heads together and came up with a plan, appointing a dedicated boat-chaperone to escort under-sixes home on the ferry each day. Lest they miss out on precious playtime on their commute, the ferry is now equipped with entertainment to continue the *børnehave* experience at sea.

My five-year-old son is near giddy with envy ('They get to *play* on a *boat*? Every day? TWICE? With no parents?! Luck-y!'). I have to agree it is pretty 'luck-y' (pronounced as two syllables. Always). The chaperone system encourages families to live on these remote islands, and when children get bigger and start school, they take the ferry on their own.

Lightheaded with excitement about our new surroundings and wobbly of leg after time on the boat, we make it to the Airbnb and settle in. The redhead is permitted to stay up past his bedtime and we sit out on wicker chairs, having big chats. Like this one:

The redhead: 'Mummy, are you scared about dying or getting old?'

Me: 'Not in that order . . .'

Him: 'Should we burn you?'

Me: 'Do you mean cremate?'

Him: 'Yes.'

Me, thinking for a minute while staring at stars: 'Sure, cremate me.'

Him: 'Cool.'

Lego Man: 'I've just realised when Gollum talks about "my precious" he means a ring . . .' The redhead and I both turn to look at him.

'What did you *think* it meant?'

'I thought it was just that he had a really nice wife or something.'

'*Extraordinary* . . .'

Eventually, we relax. Properly. Possibly up to Veteran Viking's '30 per cent'. There's a cadence to island life that's largely dictated by the ferry – from the times new people arrive, to when the supermarket gets fresh deliveries. 'Rush hour' is twice a day, when the four cars on the island (FOUR!) head to or from the ferry (and we're not talking cross-Channel here: the boat has space for six cars 'to accommodate tourists'). And so we manage to fill days with . . . nothing.

'It's like we're turning into our retired parents!' I say with disbelief, checking my watch and realising I have managed to sit still for . . . eight minutes and fifty-three seconds. *A new record!* Days are spent at the beach and once the five-year-olds overcome their indignation at not being able to watch TV, collecting *hulsten* becomes a favourite hobby. Evenings are spent barbecuing, aka spying on what the neighbours are having for dinner. 'He made a seafood platter!' I stage whisper to Lego Man as he turns a charred sausage. Still, everything tastes better eaten alfresco while watching Aperol spritz sunsets. Slowly, we fall into a rhythm and I feel a pressure valve loosening.

The smalls play with toys left behind in the house, long outgrown by the mini-Vikings who once loved them. My son goes a whole morning without asking for the iPad. My daughter takes a shine to a stuffed lemur with a long stripy tail, carrying it around with her from morning until night.

'It's Lemur's birthday,' she tells me.

'How old is Lemur?'

'Susan.'

'Sorry?'

'Her name is Susan and she's 100.'

'Goodness . . . she looks well on it . . . '

Susan celebrates her centenary with a bear named Nigel and

a one-armed action figure called Cutie-Pie. Only it turns out it's Susan's birthday the next day, too. And the one after that. On day three of 'happy birthday, dear Susan', Lego Man stands and announces that he is going to 'be alone with his thoughts'. After ten minutes of being alone with his thoughts, he decides that's quite enough of that. He proclaims he's 'finished relaxing' and leaves the summer house. A few minutes (hours? Days?) later, he hurtles back, falling through the door like a marathon runner at the end of a race. There is a reckless air about him. I feel a constriction where my Zen had been.

'What have you done?'

'Why would you say that?'

'Because I know you. What is it?'

'We're going sailing!' he tells me, triumphant.

'Are we? Why?' I tend to associate sailing with spongy-nosed men sporting luxurious bouffants and women with skin like a satchel.

'For fun! Tomorrow!'

I rather had tomorrow down as 'chill, snack, repeat'. Not 'sailing'. But the mini-Vikings are now primed for adventure and I am outnumbered. So this is happening.

A man who looks like a greyhound tells us he'll be our guide and all we have to do is 'exactly what he tells us'. The Greyhound equips us with lifejackets and even a health-and-safety briefing (not guaranteed in Denmark). Where sand trails down to the sea, we're led to a wooden, almond-shaped boat and told to 'carry it into the water'.

'Carry? A whole boat?' I appear to be the only one with reservations about this, since my children are already mid-heave. I lay my hands on the boat and am surprised to find it's hot to the touch, heated by the sun.

'First, we row until we're clear of the shore.' The Greyhound takes up an oar and hands me the other.

Me? Not Lego Man? Damn Nordic egalitarianism . . . My daughter stares at me, unblinking, watching how I'll react. It's like Elsa from *Frozen* watching me scale a tree all over again. I can't let either of them down. *Must. Channel. Inner. Viking. Am not an English Rose: am strong Shieldmaiden . . .*

It's hard going, but I remember what Lasse in Norway told me about having the arms of a 'survivor'. *I can do this,* I tell myself, pulling harder.

Lego Man is stationed by the tall pole-thingy in the middle that I'm reliably informed is 'the mast'. He is charged with 'undoing a bow' on the Greyhound's command.

That's his job? Undoing a sodding bow? And I have to row? Unbelievable.

The Greyhound tilts his head, feeling the wind. Then, wordlessly, he gives the nod: *Do it now.* Lego Man unties the knot that binds a ream of white fabric to our mast and with a swift, violent unravelling, the sail lashes outwards. It whips and cracks as it fills with air and we lurch forward, wind blasting my face. I can taste sea. The twins are yelping with joy and the redhead is waggling his limbs like one of those inflatables with waving arms outside a car showroom.

'Hold on!' I yell. Remarkably, he does, grabbing a rail wet with sea spray.

The Greyhound secures the sail and tells us how even children can 'read' the waves.

About all they can read, I can't help thinking.

'You just have to think, *Are the waves still at the same angle to the boat as they were?* and *Is the wind blowing in the same direction?*' says the Greyhound. 'When we're near shore, we look at the water and judge how flat it is to work out how shallow the sea is. Then there are swans.'

'Swans?'

'Swans. Their necks are about this long' – he holds his hands just over a foot apart – 'so if they have their butts in the air, you know the water's deep enough for a boat like this. If swans are just poking their heads under to fish, it's too shallow and you'll get grounded.'

This is my new favourite swan fact (*everyone* knows the break-your-arm one).

'All birds can help you in a boat,' says the Greyhound, 'since most fly towards land. And ravens are a sailor's best friend.' At this, Lego Man starts humming 'Diamonds Are a Girl's Best Friend' from *Gentlemen Prefer Blondes*. The Greyhound ignores the musical interlude and explains how the petrol-blue-and-black birds fly higher than most. 'It means they can see land sooner – they'll head straight for it and you can follow.'

The redhead nods gravely, storing this raven data for future Scout escapades.

'You can also use clouds – there are always more clouds over land than there are at sea,' says the Greyhound: 'And you need to *listen*.'

Lego Man stops humming 'Diamonds Are a Girl's Best Friend'.

'You can actually *hear* land. Traffic, sirens, dogs.'

All I can hear is the wind, whistling around my ears. But this is useful, too, he tells me, as we soar through surf.

'Move your head until you feel the wind blowing evenly on both ears – then you know you're facing into the wind.'

I move slightly until I can feel the wind whipping around each ear, and it works! We fly through water as the Greyhound wrenches ropes stiffened by salt. It is invigorating. *I'm having a . . . what is this feeling? Oh! I know: a 'nice time'!*

The boat grates on sand as we reach shore again and disembark, with sea legs and silly smiles. I thank the Greyhound. And then I thank Lego Man. 'For making me do the scary thing I didn't want to.'

He looks pleased. Smug, even. With notes of 'I told you so . . .'

I bring him back down to earth: 'Still, we've got to crack on with the packing and cleaning now.' I'm fun like that.

Everyone knows that packing to go home is the worst part of any holiday. But leaving a rented summer house entails an added undertaking: the clean-up. From emptying bins and eco-toilets (grim), to mopping, scrubbing, vacuuming ('floors and beds' as one recent Airbnb demanded). Most significantly in our case: going home means saying goodbye to Susan the lemur.

After tears (some) and protestations (many), we load the car and make a dash for the ferry. We are late. We are always late since having children. We arrive just as our 'loading lane' is closing and it takes all my powers of persuasion and Danglish, but we make it. After a tight game of car Tetris, we head up on deck to wave goodbye to 'our island'. And it's then that I notice our daughter looking suspiciously bulky.

'What have you got up your jumper?'

'Nothing.'

'I can see a stripy tail sticking out.'

'No.'

'Is Susan the lemur up your jumper?'

Shakes head

She continues to style this one out until Lego Man appears and immediately spots the offending article. Over the wind I hear 'not yours' and a bottom lip begins to quiver as she looks down, tracing the outline of the deck slats with her foot. I let Lego Man handle this one and compose a message to the owners of the summer house.

'*I'm so sorry . . . now on the ferry . . . I'll send it to you asap.*'

I'm just walking back when my phone pings.

Cry laughing emoji. Heart emoji. Lemur emoji.

Okay . . .

'*Don't worry, our son used to do the same. He's twenty-seven now. Tell your daughter she can keep lemur as long as she promises to give it plenty of* kram (hugs in Danish). *Winking emoji.*

Oh my . . .

There follows a parental debate in hushed tones: 'How's she supposed to learn if she gets the lemur anyway?' and 'Got any better ideas?!' We compromise on a 'teachable moment' about not taking other people's property and a 'thank you letter' since it's now technically a gift.

But I wish there was a grown-up on board to tell us what to do. Like Kitta. If she can handle prison, she can handle lemur larceny. *Stuff Mary Poppins: what would Kitta do?* WWKD? (another top-drawer tattoo inspiration . . . *makes note*). Increasingly convinced that this is the Rosetta Stone of raising Vikings, I return below deck in search of snacks. I see another message on my phone, this time from Veteran Viking. It says simply:

'*30 per cent.*'

I write back immediately: '*Congratulations! Relaxation? Crushed it.*'

What I've learned about how to holiday like a Viking

1. Keep it simple. No running water? No problem when it comes to Viking holidays (but bagsy not emptying the eco-loo). We don't have to spend a lot to have a memorable family holiday. Children don't care how many stars somewhere has or what angry men named Clive say about it on Tripadvisor. I hear from friends back home who've shelled out for trips to Dubai or the Maldives with small children and now think: *Why?* I'd much rather save to go somewhere long-haul once they're old enough to appreciate it. Or better still, get away solo once my children are teenagers and have decided that going on holiday with Mum and Dad is officially for losers.

2. Going offline, if not off-grid, helps. I *can* relax, I've discovered, but there really need to be no other options. I will happily busy myself with *anything* before sitting down and doing nothing (parent: know thyself).

3. Stones are acceptable kids' entertainment. And contrary to American Mom's assertion, an old Rubik's Cube in the summer house proved remarkably absorbing for my children once they realised that there were no iPads available. Perhaps that's what all the play research is getting at: given the time and the space, humans will just play. With pretty much anything.

4. We're all stronger than we think. Especially if there are impressionable small people watching. Children make us braver and this is A Good Thing. Update: I can row a Viking boat now. Tell *everyone*.

15

Let's Get Physical

S WEAT POOLS ABOVE the collarbone. My cheeks feel like they're melting. And . . . *could my eyeballs be sweating?* I'm in a sauna with my daughter, my mother-in-law and two mums from school. And we are all stark naked. I am trying very hard to be nonchalant about this but feeling, heat aside, distinctly *chalant.*

Chalant I shall remain, I think, *until I get out of here and get a bra on . . .*

I know, logically, that the body is just a body. That it's healthy to be relaxed about nudity. And, oddly, I'm okay about it in front of strangers. I've been naked in front of enough of them in Danish communal changing rooms by now. But naked in front of people I *know*? And am neither biblically acquainted with nor have given birth to? In a municipal swimming-pool sauna? Like I said: *chalant.*

It's safe to say that Nordics don't go in for prudishness in swimming pools, gyms and sports centres. Throughout Denmark, changing rooms, showers and saunas are separated by gender. But within those, nudity is the norm. Swimming pools all require a nude full-body soaping in a public shower room before entry. And helpful posters remind everyone to wash thoroughly, since failure to do so is akin to civic deviance in Denmark. A few favourites from my local pool include:

> *One person who has not washed is equivalent*
> *to 20 who have washed thoroughly!*

The less catchy but certainly comprehensive:

> *Soap + thorough washing WITHOUT SWIMWEAR*
> *= less chlorine + cleaner bathing water*
> *= less irritation in the eyes and mucous membranes!*

Or the short and sweet:

> *SHOWER AGAIN after TOILET!*

'Why wouldn't you wash?' says Veteran Viking when I quiz her on this. Having spent sunny days at Tooting Lido watching the water cloud with sweat and sunscreen, I admit she may be on to something. A society that values cleanliness isn't the worst thing in the world and it's no surprise that chlorine levels in UK and US swimming pools are higher than those in the Nordic countries. In Iceland there's even a song to remind tourists which body parts to scrub, led by a fictional 'Director of Spa Etiquette' and sung to the tune of 'Heads, Shoulders, Knees and Toes' ('Head, armpits, crotch and toes, crotch and toes!').[1] Nordics don't ablute staring resolutely at their shampoo, either, terrified of catching the eye of a fellow bather in a state of undress and blushing puce. Instead, they hold *actual* conversations while tackling pits and slits. Like it's no big deal #*chalant*.

'Internationals are often surprised by how relaxed we are,' says my Swedish friend Maria, 'but there's nothing sexual about it: they're just bodies. And not having wet bathing costumes sticking to your skin makes everything more comfortable.'

Being naked is just normal. Especially in Finnish saunas, I learn. Traditionally found in private homes and holiday cottages, these high-heat, wood-lined rooms are designed to make you sweat, flush out 'toxins' (allegedly), improve circulation and aid muscle recovery. The traditional hot–cold sauna cycle ends with an icy dunk, or a roll in the snow if there's any around. Finns love saunas so much that there are 3.3 million of them in a country of just 5.5 million people.[2] Emilia, the Finnish Scout leader who lives near me, explains how Finns regularly 'sauna' (it can be a verb, too) with extended family – from aunts to uncles, cousins, grandparents and in-laws.

'The first time I met Emilia's dad,' her husband Andreas tells me, 'we sat next to each other, naked, in a sauna. It was quite the first impression.'

I'll bet . . .

'Many of the older generation were born in saunas,' says Emilia, 'since it's clean and keeps the mother and new baby warm. The sauna was often the first "room" anyone built in a new house.' Babies take their first gentle sauna when they're a few months old and from then on, they never stop. Andreas and Emilia now have their own sauna at their home in Denmark to continue the tradition. And the popularity of saunas is spreading across the Nordic countries, with a sharp uptick in public saunas in Norway's capital to meet demand. Mixed-sex saunas aren't always swimsuit-free zones. 'If you're not sure, look at what everyone else is doing and do that,' says my friend who looks like Peter Schmeichel (a big sauna fan), 'but a warning – even if everyone is naked, bring a towel to sit on. No one wants to see your sweaty butt print.'

Understood.

The Nordic attitude to nudity has been profound for this former Catholic schoolgirl raised in the UK. I was in my thirties when I moved to Denmark, which means I'd been knocking around for three whole decades before I saw the full spectrum of women's bodies in their natural form. Not film stars in carefully choreographed sex scenes, or an unvarying parade of smoking-hot Nordic goddesses. I mean real bodies, naked. Tummies that pucker, C-section scars, breasts that swing, bottoms that dimple and pubic hair that grows wherever it pleases, gloriously un-coiffed. As a result of this exposure to a whole range of real bodies, I began to accept my own a little more. Lego Man assures me that 'the cock and hairy balls show' in the men's changing rooms has a similar effect. And there's a certain honesty to baring all: everyone is exposed, and everyone is equal – there's nothing funny or shaming about being naked. Now, I often feel there should be a sign outside all Danish changing rooms that reads: *Welcome to the pool: please leave your shame here.*

A survey conducted by the University of Zürich showed that Danes are the most shameless people in the world. A mere 1.62 per cent of Danes suffer from gelotophobia – fear of ridicule – the lowest proportion of the population in any country surveyed.[3] In the UK, we have the *highest* number of people with the phobia.

My own mini-Vikings have grown up with nudity. In changing rooms, at the beach, at the lakes in Sweden, or even just walking past the full-frontal Porny Pony fountain in our town. Danes are just *okay* about their bodies. From birth.

Children are allowed in either male or female changing rooms until they turn six, when pools ask that they change in the locker room of the sex with which they identify. So children get to see all sorts of bodies. And should they need more, there's always extra 'help' on hand.

Public-service broadcaster DR's show *Ultra smider tøjet* (*Ultra Strips Down*) prompted a scandal in 2020 for presenting children aged eleven to thirteen with a panel of nude adults. A scandal, that is, outside of the Nordic countries. Danes were fine about it. As clinical psychologist Erla Heinesen Højsted said at the time, 'What kind of culture are we creating for our children if it's okay for them to see "perfect" bodies on Instagram – enhanced, digitally or cosmetically – but not "real bodies"?' So Danes focus on 'real bodies' that are strong and healthy, rather than stick-thin.

'There's definitely less of a fixation on being thin in Sweden, too,' agrees my friend Niki in Malmö: 'it's about being healthy instead. So shop mannequins vary in size for a more inclusive feel. And even advertising billboards show normal-looking women. I'm really happy about this as a parent.'

Nordics 'train' rather than exercise, with sport for all, regardless of age, ability or innate skill. Simply because it feels good. I swim every Thursday and there is a septuagenarian who spends the entire thirty-minute session climbing up metal steps, then zooming down the water slide, solo. Every. Single. Week.

The emphasis on physical activity for *fun* is paramount, and girls grow up playing football as well as boys (with great success – the US Olympic gold-medal-winning women's team was coached by a Swede). Football is the most popular sport in

Denmark, with the national team earning surprising success internationally. Then there's Denmark's national sport: handball. From what I can make out by watching Veteran Viking's daughter play, this is a cross between netball, basketball and football, with players required to dribble a ball into goals instead of baskets. Denmark is officially the most successful nation at handball in the world, with a total of 104 medals.

'Is that because no one else plays?' Lego Man asks.

'No.' I tell him what Veteran Viking told me. 'Germans like it, too, actually! The sport was even played in Ancient Greece. So there!'

It gets cold in winter, so ice hockey is popular in Denmark and Sweden. Norwegians love to ski – cross country and downhill – while Swedes and Finns are fans of 'floorball' – a type of indoor hockey invented in the late 1960s where players whack around a ball with holes in it for twenty-minutes at a time (convenient for parents on cheerleading duty).

'Being active is just for everyone, it's just what you do,' says Katja from Finland, 'and there isn't so much of a car culture, which helps. In North America, friends spend two, three, maybe four hours a day driving. But in the Nordic countries, it is easier to cycle or walk. We don't drive a car to a gym to sit on a stationary bike – what is that?! Many Finns just lead a good, active life, using basic common sense.' According to the 2022 Active Healthy Kids Global Alliance report, Denmark and Finland top the polls when it comes to keeping children active. There are famously more bikes than cars in Copenhagen, and 82 per cent of Danish children 'actively transport themselves' to school twice a week, with 60 per cent doing so daily.[4] 'It doesn't matter who you are or what you look like,' says Peter Schmeichel, 'your body is there to be used.'

'And enjoyed,' adds Veteran Viking, stroking her cat, 'don't forget that.'

How could I forget . . .?

Sex education has been mandatory in Denmark since 1970, and children from the age of six are taught about their rights over their own bodies during a national curriculum 'Sex Week' every February (also week six in the calendar, or *seks* in Danish, pleasingly). Each year there's a theme – from consent to identity and 'the perfectly imperfect body'.

Eleven-year-olds take a module called 'adolescence' where they can submit questions anonymously for teachers to address. Student suggestions this year include:

'Why do some people think it's bad being gay?'

'Why does sex make a noise?'

'What is masterbathing? [sic] Is it comfy to masterbathe with your own gender?'

And my favourite: 'Do you swear more after you've been through puberty?' (Answer: 'Yes.')

'But you still have to be on top of it as parents,' says my American Mom friend, 'to check kids know when and *where* to use their newfound knowledge.' She reminds me of the time her eldest's class studied safer sex and teenagers were encouraged to 'wrap that rascal' ('which, obviously, they found hilarious and kept chanting. All. The. Time'). 'Or the year kids were given a handout of all the words for genitalia that they might encounter.' American Mom flinches at the recollection. 'Top of the list?'

Ummm . . .

'C*nt.'

Ohhh!

'Exactly! I made them promise: "Don't tell Grandma!"'

Unless she's anything like C-Bomb Ruby, the pensioner who thrashed me at Scrabble.

By the age of thirteen, Danes have covered off everything from the ins and outs of masturbation to transgender rights – in frank and open discussions. An eye-opener for those of us who learned about sex from Judy Blume's *Forever*.

Broadcaster DR supports sex education in schools with *Under dynen med Anna Lin* (*Under the Covers with Anna Lin*), where the twenty-seven-year-old host discusses young people's concerns about sex. 'I had a lot of questions [when I was growing up], and I can tell from the children who turn to me now that they do, too,' Anna Lin told DR. 'You can have doubts about everything from your body's development, to the very essential: "Who am I?"' The show is made with consultation from Denmark's version of ChildLine (BørneTelefonen) and Sex & Samfund (Sex & Society) to ensure the right tone and focus for children's needs and life stage. Sex & Society consultant Pernille Ane Egebæk told DR how sex education is 'partly a school-based task, but also a broader social task that institutions must contribute to'. This is an approach echoed in Sweden, the first country in the world to introduce obligatory sex education in schools in 1955.

'We're surprised when people – often from the UK or the US – make a fuss about the way we do things in Sweden,' says Kajsa Peters, mother of two and producer of youth content at Sweden's public-service broadcaster SVT. 'We start talking about the body and sex really early in Sweden, because isn't it better to tell kids the truth in an age-appropriate way?' When Kajsa first started at SVT, she commissioned a short video to give children between the ages of three and six an idea about the differences between male and female bodies. It was made on a shoestring, with just Kajsa, an animator and a composer, Johan Holmström.* 'We followed all the guidelines and ran it by the ministry for education,' says Kajsa, 'and it was intended as a playful extra for kids' TV show *Bacillakuten*, which airs on a Sunday. But it *exploded* . . .'

'Snoppen & Snippan' was uploaded to YouTube, classified as 'adult content', and viewed 1.5 million times by the Tuesday.

'Newspapers all over the world started writing about it. I had all these crazy messages, even threats, from the UK the US.'

So why the controversy?

The minute-long video opens with a catchy melody and rudimentary animation of a dancing penis, or *snoppen* in colloquial Swedish.

'Here comes a willy like a kangaroo,' a cheery voice sings as a dismembered phallus with big Disney eyes hops into the foreground.

O-kay . . .

'All the girls think it's excellent . . .'

A heart-shaped *snippan* (slang for female genitalia in Swedish) with enormous eyes and thick lashes whizzes by, before another *snippan* with a grey wig and a walking cane appears.

'Even graceful ladies think it's *elegant*!'

Other lyrics such as 'the vagina is cool, you better believe it!' and 'here comes the penis at full gallop' caused outrage.

Although, I think, *it can feel like a penis is coming at full gallop. Perhaps forewarned is forearmed . . .?*

'Okay, so we ended up teaching a lot of kids in Sweden the

---

* Who also composed the music to the game *Candy Crush*, downloaded by 1.7 billion worldwide. Fun fact.

word *snippan*,' admits Kajsa, 'but it's such a cute word! And it was just a fun, educational video for kids.'

Eventually, YouTube agreed to remove their 'adult classification', since the video was neither targeting adults nor 'explicit'. And everyone carried on as normal. At least, in Sweden. The Swedish Agency for Education has a policy of 'seizing every opportunity' for sex education. As well as dedicated lessons, sex ed is integrated into every subject from biology to history, art, religion, physical education, even music, 'Looking at how gender, sexuality and relationships are depicted in lyrics or music videos,' I learn from the ministry. Then there's 'the sex-ed test', containing 100 questions intended to inform pupils about relationships, love, 'sexual terms they are likely to encounter' and pornography.

Pornography is included in the curriculum in several Danish schools, too, and Denmark was the first country in the world to lift the ban on pornography in 1967. Some experts want to go further still. Sexology professor Christian Graugaard of Aalborg University has suggested that pornography should be shown in schools as a way of teaching teenagers that it's nothing like real sex. 'We know from research that a vast majority of teenagers have seen porn at an early age – so it's not a question of introducing youngsters to porn,' he told me for a UK newspaper.[5] According to one study, 99 per cent of boys and 86 per cent of girls in Scandinavia have already seen pornographic films by the time they're sixteen. Christian wants to make sure teens 'possess the necessary skills' to view porn constructively and distinguish between the media's depictions of sex and everyday life.

The Norwegian publicly funded broadcaster NRK has taken this into their own hands, publishing a sex guide of sixty different positions (that's right: sixty. What have I been DOING with my time?). This is accessible to all and modelled by real people in heterosexual and same-sex partnerships. Positions include Clamping Koala (sitting, facing one another, legs crossed at the ankle); the Speed Dump (captioned: 'Drive carefully!'); and Can I Keep My Socks On? (okay, I made that one up). At last count, the guide had six million page views – in a country of 5.4 million. NRK's editorial director explained: 'I think a lot of people share the concern about how porn affects young people's sexuality, and appreciate the Sex Guide as an attempt to give a factual, nuanced and realistic picture of what sex can be.'

Realistic sex? And honest depictions of what bodies looks like? Whatever next?

'We just take a more practical approach,' Veteran Viking tells me. 'Sex is part of life, so you may as well learn about it, early on. Right?' I wonder whether now would be the time to remind her that I'm British and attended an all-girls school.

The age of consent is sixteen in Norway and Finland, the same as the UK and much of North America. In Denmark, Sweden and Iceland, it's just fifteen. And for Icelanders, there's an added element to sex education for all ages. With a population of around 360,000, where almost everyone is distantly related, introductory questions at a bar to a prospective new beau can go something like: 'What's your name? Do you come here often? Are you my cousin?'

Fortunately, Icelanders are now able to look each other up on an app to avoid accidental incest. Technology only possible thanks to Iceland's online database holding genealogical details of almost the entire population, since most are descended from a group of ninth-century Viking settlers. The app lets users 'bump' phones, setting off an 'Incest Prevention Alarm' if they are too closely linked. Islendinga App – or 'App of Icelanders' – is promoted with the catchy slogan: *'Bump the app before you bump in bed!'*

'Well, really . . . !' is how my mother responds when I share this nugget. 'It's all very "no nonsense", isn't it?' Her tone implying that she'd prefer a modicum of 'nonsense'. But she won't find it here. Vikings don't muck about. Later that week I'm offered another decidedly sans-nonsense invitation. No koalas, apps or cousins are involved and I'm fully clothed. Although not everyone involved is.

To mark the fortieth anniversary of the definitive 1980s classic *Flashdance* (anyone else feel old?), a local school is putting on a production and would I like to come?

Would I! To see *Flashdance: The Musical*? Dialogue in Danish, songs in English? The story of Alex, welder by day, burlesque dancer by night? Yes, please. Yes, I would.

After paying twenty-five kroner for entry and a programme, sponsored by Lego Man's favourite DIY store (the one that sent him a loyalty dagger), I take my seat. As the production gets underway, it becomes clear that there are only two children with what my mother calls 'the show-off gene' in a cast of fifty. They all seem pleased to be there, but unwilling to take the spotlight or do anything solo. Some can sing. Some can dance. A few can act. But all three?

'It's hard to be a theatre triple threat this early in life,' murmurs my American Mom friend in the seat next to me. This may be true, but there is a certain irony to singing 'dancing for my life' while standing stock-still. And then there are the scenes in the strip club.

'Is this appropriate? For a school production?' I whisper to American Mom. She's here to support her son, who's in the band. His younger brothers are also in attendance. I can only imagine the scenes at school tomorrow.

'You went to a play where high-school kids stripped onstage? Yeah, sure you did . . . '

Spoiler: this is not the raciest part. That comes as another actress disrobes to reveal dollar bills sticking out of her pants. And the younger brothers' jaws hit the floor.

'Don't tell Grandma!' I hear American Mom whisper.

It all ends happily as the stripper is 'saved' by our heroine, who swaps welding for ballet, and they all pop on legwarmers and have a singalong (naturally). And what would have been the stuff of *Daily Mail* fury in the UK – a comments section aflame with indignation, a school shut down, even – is completely . . . normal.

We may not all be ready for Nordic-style liberalism just yet. But we can take steps in the right direction. To strip down, soap up and embrace our real bodies – in all their bizarre and beautiful glory.

What I've learned about how to raise body-neutral Vikings

1. Using bodies for what they're meant for helps us feel better about them. We are all a collection of bits and should chill the heck out. If we can move our bodies, we should.
2. Children shouldn't learn about bodies and sex from porn. Learning about real bodies, what they do, and our rights over them seems eminently more sensible. Sex is normal. Masturbation is normal. Everyone should have control over their own body.

3. Think 'strong', not 'thin'. How much disordered eating might have been avoided had we all grown up with this mantra? I wish I could go back to self-parent myself as a child and hammer this one home. Wouldn't it be lovely if the rest of the world caught on, so that more young people can grow up happy, healthy, safe and strong?

4. If the opportunity arises to see an eighties musical, take it.

16

Teen Viking

T HE OPENING SYNTHESISER riff sounds familiar. It's followed by a brassy sound as someone, somewhere, pounds a Yamaha. This isn't ideal, as I'm trying to wrestle five-year-olds into the bath, persuading them it's bedtime despite bright sunshine outside. Although there's near perpetual darkness October to April, come June, it's light for twenty-one hours a day. Which means no one sleeps.

'What is that noise?' the eight-year-old demands over a galloping drumbeat that sets hairs on the back of my neck on end. The music gets louder in the key of F minor as the iconic chords of Swedish rock band Europe's 'The Final Countdown' power out and a truck rolls into view. It's an open-air affair with no seats, much less safety belts, probably used for livestock ordinarily. But today the truck is equipped with massive loud-speakers and decorated with ribbons and hand-made banners. Spray-painted down the side of one of these are the words:

Hvem fuck er Macbeth?!

I do a quick translation: 'Who the f**k is Macbeth?' *What is going on?*

There's whooping and cheering as the truck pulls to a stop, brakes emitting a hissing sound. A metal ladder clanks against tarmac and teenagers in shorts and sailor caps spill out, navigating their way with sea legs (or 'beer legs', as I discover). As from a clown car, they disembark in numbers that scarcely seem plausible. *Fifteen? Twenty? More?*

They arrange themselves into two lines facing each other, then join hands to form a tunnel. A boy I vaguely recognise descends from the steps to rapturous cheers.

Is that . . .? Could that be? The chatty neighbour's son? The boy who was playing with toy diggers in the garden only two minutes ago?

In a burst of brazen glory, he runs under the hands of his friends, arms outstretched. At the end of the human tunnel, the boy takes to one knee, as a tube of plastic is lowered into his mouth . . . and a pint of beer is poured in the other end.

Good grief . . . he's not playing diggers any more, Toto.

'What is *happening*?' the redhead shouts over the regular, deafening beat.

'It's the final countdown!' Lego Man is transfixed.

'Or rather, graduation,' I add, 'Danish style.' Because for two weeks in June, the streets are full of animal transporters, tractors, old army trucks, or even horse-drawn carriages carrying high-school students. Nineteen-year-olds who have finished secondary education are driven around their hometown by a designated driver, visiting every classmate's house to celebrate. I've seen it from afar during our years of living Danishly. But this is the first time I've had a ringside view.

Graduating in Denmark is far more fun than cider and a Scotch egg in the park circa 1998 . . . I reflect on my own salad days and feel an overwhelming sense of goodwill for these young people and all that lies ahead of them. By the looks of it, the rest of the neighbourhood is experiencing a similar swell of nostalgia. Most are now out in support, raising a glass to the neighbourhood teen. I'd quite like to join this bacchanalian scene, but I have two butt-naked bath refuseniks. So instead, I watch from our balcony, like a low-rent Evita.

The smalls try every postponing ploy in their repertoire, but we finally get them to bath and bed with a mixture of Jesper Juul straight-talking and basic bribery ('Mummy and Daddy need to relax now. You can stay up late at the weekend. Yes, I'll play you "The Final Countdown" at breakfast'). Once the coast is clear, we sneak downstairs to see if we can swing an invitation to what is clearly the hottest party in town.

Strangely, no invitation is forthcoming.

'I wonder why a load of nineteen-year-olds don't want to hang out with two really tired parents in their forties?' Lego Man asks.

'Weird,' I agree.

Digger Boy's parents, however, are happy to chat – over the hedge and to the dulcet tones of 'Don't Leave Me This Way' by the Communards.

These people were born in the 2000s – how do they know the Communards?

'What's with the hats?' Lego Man asks. 'Sailor theme?'

Our Chatty Neighbour explains that when the final exam of secondary school is completed, they get a *studenterhue* – the Danish word for the cap that all students wear when they graduate. This is usually white with a black peak and a ribbon to indicate what kind of education a student has had. Red signifies the standard high-school education, like our neighbour's son and his pals. If you've studied at a specialist trade or technical school, you go blue; farmers get green; and hair-dressers, pink (*please* . . .).

I notice that many of the hats have an emblem resembling the Maltese cross.

'This symbolises the cross on our Dannebrog – the Danish flag,' says Chatty Neighbour, explaining that in more inclusive and enlightened recent years, students can also opt for the Star of David or the Islamic crescent instead. She tells me it's customary for students in the year below to decorate the truck.

'And so . . . Macbeth?' I point at the banner.

'They studied it. Some of the kids had a hard time getting with Shakespeare.'

Lego Man nods knowingly.

'But that's all over now,' says Chatty Neighbour.

'Now: we party,' her more taciturn husband raises his glass.

The partying starts early at 8 a.m. Trucks pick up students to drive about, honking horns, singing, dancing, drinking and stopping at each classmate's house for a minute mini-party with family and family friends. The last house on the route hosts the 'afterparty', then the bus drops everyone home. This ritual ride is thought of so fondly that it has even been described as an expression of Danish civil religion.[1]

Because it's Denmark, there are rules attached, obviously (#rooligans). These vary from school to school, but my neighbours – and various teens who lurch up to say '*hej*' – fill me in on key protocols.

'If you have the biggest hat, you have to give everyone in your class a beer; if you have the smallest hat, you have to give everyone in your class a beer. If you have the highest grades, you have to give everyone in your class a beer. And if you have the lowest grades—'

'Let me guess: you give everyone in your class a beer?'

'How did you know?'

'Just a hunch. So basically, in most scenarios you have to give everyone in your class a beer.'

She grins. Tousled youths stumble over each other like drunk puppies, finishing each other's sentences in increasingly slurred Danglish. Most Danes speak excellent English, having learned it at *folkeskole*, but no one expects fluency after funnelling beer since 8 a.m.

'If the party lasts until sunrise—' a blonde in bunches tells me.

'You cut a triangle in the sweatband!' a girl in a bikini top butts in.

'And if you have *sex*—'

'You cut a lightning bolt in it!' a reed-thin boy yells to be heard over the din. 'But if you score with a teacher, you tear the white cover off your cap!'

There is a hiatus in the music (Wham! – thanks for asking). We all look at him.

'Has that *ever* happened?' Lego Man is suspicious.

'My brother knew a guy whose *cousin* once did.'

Taciturn Neighbour shakes his head and calls it: 'Bullshit.' We all nod in agreement and Andrew Ridgeley starts up again.

'Oh, and there's one more,' Chatty Neighbour adds, pointing at the brook running past the end of our garden. 'If you jump in the water with only the student cap on, you cut a wave in the sweatband of the cap.'

'Like that guy?' Lego Man asks.

'*Halløj,* sir!' A naked youth addresses him from the river, beaming.

Within moments, there's another. And another. And another.

I haven't seen this many nineteen-year-old boys' bottoms since . . . well, we've all had our fun summers. I spot the neighbour's son and try to keep my eyes above waist level.

The fat-cheeked boy who used to play with toy diggers in the front garden now has a six pack?

It's true what American Mom always says about parenting: the days are long but the years are short.

When did this happen? And how long before it happens to my kids? The redhead is already eight. How long until I'm dealing with teenagers?

'Couple of years. Three, tops,' Taciturn Neighbour shrugs. My alarm must be evident, as Chatty Neighbour sends her husband away in search of 'the good scissors' ('to cut the waves'). But the question of when mini-Viking tips into 'teen' preoccupies me. In bed that night, I stare at the ceiling, pondering, eventually dropping off before the birds begin their morning chorus at 3 a.m. Like sadists.

When does 'teenaging' start? My worry-machine begins again.

'When they're confirmed,' says my Veteran Viking mother-in-arms at school drop-off. Despite being a largely secular country, Denmark has a state Lutheran church to which 74 per cent of the population belong. In seventh grade – age thirteen or fourteen – teens are invited to *gå til præst* or 'go to the priest' to learn about the Bible and chat about life's big questions. But there's no pressure to actually believe, since the Danish ceremony is about God saying 'yes' to you and not the other way around. Once teens have genned up on the Good Book, there's a church ceremony with boys in suits and girls in fancy frocks. After this, there's a lunch for family and friends where the newly confirmed give heartfelt speeches. A crippling prospect for most thirteen-year-olds but one that Danish teens take in their stride. And then? The main event: swag. Because guests gift *generously*.

The average teen will receive confirmation gifts worth around DKK 17,000 (or £1,980), according to a survey by Danish bank Nordea. Popular 'wish-list' items include iPads, laptops, cameras or phones, but teens also accept cold hard cash.

'The amount you give as a guest should be the amount spent on entertaining you,' says Veteran Viking, adding that the closer you are to the family, the more you're expected to give. The gifting part of confirmation culture in Denmark is so entrenched that teens get the day off school after their confirmation ceremony to go on a shopping spree. I comment that this all sounds mercenary, but another parent who runs a clothes shop shuts me down. She tells me *konfirmander* – the newly confirmed – are a big driver of the local economy. She's already ordered in extra stock in anticipation of 'Blue Monday', as it's known.

'Okay, so they've shopped. They've had their first young adult initiation, what next?'

Veteran Viking looks at me as though I am an idiot (again). With a deep sigh that suggests this is the most obvious thing in the world, she replies: '*Efterskole*, of course.'

Of course.

This is the uniquely Danish boarding school her middle child has been attending for the past few months that sounds like a cross between a hippy commune and Hogwarts. So I start investigating.

'*Efterskoler* have been around for about 150 years and they're something Denmark does really well for its teenagers,' says Jakob Clausager Jensen. Jakob works for Denmark's *efterskole* association, but he also attended one in his youth, taught at one for eight years and is currently sending his daughter to one (so he's a fan). Jakob tells me that a quarter of all Danish teenagers attend *efterskole* between the ages of fourteen and sixteen between their *friskole* or *folkeskole* (normal school) and *gymna-sium* (the one with the sailor hats) as a sort of optional year or two out. Although they offer general education, the primary task of *efterskole* is to prepare you for life. 'You're there 24/7, so you have to be yourself,' says Jakob. 'You figure out who you really are.'

Working out who you really are at sixteen? Just think of the decades of therapy saved if we all took this path.

'It's not like an English boarding school, either,' says Jakob. I only need to walk around the light and airy yet simultaneously intimate *efterskole* near me to pick up this vibe. 'At *efterskole*, everyone is equal.' Each member of staff has ten students for whom they are contact teacher, together from the time they awake to the time they go to bed. 'So saying "good night" can take a long time, as students like to talk and often have questions right before sleep,' says Jakob, 'but this means teachers have to be their authentic selves, too. And they get to teach their hobbies or specialisms. Both sides benefit.'

Independence is celebrated and students are encouraged to be self-reliant, working things out with their peers or their 'contact teacher' rather than parents. 'We're trying to prepare them for life,' explains teacher Michelle Brogaard from Fjordvang Efterskole in West Jutland. 'So we'll say, "Is this something you can work through with your contact teacher? Or with one of your friends?" If it's not, then they're welcome to call home, but often they feel proud that they handled something by themselves. They feel a sense of mastery and confidence – and they know for next time.' (#mastery)

'Often for the first week or even the first two months there's a no-phone policy,' says Jakob. 'Kids may find this annoying for the first day, but after two months they say, it's "amazing" – they've never felt so free.' After my depressing deep dive into Denmark's digital blind spot, I believe him.

'You can go home at weekends if you want,' says one of Michelle's 'contact students', 'but actually, you make friends quickly and have this great environment, so often we don't. You know your contact teacher is there for you if you need them. And you learn to do a lot for yourself.'

Students take turns to clean the school and feed around 150 pupils daily. It was at *efterskole* that Trine Hahnemann cemented her love of cooking. 'We would do it in rotation, normally,' she tells me, 'but I found I really liked it and I was good at it. And *efterskoler* are very democratic . . . so everyone took a vote, and it was decided that I should cook every day. That was quite something, age sixteen, cooking for 150 kids daily!'

I ask if it's too early to sign up an eight-year-old ('or five-year-old twins?').

How much you pay for *efterskole* depends on how much you earn, with the remainder paid for by the government. On the average Danish salary of DKK 540,000 – around £62,000 – parents pay around DKK 60,000 – or £7,000. 'But that's for the whole year, including boarding, lessons, food, school trips – everything,' says Jakob. This is still a significant outlay, but nothing like the amount you might pay elsewhere (oh hi, Eton, at £46,296 per year). And it's clearly accessible to many Danes. A quarter of them, in fact.

Studies show that *efterskole* students are more likely to complete upper secondary education (with 16 per cent less risk of dropping out) and there's a 'schoolmate effect', where stronger students lift weaker students up. 'Which is probably why the Danish government keep funding it,' says Jakob.

There's now interest in setting up *efterskoler* overseas. 'From Japan and Korea especially,' says Jakob. 'I get about 25 groups of Korean educators each year coming to Denmark, and Korea is building 500 *efterskole*-inspired schools. These are in opposition to the results-focused, high-pressured, disciplined academic schools Korea is so famous for.' Parents from overseas can also enrol children in Danish *efterskoler*, two of which are completely in English. 'There's no pupil subsidy for international students, but the price isn't more expensive than private schools around the world,' says Jakob.

My teacher friend Anne from choir tells me she can always spot *efterskole* alumni in her *gymnasium* class at the start of each year. 'They're much more grounded and mature. You just become centred at *efterskole*. Not self-centred but centred. *Efterskole* is like adult life with training wheels. You have someone to show you how to do your washing – and then you *know* how to do your own washing, age sixteen.' I once knew a thirty-year-old who didn't know how to do his washing. So this sounds brilliant.

The next step in state-funded education for teens with more practical aptitudes or interests may be a trade school to train in skills like metalwork, electrical engineering or mechanics. Then there are business schools where you specialise in anything from software to accounting. All completely funded by taxes. More academic students opt for *gymnasium* – where students continue their general education with obligatory subjects but also choose fields of study to prepare them for university. These range from maths and sciences to languages, social studies, music and arts. The student day starts at 8 a.m.

until 3 p.m. or 3.30 p.m., but homework ramps up to one and a half to two hours a day and ten hours a week for written assignments.

Danish *gymnasiums* are often a culture shock after a cosy *folkeskole*. They're big, for starters, with vast atriums, extensive technical facilities and common rooms with more microwave doors pinging than can possibly be necessary for an army of ravenous teenagers. Students starting *gymnasium* after years of laid-back Scandinavian schooling can find the academic escalation demanding.

'These kids may have been the best in their *folkeskole*, with the highest grades, but now they're at *gymnasium* with other kids who were best in *their* school, and that's tough for many,' says Anne. 'We try not to dramatise the impact of grades – in the first year you don't get a grade at all until the end of the year. But statistically, they can't all get good grades. So there's a learning curve.' As local teacher Louise explained, graduating teens are given a grade between -3 ('not so good') and 12 ('the best'). It's hard work, even for those getting a double zero – or 'the glasses grade'. So afterwards, they go *bananas*.

As another truck of beer-swigging students passes by the end of the street, I ask Anne: has being a teenager in Denmark always been so boozy?

She laughs: 'Danes do tend to drink . . . with enthusiasm, shall we say. And we start early.'

Danes are legally allowed to buy alcohol up to 6 per cent proof from the age of sixteen. For anything else, it's eighteen. Swedes and Norwegians can go to bars from eighteen, but the only way to buy anything stronger than a light beer for home consumption is by going to a state-run shop – a *systembolaget* in Sweden or a *vinmonopolet* in Norway. These have limited opening hours and shut on Sundays. So although Swedes and Norwegians love a drink, buying alcohol isn't easy. Finns have to wait until they turn twenty to drink legally. In the US, it's twenty-one – and parents can be charged if they give their children alcohol under age.

So why are Danes so accepting of teenage drinking?

Efforts to raise the legal age in Denmark to eighteen for all types of alcohol have met with resistance. Predominantly because older adults recall their own youthful intoxications with such fondness. 'Being a young person in Denmark is and will be inextricably linked to alcohol and drinking. It's part of who we are,' wrote anthropologist Maja Gildin Zuckerman in the newspaper *Weekendavisen*: 'We toast with them when they are fifteen and pick them up at the emergency room after their stomachs are pumped when they are sixteen.' She's not joking: a WHO report found that Danish fifteen-year-olds consumed alcohol at double the European average.[2]

'We learn from our parents!' slurs a beery-smelling boy in a sailor's hat when he hears me talking teen liquor with my American Mom friend.

We're at a coffee shop in the Porny Pony town and the boy has long curly hair escaping either side of his cap. His eyes look familiar. Then I notice a love bite on his neck.

Love Bite? The pool-dangling 'coach' from the twins' Splash 'n' Play swim class? He speaks!

He seems to have clocked me at the same time.

'Oh, hi!'

'Hi! Sorry, I didn't recognise you with your clothes on.'

American Mom's eyebrows raise and coffee sloshes over the side of her cup.

'Swimming,' I manage to mumble, 'teacher.'

She flashes him a Whitestrips-bright smile. He gives a wink and lurches off.

American Mom fans herself and asks if they need any more 'helpers' at swimming.

I tell her 'no' unless she's into bin bags. But his observation gets me thinking. Danes have the highest rates of 'heavy, episodic' drinking of any country in the EU, as well as the highest proportion of those who would categorise themselves as 'drinkers' (97.1 per cent of men and 95.3 per cent of women). Danish director Thomas Vinterberg explored Denmark's drinking culture in his 2020 film *Another Round*, or *Druk*, as it's called in Danish. *Druk* translates as 'binge drinking'. And yes: the fact that Danes have such a short, catchy word for a complete bender speaks volumes.

In the film, four teachers at a *gymnasium* in Copenhagen are inspired by the Norwegian psychiatrist Finn Skårderud's theory that people have a 'natural alcohol deficiency'. Skårderud speculated that a blood alcohol content of 0.05 per cent could rectify this, making us more creative and relaxed. The four friends decide to try it, staying moderately drunk at all times and citing Hemingway and Churchill as inspirations (although Hemingway regularly let a cat babysit his son. So the red flag was there).

Everyone in the film is having a lovely time ('I haven't felt this good in ages!' says Mads Mikkelsen's Martin). But things don't stay that way. Because, sadly, micro-dosing alcohol to improve performance doesn't work. Studies now show that analytical problem-solving skills suffer across *all* levels of alcohol consumption, and 'micro-dosing' soon turns to 'macro-dosing' as we drink more to maintain blood-alcohol concentration. But the film sparked debate. Both globally, and in my living room.

'Good or bad?' Lego Man stared at the screen, then at his wine glass, then at me. 'Drinking: good or bad?'

'I don't think it's as simple as that . . .' I began, but he was already searching for 'answers' on his phone.

'American reviewers say "bad".'

I peered over his shoulder at review upon review from North America discussing the film in terms of an anti-alcohol polemic. But to me, it seemed largely . . . joyous.

I know what you're thinking: 'Is this because she's a wild party animal? A debauched hedonist? A hell-raiser?' To which the answer is 'no'. I am a tired parent of small children. Someone who *used* to drink but now delivers bin bags for ballet club. If anything, I am a hell-*lowerer* these days. I'm the person at a wedding who says: 'Why don't we all get in a water round!' or 'Who's for Berocca?' But at the start of the *Druk* film, all four men are stuck. They embark on the experiment, have a great time, until one of them – who was unhappy before – stops having fun. It's a trajectory I don't think I'd mind. This could be my fatalistic Catholic upbringing, but still.

'Or maybe you're becoming more Danish,' Lego Man speculated.

I wonder . . .

Thomas Vinterberg spoke to the *New York Times* about Danish drinking, saying: 'We have this very constant, very chaste debate about alcohol. But we also drink like Vikings. Whether it comes to sex or fighting,' he added, 'it helps us lose control.' Most Danes, when sober, are pretty controlled. So I can see where he's coming from.

The UK has its own issues with alcohol. Brits abroad have quite the reputation and teenage drinking has been a rite of passage for generations. I drank on a weekly basis from the age of fourteen, which horrifies me now but wasn't unusual at the time. Whereas my American Mom friend grew up in the US with breathalysers before every dance in high school. 'Also: it wasn't cleaned in between students. And we wondered why we all got sick after! *But in Denmark?* Everyone drinks!'

As well as Denmark's established drinking 'traditions', there's a new craze most of us didn't grow up with. 'The beer-bong trend scares me,' says Line, mother of three. These are the long tubes of plastic that I saw our neighbour's son subjected to. *Ølbong* – or beer bongs – are available in supermarkets come graduation, and a popular online shop called Party Vikings has Europe's largest selection, describing *ølbong* as 'an integral part of the Danish party culture'.

'It wasn't like that when we were kids,' reflects Veteran Viking, 'but there was a lot of drinking. We feel like hypocrites if we're strict on this.' So she isn't. Neither are many Danish parents. 'Instead, we talk to our kids about how much to drink,' says Line, 'what drinks to be more careful of, to look after their friends, call us if they get in trouble.' And, presumably, hope for the best.

I think about some of the messes I got myself into as a teenager. *And in my twenties. And my thirties* . . . Experimenting is part of growing up. We all do daft things and learn from them, hopefully. But I'd rather my kids didn't do the daft things after five beer bongs.

Binges aside, drinking culture is slowly changing in Denmark. A study from Aarhus University found in 2021 that alcohol-related liver disease has actually been declining in Denmark for the past twenty-five years.[3] Generations born after the 1960s are more aware of the risk factors of episodic drinking and more health-conscious. And global data on deaths from alcohol-associated liver disease (cheery reading) now puts Denmark on a par with the US and the UK – far lower than Germany, Russia and parts of Asia.[4]

Guidelines on alcohol consumption vary, and the UK government advise no more than fourteen units a week. In the US, it's fourteen for men and seven for women. The Danish health authority changed its guidelines in 2022 to recommend that adults consume no more than ten drinks a week – whatever their gender. Young people under the age of eighteen are advised not to drink *at all* under the new guidelines. And since 2023, under 18s have been banned from buying alcohol in nightlife areas after 10 p.m.

Line's middle child recently graduated, and she hosted the afterparty for all of his friends. 'Those young people were just awesome – so kind and polite, even later in the evening. They complimented our garden, the food we served, my dress. They apologised for spilling stuff and came running to tidy up. They asked if we needed help, and turned the music down when we asked them to. They looked after each other and laughed and sang the night away. I know this is not always the behaviour of all Danish youth – I just think these young people give me hope for the future.'

Parents enjoying the company of well-behaved teenagers? What mischief is this? Perhaps Danish teenagers are just nicer. Does all this freedom actually pay off?

'Danish parents can seem super-loosey-goosey when it comes to teenagers,' says Marie, the psychologist. 'They allow alcohol at ninth-grade parties, let their dating teens co-sleep, and have very little after-school supervision. At the same time, they expect teens to hold a conversation with adults around the dinner table, be polite when visiting their friends' houses, and take responsibility for their school projects. Permissiveness paired with responsibility might be the way to go – maybe it makes for really good people in the end.'

Line thinks so: 'My children are now sixteen, nineteen and twenty-two, and it has never been more wholly joyful to be their parent.'

Everyone back home who I later recount this to will roll their eyes in disbelief, or look as though they're about to vomit. Cynics that we are. But for Danes, it's the truth. 'In the last seven or eight years I have just found it even more intensely gratifying to spend time with them and talk to them,' says Line. 'I didn't expect this at all – it's a surprise and joy after always hearing how horrible teenagers are.'

'It's the same in Sweden,' says Lisolette in Uppsala, 'teenagers get a bad reputation. Everyone is always asking me, "How were the teenage years as a parent for you?!" They're expecting the answer to be "a nightmare", but no, they were lovely. Easy, even.'

Just one criticism is levelled, again and again, at teens who haven't been to *efterskole*.

'They can't mop for shit,' Peter Schmeichel tells me.

'Sorry?'

'Have you asked an eighteen-year-old intern to mop something recently?'

I shake my head.

'I have: they can't!'

I mention this to prison-guard-turned-pedagogue Kitta at *børnehave* pick-up. 'That sounds right,' she says. 'I see a big difference in the young helpers who come to work with us now to, say, ten years ago. Back then a young person could see what they needed to do and just do it. They could take the initiative. But an eighteen- or nineteen- or even twenty-year-old these days? No! They are babied for too long!'

Chef Jacob Holmström tells me about the student helpers he works with at his restaurants in Sweden. 'These kids are eighteen or nineteen, and they have no idea how to iron a shirt or vacuum or mop! At the restaurant, you iron your own chef's uniform – and they don't know how to do it! I will say to them, "Is this the first time you're doing this?" They'll nod. I'll say things like: "Okay, today I will show you how an iron works. Tomorrow, we'll move onto mops . . ." My parents would never have allowed that!'

I vow here and now not to let my mini-Vikings get away with it either.

Back on the street where I live, the neighbours and a few surprisingly spritely teens are clearing up after last night's festivities. Garden furniture gets stacked, gazebos dismantled and bottles collected, until all is neat and ordered once more. The day is overcast but my neighbours are wearing sunglasses, moving slowly and lowering chairs with care to avoid a 'clang'.

Ouch, that must hurt. A hangover when you're fifty is very different from a hangover when you're nineteen.

I see Digger Boy – now, thankfully, clothed – and announce to my family: 'I'm buying a mop.' Four faces turn to me. 'For the neighbour's son! He didn't go to *efterskole*, so he needs to learn how to use one before university!' My family look at me in horror.

'That's a terrible idea,' the redhead announces.

Lego Man nods in agreement.

'What? I'll put a bow on it . . . He'll be leaving home soon; his flatmates will thank me. As well as any future partner.'

There is debate. We settle on a mop *and* an Apple Music gift card. Everyone's happy. I pop to the shops after dinner, then the redhead and I troop around to deliver our bounty.

Chatty Neighbour answers the door slowly. Still wearing sunglasses. 'Hiii,' she croaks. 'Coffee?'

It's 6.30 p.m.! Who does she think I am? Pete Doherty?

'No, thank you, we just wanted to pass on this.' The redhead proffers the present and a polite if baffled teen is summoned.

'Err, thanks?' He looks at the mop, and then the printout of the gift card: 'Wow, thanks!'

On the way back, my son takes a final lingering look at the truck. It belongs to a family friend, so there's less of a hurry to get it back than usual. Several stragglers are now taking selfies with it while the redhead watches with interest.

Presently, he points to the banner hanging on the truck.

'Mum?'

'Yes?'

'Who the fuck *is* Macbeth?'

Oh, so NOW the kid can read? Great. Just great.

What I've learned about how to raise a teen Viking

1. Let them do what they want and try not to panic – they'll probably turn out quite nice. This feels radical, both in terms of permissiveness and the idea that teenagers aren't total nightmares. But perhaps they don't have to be. Perhaps, if we expect them to be polite, engaged, thoughtful human beings, they'll step up (that, or take up joyriding . . .).

2. Adolescents are allowed to hate us and push all the boundaries, but they also need to feel that they can talk to a trusted adult when they want to. When the faecal matter hits the rotary impeller – and it will – we need

to be there. I have no desire to be one of those 'cool parents' (why break the habit of a lifetime?). But I can *listen* when they need me and/or deign to speak to me. Not just for my kids but for my friends' kids and my kids' friends. I could have done with this as a teenager, so I'm all in for the next generation.

3. Teach teens how to mop, iron, clean and do laundry. Future employers, partners, flatmates and the general cosmos will thank us for it.

Epilogue

T HE LIGHTS ARE off and there's fidgeting in anticipation. I'm glancing sideways at silhouettes in the
twilight, when a clear note breaks the silence: the plinky-plonky
opening of Chris Rea's 'Driving Home for Christmas'. The
redhead has turned on the radio and lo! By a festive fluke! It's
Chris. Again. It's December, when Danes can't get enough of
'Driving Home for Christmas', despite the fact that the country
is so small, even the most ambitious journey tops out at around
four hours. 'Or sixty plays of "Driving Home for Christmas",'
says Lego Man. He recently discovered that Chris Rea also hails
from his hometown of Middlesbrough and has taken him to
heart like a long-lost uncle.

'Okay, here goes . . .' I announce, plugging in fairy lights
and *ta da!* Nothing happens. The fuse has blown. Again. We
live in an old house, so this is par for the course. I make my
way to the understairs cupboard to flick on the power but notice
how beautiful it is in the darkness. A sprinkling of powdery
snow is falling outside and our neighbours' houses are lit by
candles. Wafts of *gløgg* – Danish mulled wine – fill the street

whenever a front door opens. And this happens regularly, since there seems to be a near-constant stream of comers and goers. Because this is 'peak visiting season'.

'Christmas in Denmark is all about the family,' says Danish cultural sociologist Emilia van Hauen. 'We celebrate on the twenty-fourth, but really the whole of December is considered a special family time.' In the UK, Christmas is cited as a source of major stress, up there with divorce and moving house, supposedly. But Danes deck the halls with family all month long. Seeing more of them in the run-up to Christmas counter-intuitively reduces stress on the big day. 'It's less of a shock to the system,' explains Veteran Viking. Familiarity can breed *content*. 'So if you have a difference of opinion with a family member, you're likely to have dealt with it at some point during the year before Christmas.'

My mother comes to stay ('You look tired, darling!' 'Thank you!') and everyone mucks in to lay the table and peel potatoes. Danes eat duck or pork with a dash of cabbage and potatoes two ways: boiled and caramelised (hence the team effort on peeling). Once we've eaten, it's time for *pakkeleg*. This a high-octane form of pass-the-parcel where everyone brings a wrapped gift, throws a dice for the chance to win one, then throws *again* to steal other people's, stockpiling as many as possible for themselves. An early lesson for the children in life's harsh realities from the nation that brought us Nordic Noir.

'Then you light real candles on the tree and everyone holds hands and dances around it. *Carefully*,' Veteran Viking emphasises. I have form here: early adoption of this tradition in our first year of living Danishly necessitated a fire extinguisher. Clever Danes leave their trees outside until Christmas Eve. I, however, get overexcited and crack the first time I hear 'Driving

Home for Christmas' on the radio. Our tree is fully lit come 1 December and dry as an IKEA flatpack furniture manual come the 24th. So we dance 'carefully' and stick with tradition by singing a few songs from the ubiquitous *High-School Songbook*. All manner of *hygge* ensues, before presents.

Christmas gifting can be another source of stress for those of us who aren't naturally talented shoppers (me. I mean me. Sorry). There's also the angst of ingratitude and fake enthusiasm for giftees ('What am I supposed to do with this cat bowl? I haven't got a cat.' 'Why have I been given a Lush bath bomb? It isn't 1995,' etc.). I read a study telling me that people in the UK spent £2.6 billion on unwanted gifts, but Danes do things differently. 'There's no sentimentality – if we don't like something, it's perfectly normal to take it back,' says Veteran Viking. 'Don't you have a saying in English, "It's the thought that counts"?'

'We do. We just don't tend to *mean* it.'

But Danes are more honest (or brutal), reducing stress all round. Most items bought from November onwards come with a 'gift return sticker' over the price to show where it came from but avoid any awkwardness over receipts. This way, everyone gets something and can exchange it for what they really want after Christmas. A gift-shift that makes my festive season about 50 per cent more enjoyable.

In Denmark, the big guy in the red-and-white suit comes bearing gifts for children on Christmas Eve. But there are no middle-of-the-night magic chimney antics – whichever family member fits the *Julemand* ('Christmas Man') outfit just dresses up and chucks some presents around. By this stage, Danes have already hosted enchanted mythical creatures for almost a month in the form of a *nisse*, the original 'elf on the shelf'. Mercurial and mischievous, Danish *nisser* wreak havoc on homes from 1 December. At least, they do if you install a *nisse* door, a miniature ladder and furniture (available at all good supermarkets). According to tradition, if *nisser* are treated well, they protect the family from misfortune and help with housework. In my experience, you can treat *nisser* like kings and they'll still trash the place daily. Pranks vary according to who gets to *nisse*-duty first of an evening at my house. Last year's gems included: removing all furniture (Lego Man's work); covering the house in loo roll (ditto); dyeing the milk blue with food colouring (guess who?); and leaving the kitchen table strewn with underpants (honestly, it's exhausting . . .). They also made snow angels (adorable); lovingly crafted an Advent calendar (ditto); and left heartfelt notes to each child (me, obviously).

Yuletide traditions differ across the region, with Swedes gathering around at 3 p.m. on Christmas Eve every year to watch *Donald Duck and His Friends Wish You a Merry Christmas*. A habit that took hold in 1958, now observed by 50 per cent of Swedes.[1] 'And no, no one knows why!' says Niki in Malmö. As the credits roll, there's a knock on the door to reveal . . . *Tomten* – 'Santa' in Swedish. Sadly, a male member of the family will usually be missing at this point, having made an untimely trip to the loo . . .

For those without any Santa-esque relatives, Stockholm's biggest taxi company offers 'extra services' come Christmas. Jouni Talso is one of twenty-five 'kindly old gentleman' pre-approved for the prestigious role of 'mobile' *Tomten*. For the past twenty years he's dressed up in red and white on 24 December to make house calls and spread good cheer. 'Their faces light up when they see Santa, actually on their doorstep!' says Jouni. Word to the wise for anyone tempted to *Tomten* it:

this tradition does mean that Swedish children stop believing in Santa earlier, at 'around six or seven years old', Jouni tells me. 'Children from the US and the UK tend to believe for longer, as they never see him – he comes at night and they think he lives far away, so they've always had to just "believe". But Nordic children see Santa every year in the flesh, and they know that Santa comes from near where they live. There's less mystique, so it's over quicker!'

I don't want it to be over quicker. As American Mom keeps reminding me: 'The days are long but the years are short!'

Couldn't the days be slightly shorter? The years a tad longer? Would that be too much to ask?

Yesterday, my daughter had her first sleepover. I ate two rounds of jam and cheese on rye bread and rewatched *The Killing* to stave off tears. My son still calls his front teeth his 'smilies' and I never want him to stop. His brother starts each day by playing C+C Music Factory's 'Everybody Dance Now' and throwing some phenomenal shapes (that he definitely hasn't inherited from his parents). I would happily take this as my wake-up call for the next decade.

The neighbour's son, Digger Boy, is home from his first term at university. While our couple-about-town neighbours on the other side are expecting.

'Expecting . . . Santa?' The youngest's eyes widen.

'No, darling, a baby,' I explain.

He looks disappointed. But I realise that in the space of three homes on our street, the span of all childhood is here – a selection of Vikings at various stages of their lives.

'Give me a child until they're seven and I'll show you the adult,' as Aristotle should have said (he didn't: he just banged on about boys). I know that the foundational elements of childhood are happening. Right now. They may have happened already in the case of the eight-year-old.

So how to make the most of the childhood they have left? I wonder, folding too-small snowsuits from the clean laundry to pass on, keenly aware that Christmas marks the passing of another year. I want to imbue my children with *sisu* like the Finns; *friluftsliv* like the Norwegians; a healthy approach to bodies like the Swedes; an Icelandic love of books; and a hefty dollop of Danish *ramasjang*.

'You're doing it! You're here, aren't you?' American Mom has dropped by to deliver Christmas gifts (complete with return stickers) and join us for a festive drink. 'Growing up here, it changes them. No matter where they go or what happens next.'

I wish I could be so confident ('or just "American"?' Lego Man suggests). I wish I could bottle a little of that Viking spirit and export it. I know that the package of ideas can't be shipped wholesale, but there are elements we can strive towards. Like better parental leave, not only for the impact this has on parents, but on children and future generations. The Nordic model is based on the idea that both parents work, so affordable, high-quality childcare is a necessity.

'But in the US and the UK it's increasingly necessary to have two incomes,' as Trine Hahnemann points out, 'only there isn't the childcare in place.'

Remember the stats? Every pound invested in early child-hood education yields a 150 per cent return. Minimum. Childcare pays for itself. And planning for a 'good childhood' is better (and cheaper) than 'fixing' things later.

Rather than an obsession with left-hemisphere schooling, Nordics take the whole person into account. I've warmed to the idea of letting children play for longer and starting school later – in the hope that they'll carry on learning throughout their lives, should they choose. This helps to future-proof the next generation. By 2050, economists predict that 40 per cent of current jobs will be lost to automation.[2] We don't know what jobs our children will be doing yet. But we know they'll need adaptability, curiosity and open-mindedness to do them. Learning how to think – rather than *what* to think – feels more important than ever.

Higher education in the Nordic countries is free, so young people don't typically choose a university course based on any future income it may bring – they choose it because they're interested. Danes are even paid to study with monthly state educational support known as SU (Statens Uddannelsesstøtte), from DKK 1,024 a month if you live at home (£118), to DKK 6,589 if you don't (£759). Parents aren't obliged to remortgage or sell a vital organ to fund university, so there's greater opportunity for social mobility in the Nordic countries than elsewhere. The UK and the US score shamefully in terms of social mobility, and the earnings of American men are more closely tied to the earnings of their fathers than men in any other country in the world.[3] Whereas in Denmark? Not so much.

'So, you know, a good reason to stick around,' as American Mom always says. She's here for the long haul and thinks I should be, too. And a lot of things look better on paper in Denmark.

Mini-Vikings are given freedom. With this comes responsibility and a degree of self-sufficiency that I've come to cherish. 'The self-governing way we treat and raise little people is something I think Denmark gets right,' says Professor Ning. 'Take the snowsuit.'

Not what I was expecting, but go on . . .

'The snowsuit is a major emblem of Danish childhood.'

I think about this. Snowsuits don't come cheap in Denmark – costing upwards of £100 – and they usually have to be replaced each year as the child grows. But every parent in Denmark will make the investment or borrow one for their child, then pass it on once they've outgrown it. As I'm doing now. A snowsuit is seen as something to prioritise. And this is how it should be, according to Ning. 'It means you can be outdoors all day. Children can get it on and off by themselves. No rain or snow or sleet can hurt them. And they've been designed with children in mind, so there will be big zips, on both sides if needed, for whichever side is easiest for that child. I know that there are lots of issues, but we do think about children for the most part in Denmark. There is respect.' It's rare that you see a wealthy society where children are taken seriously. But in Denmark, they are. By everyone. Mini-Vikings have a voice and they're taught to use it.

'You have to speak out,' says Peter Schmeichel. 'You have to. Otherwise—'

I know what he's going to say: '1940?'

'Exactly.'

Denmark's occupation still looms large in the public consciousness, and the Second World War has influenced the way my children are being raised in ways I could never have foreseen. Growing up with grandparents' tales of wartime valour, there wasn't much thought given to how the Nordic countries fared. But the legacy of war is everywhere. I live opposite an old bomb shelter. Last week, we found the shell casing from a Second World War tank in the woods. Writing at a time of the war in Ukraine and hearing first-person stories – never far away when you're on mainland Europe – brings home the realities of conflict. War lives on in our collective memory and Danes aren't afraid of talking about it. They're not afraid of talking about anything – or appearing vulnerable. 'Not like when I was growing up.' American Mom pings her empty glass and reaches for a refill.

US football icon Abby Wambach relates her own introduction to the Viking way when Swedish coach Pia Sundhage took over the US Women's Team. On their first meeting, the Swede pulled out a guitar and began singing as the team sat, dumfounded. Abby recalls thinking: 'She has absolutely no idea what she's doing. We are screwed.' (*Wolfpack*, 2019.) This was the first time they'd seen 'a leader making herself vulnerable'. But sharing vulnerability brought the team closer and helped them to be more collaborative. This new, more generous mindset worked wonders, and the Swede led the US team to two Olympic gold medals and a silver medal at the World Cup.

I'm not expecting my children to become World Cup champions or Olympians (though I promise I'll give two hoots about football if they do). But I hope they grow into useful, kind members of society. With *samfundssind*. And a robust sense of the ridiculous.

'They'll need it in this family,' Lego Man mutters, giving his daily impression of someone stacking a dishwasher as our sons go outside to 'drink icy water' from the hose. We bumble through Christmas, eating, talking, walking. Celebrating Susan the lemur's birthday and playing Sylvanian Family Police Raids. I take my mother to the airport on Boxing Day and just as I'm pulling into the kiss-and-fly zone, she tells me, without warning: 'They're really nice, interesting children.'

I stop the car.

Shouldn't this declaration come with some kind of klaxon? At the very least a trumpet? A kazoo?!

My mother isn't one to praise unless absolutely necessary (she recently reviewed a BBC radio documentary I presented as 'nasal'). So this is big.

'Thank you,' I manage, heart lodged in my throat.

'You do look tired though, darling . . .'

'Okay, thanks.' I pull on the handbrake.

'Pallor like guacamole . . .'

Just the look I was going for . . . I hug her goodbye. 'Cheerio!'

Once I get home, I find that Lego Man has togged everyone up for 'a much-needed long walk' (allegedly). We head to the beach for our customary post-mortem of any family gathering and I tell him what my mother said. He's rendered momentarily speechless. Wind presses clothes against our bodies and the dog tows us as we're buffeted by the elements, sea on one side, trees stripped bare on the other. The small people run ahead to explore an abandoned mobility scooter.

'A second Christmas miracle!' says Lego Man.

'What was the first?'

'That we might be doing something right as parents!'

We sink back into silence as if by mutual agreement.

Me: thinking about the improbable turns of events that have led us here and how children are like weather, changeable and impossible to control.

Lego Man: probably thinking about Chris Rea again.

It was only ever meant to be a year of living Danishly. Then I got pregnant. Then Brexit. Then IVF. Then twins. And puff! Ten years have gone by in a heartbeat. So am I a Viking now? *I've potty-trained twins. I'm basically bulletproof.*

But I miss my mum, notwithstanding guacamole compliments.

And the rest of the family elders, who won't be around for ever. And cousins who, in lieu of siblings, are important to me and who I'd like to be guiding figures in my children's lives (no pressure). I miss old friends. Godchildren. People I love who are not where I am. I miss family, both genetic and gathered, in a country where everything is centred around family. And so, I don't think we'll be here for good.

If only we'd been born Danish, I lament, often. *If only one of us had. Why was Lego Man born in Halifax instead of Hellerup?* (a particularly leafy Copenhagen suburb). Had at least one of us been born and bred in Denmark, I would happily stay in perpetuity. But we weren't. And no amount of *snegle* can change this. Which is why it's been even more important for me to learn all I can from the Nordics about how to build a Viking from the ground up. To find out what they do differently and how the rest of us can copy it, exporting it to use elsewhere.

I know I'm lucky to have had these experiences. This period of my life will mark me. This period of their life will mark my children, too. For ever. And Danes do 'kids' well. Raising children Viking style from single cell to around age ten now seems, from all I've learned, foolproof. I love the emphasis on democracy and speaking out, since children growing up in the AI world will have to know how to analyse and interrogate information, rather than just repeating it. I like the way the Nordic system nurtures independent thinkers who can work together. I maintain that the approach of utter liberalism and freedom above all else when applied to digital devices seems mad – and counter to all the latest science. I'd like proper guidance on this, so it's not just up to individual parents. But the rest of the Nordic approach? It just makes sense.

'It's like a nice lunch,' says Lego Man.

'Sorry?'

'You don't always want the set menu. Sometimes, you want to go *à la carte*,' is how Lego Man puts it, only in a particularly pronounced Yorkshire accent. 'That's okay, isn't it? If we've gone Viking for the first ten years of their life and "home" is on the menu for when the kids get older?'

Choosing where to live is a privilege and we're all subject to the winds of change, bureaucracy and corporate restructures. But for now, I suppose, 'yes'. Home could be back on the menu.

Lego Man and I have never been able to agree on where 'home' should be, historically. We could never agree on many things, which felt like a problem. The unspoken conversations became clamorous. But actually, the Danish way has taught me that you can get along even when you don't agree. I remember what Morten from DR told me about how kids in Denmark grow up understanding that relationships are difficult and there is conflict – 'and that's okay'. There's still love. Two stubborn, avoidant people are, somehow, making it work. Like a fractionally more mature *Bamse og Kylling* – Bear and Chicken (and I mean 'fractionally').

I look over. Lego Man is saying something, but his voice is snatched away by the wind. I cup an ear: 'Sorry?'

'What I said was . . . "Did you know that Chris Rea had six siblings?"'

'I did not know that.'

He looks pleased.

In the middle distance a trailer arrives to pick up the mobility scooter and the driver gives us a cheery wave: 'Battery flat!'

Lego Man looks disappointed. 'No Christmas miracle then?'

'Just the one,' I tell him, pointing at the small people up ahead.

The redhead has picked up a stick and is giving it an experimental whack as our youngest asks questions about asteroids. My daughter is making pictures in sand, using seaweed for hair and shells for eyes. The wind blows ribbons of hair across her face and I feel a tug – the invisible thread between us, between them. Always.

Another kind of tug jerks me out of this reverie as the dog strains at his leash. A few youths with a puppy are ambling from the other direction. One has dark curls twisting out from under a beanie. A down jacket is zipped to the clavicle, but there's no denying the still visible—

'Love Bite!' Lego Man starts.

Just when you thought it was safe to get back in the water . . .

'*Hej!*' Lego Man gives an exaggerated wave at the pool-noodle-dangling lothario. 'I nearly didn't recognise you with your clothes on!'

My face twists with the supreme exertion of willpower required to avoid laughing. Our daughter runs over, ostensibly to greet her 'teacher' but really to get a look at the puppy. Her cheeks are pink with cold and she takes mittens off to blow on icy fingers.

'You want Gore-Tex gloves.' Love Bite nods towards my daughter's hands.

I hear a sharp intake of breath from Lego Man: 'That's what I always say!' Pool-noodle-dangler has just gone up several notches in his estimation.

'I don't know if you've heard . . .' Love Bite continues.

Goodness! Silent for months and now he's a regular Chatty Cathy . . .

'But we have this saying in Denmark . . .'

Okay, here we go . . .

'There's no such thing as bad weather, just the wrong—'

Lego Man finishes his sentence: 'Clothes!' He beams, regarding the younger man with unconcealed admiration.

'That's it!' Love Bite points to the communal fire pit, where another teen is stationed, giving a pyre a desultory poke. 'We're just here grilling some *pølser*.'

'Sausages? In the snow?' Lego Man is now smitten.

'Can we have sausages, too? *Please?*' the other mini-Vikings plead as they shuffle in snowsuits to pet the puppy/stare into the hazel eyes of their swimming teacher. Starstruck by the combination of puppy *and* pool-dangler ('wearing *clothes!*'), it takes a while to peel them away. But the light is fading, so we say goodbye and head home to commence the glide path of getting smalls fed, read and put to bed.

Finally, they sleep. All is silvery still. In the night I wake and pad blindly to the bathroom to find Lego Man already there. Brought together by the shared human need to urinate, I wait, in a queue of one. From the skylight on the landing, I see stars out in force. The moon shines like a sickle. And then, I hear it. The distinctive peal of a newborn's cry. Plaintive. Urgent.

Lego Man emerges, blue eyes bleary with sleep, reacting to the sound with some sort of Pavlovian muscle memory. 'Who needs what?' he croaks. 'Nappy? Milk? Both?' I hear panic rising.

'No one, it's okay: it's not ours! We've done that part!' I hold a finger to my lips and point next door: 'Listen!' There it is. Again. 'It's here – the neighbours' new baby!' I feel clammy, heart racing as I'm taken back to that day, years ago, when we first became parents. *Clueless*, I think, *completely clueless*.

I wanted a family so badly. I thought parenting was all about having a baby, then loving it, through each of its life stages. And it is. But there's much more to it than that. I wasn't prepared for questions beyond my own comprehension (see 'asteroids'). Or fights about shoes. Or iPad negotiations. Or playing peekaboo for the same amount of time it takes to get a pilot's licence. But we did it. We're doing it. With the best possible teachers around us: Vikings.

Everyone is doing their best when it comes to raising small people. And every day when things go wrong (see: unicorn bubble machine, Chapter 8) we try again the next day (see: shoehorn, Chapter 8). And we try again the day after that. We keep on trying. Like they will be next door with a squalling newborn. Like Digger Boy's mum and dad on the other side, whose mud-magnet child, grubbing about in the dirt, has somehow become an undergraduate.

The unmistakable new baby wail rents the air again. I spot our neighbour at the window. He looks up and I see the fear in his eyes. The same fear I had all those years ago. I give a nod – an acknowledgement of understanding. He gives me a wave before realising he hasn't yet learned how to hold a child with one hand. He resumes cradling his precious bundle with the clutch of a drowning man as I smile back in solidarity: *You've got this. We've got this.*

And it starts all over again.

BONUS CHAPTER

How to Party Like a Viking

TILLYKKE! (CONGRATULATIONS!) YOU'VE read the book, you've salivated over *snegle*, you've heard how they do Christmas, but happily, there's always an excuse to celebrate in the Nordic countries. On days when you or your small people have run out of reasons to be cheerful, why not borrow a few Viking traditions? Introducing the Nordic party line-up – or 'national excuse for cake' days, as they're affectionately known in our house.

1 January *Kransekage*. As the clock strikes midnight to usher in the New Year, Danes slice into a tower of eighteen or more ring-shaped layers, made from almonds, eggs and sugar (start as you mean to go on). Once everyone's surfaced at a more respectable hour, there's *vinterbadning* or 'winter bathing'. Locals do it in the nude near me, with a veritable buffet of bare bottoms, breasts and dangly bits on show. But I wear a swimsuit and a woolly hat (because: British). Pack plenty of towels, extra socks (the redhead requires two pairs after an icy dip), and flasks of coffee/hot chocolate as a reward afterwards.

25 January (or thereabouts) *Sólardagurinn* or 'sun day'. Icelanders of Ísafjörður don't see the sun *at all* for two months a year, thanks to high mountains surrounding their village. When the sun makes an appearance at long last and rises high enough to be seen, Icelanders celebrate with a *sólarkaffi* or 'sun coffee' and pancakes to symbolise the sun.

5 February J. L. Runeberg Day. Finns love all their poets and novelists, but few get their own pastry (#writergoals). So just when winter feels like it's dragging, Finns celebrate the poet Johan Ludvig Runeberg (1804–77) with Runeberg's torte. A jam-topped cylindrical cake with almonds and rum or arrack, which he ate every day for breakfast, so the story goes. Johan's wife and fellow writer Fredrika Runeberg came up with the recipe and was also a pioneer of historical fiction and the first Finnish author to critically analyse the status of women. Oh, and she had eight children. Unsurprisingly, Fredrika Runeberg has been chronically overlooked historically. So let's start a new campaign to rename 5 February simply 'Runeberg Day' – celebrating both of them.

14 February *Ystävänpäivä*, or Friends' Day. Forget St Valentine, Finns dedicate today to friends, family, neighbours and even colleagues with cards, flowers and chocolates. Tell your pals.

Seven weeks before Easter . . . is *Fastelavn*, the Danish holiday with the second-best cake ever: chocolate-topped, marzipan-filled buns called *gammeldags fastelavnsboller.** *Fastelavn*

---

* In first place is Trine Hahnemann's *brødtorte* chocolate rye-bread cake. Fact.

originated from the Catholic tradition of a foodie blowout before Lent, but after Denmark's Reformation, Lutheran leaders weren't mad about a Roman ritual, so the celebration became secular. This meant Danes could stuff their faces with no obligation to deprive themselves afterwards.

Traditionally on this day, farmers shored up good fortune for a successful harvest by banishing cats – maligned as the embodiment of bad luck. Cats were sealed in barrels that were beaten with sticks until they splintered open and the cats escaped. 'Thankfully, we just use pictures of cats now,' lifelong cat lover Veteran Viking assures me. Cat-themed balsa-wood barrels are thwacked by children in fancy dress until they explode, like a piñata, showering everyone with sweets. The child who knocks a hole in the barrel is crowned 'King' or 'Queen of Cats'. Afterwards, smalls tout for treats door to door, singing: 'Buns up, buns down, buns in my tummy. If I get no buns, I will make trouble.' Loudly. Until neighbours give them more sweet treats.

In Iceland, they cut to the chase, calling this pre-Lent gorge simply *Bolludagur* or Bun Day. Everyone stuffs their faces with cream puffs and children make wands to smack their parents on the bum while yelling *'bolla, bolla, bolla'*. For each spank, they get a bun. And no, I have not made this up.

24 February *Konudagur* or Women's Day. Icelandic custom dictates that women be utterly spoiled and treated to flowers, coffee and cake on this day. *Marks date in diary, sends invite to all contacts*

1 March *Bjordagur* or Beer Day. Icelanders commemorate the end of prohibition after a seventy-four-year booze ban from

1915 to 1989 by raising a glass to celebrate ('You need a whole day for this?' I ask Icelandic friends. 'Yes,' they say. In unison).

25 March *Våffeldagen* or Waffle Day. Swedes eat heart-shaped waffles topped with cloudberry jam and cream to celebrate the Virgin Mary (I know: bear with me . . .). According to the Gospels, 25 March is the day when the Archangel Gabriel came down to Earth and told Mary that she would give birth to Jesus. Swedes already celebrated Our Lady's Day (*Vårfrudagen*), and thought it sounded a little like *våffeldagen*. So, they combined the two. Practical and delicious.

Easter Time to exchange *gækkebreve* or Easter letters. Danish children make what look like doilies from the 1980s but are in fact anonymous letters to 'tease' recipients into giving them chocolate. Shapes are snipped out of paper to create a snowflake-esque design, then a dot is used for each letter of the sender's name. If the recipient guesses who sent it before Easter, they receive a chocolate egg. If they don't? The sender can demand a chocolate egg from the recipient.

Palm Sunday Finnish children dress up as witches and go from door to door with decorated willow twigs, offering neighbours a 'magic spell' promising good health in exchange for sweets (sensing a theme?). This dates back to Finland's pagan days when agrarian workers believed witches determined whether or not crops would thrive or fail.

15(ish) April Dancing Cow Day. Organic cows in Denmark are kept inside during the long, cold winter before being let out to pasture in mid-April. They're so happy to be back on grass that they hop, frisk, buck, gallop and look a lot like they're dancing. Farms countrywide invite visitors to watch the spectacle and serve up dairy-based snacks for *økodag* or 'organic day'. But we all know why we're really there and it's the Anchor Butter-style cow-dancing. Outstanding.

21 April The first day of summer. Old Norse calendars were based on only two seasons: summer and winter. So essentially, this celebration means 'not winter any more'. Villages, towns and cities throughout Finland celebrate with parades, outdoor games and community BBQs. Followed by a sauna.

30 April *Valborgsmässoafton* or Walpurgis Night, when Swedes celebrate the eighth-century abbess St Valborg (also known as St Walpurgis, Walborg or Walpurga or Walburga). Born in Devon, she opted for a holy life in Germany. So naturally, *Swedes* celebrate by lighting big bonfires, setting off fireworks and singing.

April is also the month for *utepils* or 'outdoor beer' – the ultimate reward for Norwegians after a long, dark winter. Whatever day everyone agrees that the weather is clement – if not 'warm', then 'slightly less cold' – it's time for *utepils* and nationwide festivity ensues. Newspapers fill with pictures of people enjoying their first outdoor beer of the year.

1 May May Day or Labour Day is a celebration of spring (and labour . . .) throughout the Nordic countries. Finns celebrate with 'funnel cake' constructed from deep-fried lemon-flavoured batter that looks like worms but tastes surprisingly good. Best served alongside *munkki* – a Finnish doughnut – and *sima*, a lemony drink.

17 May Norway's Constitution Day, also known as Norwegian Independence Day, is one of the biggest festivals in the country. Cue mass merrymaking on the streets of Norwegian cities. And sausages. And perhaps a *ventepølse* – or 'waiting sausage' – while you wait for the main-event sausage to cook.

Also in May . . . Norway's World Beard and Moustache Championships, where the follically fortunate travel from all over to show off impressive facial hair in categories including partial beard, natural moustaches and 'freestyle'. Hr. Skæg, aka Mr Beard, would be a shoo-in.

5 June Danish Constitution Day, when many businesses and shops close, buses fly the Danish flag and Danes celebrate democracy with *fællessang* (group singing), open-air gatherings, *pølser* and beer.

6 June Sweden's National Day commemorating Gustav Vasa's coronation as king in 1523 and the Swedish constitution, adopted in 1809. Nationwide merriment, plus hotdogs.

17 June Iceland's Independence Day marks the anniversary of the country's freedom from Danish ties in 1944, and the birthday of Jón Sigurðsson, who campaigned for Icelandic independence in the nineteenth century. Icelanders lay wreaths at the base of his statue in Reykjavik and there are concerts and a parade. And sausages.

19–25 June *Midsommar*. Swedes commemorate midsummer on a Friday between 19 and 25 June. Traditionally considered a time of magic, when plants acquired mysterious powers and strange things could happen. You're welcome, Shakespeare. Young Swedes pick seven different kinds of flowers and put them under their pillow to dream of their future loves. Flowers are picked in silence, otherwise the magic is broken (and your neighbour knows you're raiding his begonias). Walking barefoot in the dew as night turns to dawn and wearing a wreath of flowers in your hair ensures health, fertility and wet feet. Swedes play games like croquet or *kubb*, where you knock down wooden blocks by throwing sticks. Then they feast. Herring, shrimp and salmon are all on the menu, toasted and washed down by shots of *snaps* – akvavit, vodka or other liqueurs in Sweden. For each toast, a new song is sung (Swedes have more than 12,000 *snaps* songs, according to the Museum of Spirits in Stockholm).

23 June *Sankt Hans Eve* or the eve of St John the Baptist is combined with the summer solstice in Denmark. It's marked by singalongs around a community bonfire, where an effigy of a witch is burned, historically to 'banish evil spirits and send them to the mountains in Germany' (sorry, Germany). In our neighbourhood, there are also speeches, sausages and *flødebolle* for the children – a biscuit base topped with mallow and coated in chocolate (or 'a posh Tunnock's Teacake' as Lego Man maintains).

July is *Jordbærkage* season. Danish strawberries are full of flavour come July so summer is celebrated with *jordbærkage* – vanilla crème in a chocolate-coated pastry case, topped with fresh strawberries. Like eating summer and to be enjoyed at every opportunity in the name of 'seasonal eating'.

29 July St Olaf's Day. Norwegians celebrate their patron saint (originally their king) with festivals of singing and dancing. And sausages.

August *Kräftpremiär* aka 'Swedish crayfish party season!' For most of the twentieth century there were strict rules about when crayfish could be fished in Swedish waters to help the population recover to healthy levels. When the restrictions were lifted towards the end of summer each year, Swedes let loose and began celebrating with outdoor feasts. Diners put on party hats and huddle around a long table decorated with streamers to tuck in. Noisy slurping is considered a sign of appreciation and bibs are essential (it gets messy).

September A quieter month when Vikings catch up on garden maintenance (rock 'n' roll). Peter Schmeichel assures me that this is the time to 'cut back dead perennials' and – big news – the DIY shop has at last sent him a pair of loyalty secateurs. He's over the moon ('next level: the dagger!'). For everyone else, it's chill time. Unless it's your birthday, your anniversary or a Wednesday (see below). Or you're in Iceland.

Icelanders countrywide take part in September's major social event: shepherding. Locals ride horses to round up 800,000 sheep from the countryside. Some tour companies even allow tourists to participate (sign me up! who's with me?).

October Week forty-two of the year is *Kartoffelferie* or 'potato holiday' – Denmark's far-cooler rebrand of half-term with extra appreciation for spuds.

1 November *Jólabókaflóðið* or 'the Christmas book flood' begins in Iceland, when the list of newly published books is announced. Icelanders exchange books on Christmas Eve and every home gets a free catalogue of all the new publications, called the *bokatidindi*. My mate Siggi remembers spending hours circling the ones he wanted ('Like me with the Argos catalogue,' says Lego Man. Me: 'Err . . . sort of . . . ').

The first Friday of November *J-Day*, when the special Christmas beer, or *julebryg*, goes on sale in Denmark at precisely 8.59 p.m. Over time, *J-Day* has become a Christmas tradition celebrated in bars and pubs around the country (one for the grown-ups). But why not start your own tradition? John Lewis Christmas Ad Day? Pret Roast Turkey and Trimmings Sandwich Day? The list is endless.

10 November *Mortens Aften* or Saint Morten's Day is marked in Denmark by everyone eating duck or goose in honour of Saint Martin of Tours (*Morten Bisp* in Danish). The story goes that Martin was so good at healing the sick that locals wanted him as their bishop, but Martin wasn't keen. So he hid. Not somewhere sensible and quiet, but in a flock of geese. Unsurprisingly, their honking gave him away and Martin was so incensed that he made everyone slaughter and eat goose as a punishment for their treachery. Danes have stuck to this strange tradition – first documented in Denmark in 1616 – only allowing duck as an acceptable alternative in recent years for anyone finding a goose hard to come by (or to fit in the oven).

1 December *Juleboller* go on sale in Denmark. A soft, sweet and spicy delight, similar to a hot cross bun, without the cross. Best eaten with a good layer of *tandsmør* or tooth butter – the Danish term for a layer of butter so thick you see teeth marks in it after biting. Hard recommend for maximum Christmas cheer.

Advent There are plentiful opportunities for pre-Christmas bonding, but the most popular in Denmark is baking. Early in Advent, families get together for a 'baking day' to stock up on Christmas standards, including *pebernødder* spiced biscuits and *æbleskiver* – spherical pancake/doughnut hybrids of pure deliciousness. The only thing Vikings don't bake at this time of year is a fruited Christmas cake. Danes put their raisins in wine instead, along with sliced almonds. Nordic *gløgg* is like mulled wine, only with the added jeopardy of 'bits' in every gulp, so that you think you're about to choke. Ding-dong merrily on high!

Christmas craft day comes next – or *julpyssla* in Swedish. Vikings whittle and forage and cover their house with a medley of lichen and sprigs. Children are charged with making a *juledekoration* candle centrepiece at school or kindergarten, wedging pinecones, spruce branches, moss and general garden detritus into a lump of clay with an Advent candle in the middle. Or *julehjerter*, the white-and-red woven hearts that Kitta taught all my children to make but that I still can't master (total respect to all who can).

12 December The first of Iceland's Yule Lads arrive. These half-troll Santa-substitutes come down from the mountains to play pranks on children until Christmas, with names like Spoon-Licker, Door-Slammer, Doorway-Sniffer, Window-Peeper and Sausage-Swiper (did I mention Vikings love a sausage?). If you think this sounds creepy, there's also the Christmas Cat, who eats children who don't get new clothes ('It seems harsh now, but I think it was to encourage parents to knit a new sock,' says my friend Birna #NordicNoir).

13 December Santa Lucia Day. Commemorating the third-century Sicilian who wanted to devote her life to God at a time when Christians were persecuted. According to legend, the Roman emperor commanded that Lucia be taken to a brothel, but by divine intervention no one could move her. The emperor tried to burn her at the stake next, but she survived. So she was stabbed *and* beheaded. Just to be sure. To honour Santa Lucia today, Swedes, Danes, Norwegians and Finns bake saffron buns and have a procession where a girl in a white dress wears a crown of candles on her head (Lucia liked to be hands-free). She's followed by candle-bearing girls and boys, also in white dresses (or, at my *børnehave*, sheets). They sing a translation of the Neapolitan song 'Santa Lucia' and by the end of the procession, there isn't a dry eye in the house.

25 December Since Vikings celebrate Christmas on the 24th, on the 25th you can just kick back, eat chocolates and watch TV . . . oh no, wait, that's in my old life: these days we have to go on another 'lovely long walk', as Lego Man puts it. *Sighs* Fortunately, he makes sure we're all kitted out for it ('You know what they say? No such thing as bad weather—' 'Yes! We *know*!'). And on Lasse the *friluftsliv* fanatic's advice, I pack ALL the leftover Christmas chocolate.

31 December New Year's Eve. Young and old enjoy home firework displays throughout the Nordic countries (safety goggles advised). Icelanders also sing songs and dance by the light of a neighbourhood bonfire. Finns melt miniature horse-shoes on a spoon over a flame (less *Trainspotting* than it sounds), then throw the contents over snow or ice to see what shape it takes. This will 'tell their fortune' for the year ahead. A heart means love; a coin, success; a ship, travel.

Swedes enjoy a recitation of Alfred Tennyson's old poem 'Ring Out, Wild Bells' ('*Nyårsklockan*'), a tradition no one seems able to explain but one that has been in place since the 1890s.

Then everyone watches *Dinner for One*, a British two-hander comedy sketch from 1962 that has, inexplicably, become essential viewing in Denmark, Sweden, Norway and Finland (as well as Germany, Austria, Switzerland and Estonia). In the sketch, an upper-class Englishwoman has a dinner party for her ninetieth birthday – only all her friends are dead. So her butler pretends to be each of them in turn and drinks for them all. Despite being largely unknown in the UK, it's aired every year in Denmark since 1980 and in Sweden since 1969, save for a hiatus 1963–69, when it was banned due to the depiction of heavy alcohol consumption.

After that, there's more food and more drink, possibly coffee (at night! I know!), then Danes jump off the sofa as the clock strikes twelve to symbolise 'jumping into the new year'. And then? Then, you tuck into the *kransekage* and start the cake calendar again.

But there are also Viking party perennials. Like 'Wednesdays'.

Wednesdays Liven up hump-day by observing the Danish custom of eating cinnamon buns called *onsdagssnegle* ('Wednesday snails'). Some bakeries sell these at reduced prices to 'celebrate' . . . um . . . Wednesday.

Birthdays According to Danish tradition, you're responsible for the weather on your birthday. If it's sunny, it means you've been 'good' all year and everyone thanks you for the lovely weather. If it's raining? You've done something dire and now everyone knows it. It's a meteorological *Picture of Dorian Gray*, only with the chance of a do-over each year.

The flag is flown on birthdays but if you don't have a flag-pole (embarrassing for you), a flag outside your door will do. Most important is the mini-flagpole to decorate the 'birthday table' at mealtimes and make you feel special – regardless of your nationality, since the flag symbolises celebration. I recently learned that Swedes get breakfast in bed on their birthday, too, so if any of my family are reading: I want this.

Birthday cakes for children in Denmark tend to be *kagemand* or *kagekone*, three-foot-long mega-pastries in the shape of a person, decorated with marzipan, *slik* (sweets) and liquorice strands for hair. The birthday girl or boy cuts the cake by slicing through the jugular, whereupon everyone screams. Because nothing says 'kids' party' like decapitation or a pastry-themed slasher film.

If you're over the age of ten and feel too grown up for a *kagemand*, Danes opt for a layered sponge with cream between and berries on top. And you bring your own birthday cake, which means everyone's spared any 'oh shit, we forgot!' embarrassment. It's impossible to 'forget' somebody's birthday when they're standing in front of you holding a three-foot cake-person. Other than cake, celebrations tend to be low-key, except for milestone birthdays, when things ramp up.

'When you turn twenty-five, you get cinnamon-d,' Peter Schmeichel tells me. 'I got it thrown at me from the moment I woke up. I tried to wash it off, but every time I got out of the shower, they'd attack again. I went outside, but they tied me to a lamp-post and gave me swimming goggles to wear and threw more at me.' *Why?* 'Good question! Well, a very long time ago – sixteenth century, maybe – spice salesmen were so busy travelling that they had no time for dating and became known as *pebersvends* or "pepper journeymen".' Since then, unmarried Danes turning twenty-five have been showered with spices. Few Danes are married by twenty-five, so this has nothing to do with derision of the unwed and everything to do with 'tradition'.

When you hit thirty, if you're still not married, you're upgraded to a pepper dousing and may also receive a sculpture of a 'peppermill' made from stacked oilcans. At least 'pepper-mill' was the original custom – today they're often made to look like horses or genitalia. Many happy returns!

'Round' birthdays, when your age can be divided by ten, are also special, celebrated with a bigger party for family and friends. And big *halvrunde* ('half-round') birthdays like seventy-fifth birthdays also warrant celebration and singing. Traditionally, Danes give speeches and write special song lyrics for a big birthday bash.

Weddings Viking nuptials include a lot of speeches and kissing on demand. When guests stamp their feet, newlyweds have to get under their table and kiss. When guests clang cutlery, newly-weds must stand on their chairs and snog. When either of the newlyweds is out of the room, guests dash to kiss the lone newlywed throughout Denmark, Sweden and Norway (sounds problematic, but apparently Vikings are okay with it).

In Sweden, bride and groom walk down the aisle together and men get engagement rings, too. And photos are taken before the ceremony, so guests don't have to hang around afterwards. Let's all agree to do Swedish-style wedding photos from now on.

In Norway, brides get a crown (vow renewal in Oslo, anyone?). The *brudekrone* or 'bride crown' is often a family heirloom passed down through generations ('Mum? Yes, I know I look tired, but quick question: any *crowns* knocking around?'). Post-wedding, the couple plant a fir tree either side of their front door to signify the children they plan to have and/or their growing relationship.

Anniversaries In Denmark, neighbours, family and friends make a floral arch around your front door to celebrate twelve and a half, twenty-five and fifty years of married life. For a twelve-and-a-half-year 'copper anniversary', the arch is half height, so there's some ducking required. Then between 6 and 7 a.m., family, friends and neighbours gather outside the arch and start singing for the anniversary couple to materialise before breakfasting together. There'll be bread rolls, *snegle* (of course), coffee, and possibly something stronger to toast the still-married couple having survived thus far.

So there you have it. Raise a glass (of anything you fancy) and *skål!* or 'cheers!' Congratulations, you're a Viking now.

Acknowledgements

To all the small people who have made this book possible, thank you. From sharing stories to fetching 'warm paper' from the printer and making 200 paper airplanes with my penultimate draft, *tak* ('thank you' in Danish).

Thank you to Anna Power for always believing in me and to Louise Haines, Anna Michels and Liv Turner, who let me write books for a living and be a part of that magical place where ideas can wrestle it out.

To the team at Harper Collins UK – Victoria Pullen, Mia Colleran, Nicola Webb, Eve Hutchings and Kate Quarry. A huge thank you to all at Source Books and Penguin Random House in the US and to the Johnson and Alcock crew – Michael Alcock, Anna Dawson, Helene Butler, Saliann St-Clair and Kroum Valtchkov.

Thank you to all the experts named in the book for their generosity and to all those who helped me to get to them, including Denise Lauritsen, Bryony Lester, Lasse Ribergård Rasmussen and Neeni Lomborg. To Pia Nielsen and Kitta Pust, the best pedagogues in town.

To all the Viking parents for their support, especially Camilla Bjerre, Rikke Bruntse Dahl, Camilla Uhre Fog, Kimie

ACKNOWLEDGEMENTS

Sandborg Randorf, Johanne Lucie Ertok, Sille Aarlit Jensen and Maria Gustavsson (as well as honorary Viking dads John Hassall and Tracii Guns).

Special thanks to Sanne Moth and Annika Friis for fellow twin mom sanity checks and early reader excellence. And to my mum, for raising me.

To fellow 'outsiders', Tim, Amy, Sean, Graham, Louise, Viv, Ian, Jono, Fee, Chesney and Nichole for sharing insights and observations. To Tara, for keeping my children in rollerblades (crucial) and Fen for invaluable early brainstorming.

I am ever grateful to my UK crew – Ali, Caroline, Chrissy, Emily, Sarah, Kate, Katie and Jill for helping to turn off Shit FM if the volume ever gets too loud.

And to you for reading. Thank you.

Endnotes

The abbreviation 'n.d.' in a note indicates that no publication date was available.

Introduction: The Accidental Viking

1 K. M. Sonderskov and P. T. Dinesen. 'Danish Exceptionalism: Explaining the Unique Increase in Social Trust over the Past 30 Years' *European Sociological Review* 30 (6). 2014. 782–95. https://doi.org/10.1093/esr/jcu073.

2 Marc J. Hetherington. 'The Political Relevance of Political Trust' *The American Political Science Review* 92 (4). 1998. 791–808. https://doi.org/10.2307/2586304.

Jack Citrin and Laura Stoker. 'Political Trust in a Cynical Age' *Annual Review of Political Science* 21 (1). 2018. 49–70. https://doi.org/10.1146/annurev-polisci-050316-092550.

'Trust in Government, UK: 2022' Office for National Statistics. 13 July 2022. https://www.ons.gov.uk/peoplepopulationandcommunity/wellbeing/bulletins/trustingovernmentuk/2022.

'Trust in Government' Organisation for Economic

Cooperation and Development. 2022. https://doi.
org/10.1787/1de9675e-en.

   'Public Trust in Government: 1958–2022' Pew Research
Center – US Politics & Policy. 6 June 2022. https://www.
pewresearch.org/politics/2022/06/06/public-trust-in-
government-1958-2022/.

3 '2022 Corruption Perceptions Index' Transparency
International. 2022. https://www.transparency.org/en/
cpi/2022.

4 Charlotte Edmond. 'These Are the Countries Where
Children Are Most Satisfied with Their Lives' World
Economic Forum. 4 September 2020. https://www.weforum.
org/agenda/2020/09/child-well-being-health-happiness-
unicef-report/.

5 'The State of the World's Children 2021: On My
Mind – Promoting, Protecting and Caring for Children's
Mental Health' United Nations Children's Fund.
2021. https://www.unicef.org/reports/state-worlds-
children-2021.

6 'Any Anxiety Disorder' National Institute of Mental
Health, 2017, www.nimh.nih.gov/health/statistics/any-
anxiety-disorder.

7 'Divorces' Statistics Denmark, https://www.dst.dk/en/
Statistik/emner/borgere/husstande-familier-og-boern/
skilsmisser.

8 CNN, Bill Weir. (n.d.) 'Is Marriage Becoming Totally
Outdated in Iceland?' CNN. https://edition.cnn.com/travel/
article/wonder-list-bill-weir-iceland/index.html.

1. Congratulations! It's a Viking!

1 Daniel Rosenkjær, Allan Pacey, et al., 'Effects of Virtual
Reality Erotica on Ejaculate Quality of Sperm Donors: A

Balanced and Randomized Controlled Cross-over Within-Subjects Trial' *Reproductive Biology and Endocrinology* 20. Article 149. 2022. doi.org/10.1186/s12958-022-01021-1.

2 'Volunteering in Denmark' Frivilligjob.dk. Accessed 7 July 2023. https://frivilligjob.dk/Volunteering-in-Denmark-People-culture-and-history.html.

3 Bjørn Bay, Peter B. Larsen, et al. 'Danish Sperm Donors Across Three Decades: Motivations and Attitudes' *Fertility and Sterility* 101 (1). 2014. 252–7. https://doi.org/10.1016/j.fertnstert.2013.09.013.

4 'Households and Families' (n.d.) https://www.dst.dk/en/Statistik/emner/borgere/husstande-familier-og-boern/husstande-og-familier.

5 '"There's No Stigma": Why So Many Danish Women Are Opting to Become Single Mothers' *Guardian*. 14 September 2015. https://www.theguardian.com/lifeandstyle/2015/sep/14/no-stigma-single-mothers-denmark-solomors.

6 'Adoption' Familieretshuset.dk. Accessed 7 July 2023. familieretshuset.dk/en/your-life-situation/your-life-situation/adoption.

7 'Intrauterine Insemination (IUI)' NHS Choices. 2019. https://www.nhs.uk/conditions/artificial-insemination/.

8 Cryosinternational.com. 2022. https://www.cryosinternational.com/da-dk/dk-shop/privat/blog/alt-du-skal-vide-om-at-faa-et-donorbarn/.

9 Susan Golombok. *Modern Families: Parents and Children in New Family Forms*. New York. Cambridge University Press. 2015.

10 Anna Barbuscia, Mikko Myrskylä and Alice Goisis. 'The psychosocial health of children born after medically assisted reproduction: Evidence from the UK Millennium Cohort Study' *SSM Population Health*. 7:100355. 14 January 2019. doi: 10.1016/j.ssmph.2019.100355.

11 Hanna Remes, et al. 'The Well-Being of Adolescents Conceived Through Medically Assisted Reproduction: A Population-Level and Within-Family Analysis' *European Journal of Population*, 38, 2022. 915–49, SpringerLink. 11 April 2023. https://link.springer.com/article/10.1007/s10680-022-09623-6#citeas.

    E. C. Ilioi and S. Golombok. 'Psychological Adjustment in Adolescents Conceived by Assisted Reproduction Techniques: A Systematic Review' *Human Reproduction Update*. Jan–Feb 2015. Accessed 16 June 2023. https://pubmed.ncbi.nlm.nih.gov/25281685/.

2. A Viking is Born

1 'Finland (FIN) – Demographics, Health & Infant Mortality' (n.d.) UNICEF DATA. https://data.unicef.org/country/fin/.
    'Child Mortality' UNICEF DATA. December 2021. https://data.unicef.org/topic/child-survival/under-five-mortality/.
2 'Guterres Calls for "Coalition of the World" to Overcome Divisions, Provide Hope in Place of Turmoil' United Nations. (n.d.) Accessed 22 August 2023. https://www.un.org/en/desa/guterres-calls-coalition-world-overcome-divisions-provide-hope-place-turmoil.
3 'Kvinde Fødte Barn På Motorvejen – Mens Far Kørte Med Civil Udrykning' (n.d.) TV2 Østjylland. Accessed 26 August 2023. https://www.tv2ostjylland.dk/aarhus/kvinde-foedte-barn-paa-motorvejen-mens-far-koerte-med-civil-udrykning.
4 'Taxing Wages 2023: Indexation of labour taxation and benefits in OECD Countries' OECD Publishing. Paris. Accessed 16 June 2023. https://www.oecd.org/tax/taxing-wages-20725124.htm.

5 The Organisation for Economic Co-operation and Development (OECD) is an intergovernmental organisation with thirty-eight member countries, founded in 1961 to stimulate economic progress and world trade. OECD. 2023. https://www.oecd.org/.

'The Average Dane' (n.d.) dst.dk. https://www.dst.dk/en/Statistik/laer-om-statistik/gennemsnitsdanskeren.

6 'Income Tax Calculator 2023 – Denmark – Salary after Tax' (n.d.) talent.com. Accessed 7 July 2023. https://dk.talent.com/en/tax-calculator.

7 'Cost of Living Comparison Between Denmark and United Kingdom' NUMBEO. (n.d.) https://www.numbeo.com/cost-of-living/compare_countries_result.jsp?country1=Denmark&country2=United+Kingdom.

8 'Average Usual Weekly Hours Worked on the Main Job' OECD. 2018. https://stats.oecd.org/Index.aspx?DataSetCode=AVE_HRS.

9 Shigehiro Oishi, Selin Kesebir and Ed Diener. 'Income Inequality and Happiness' *Psychological Science* 22 (9). 2011. 1095–1100. https://doi.org/10.1177/0956797611417262.

10 Richard Wilkinson and Kate Pickett. *The Inner Level*. Penguin. 2019.

3. Baby Dane

1 M. Tourula, A. Isola and J. Hassi. 'Children sleeping outdoors in winter: parents' experiences of a culturally bound childcare practice' *International Journal of Circumpolar Health*. 67 (2–3). June 2008. 269–78. doi: 10.3402/ijch.v67i2-3.18284. PMID: 18767347.

2 'The Smart Economics of Norway's Parental Leave, and Why the U.S. Should Consider It' *Washington Post*. 11 January 2016. https://www.washingtonpost.com/news/

parenting/wp/2016/01/11/the-smart-economics-of-norways-parental-leave/.

3 Grant Thornton. 'Number of Women in Senior Management Positions Reaches New High' https://www.consultancy.uk. 8 March 2022. https://www.consultancy.uk/news/30635/number-of-women-in-senior-management-positions-reaches-new-high.

4 'Quick Take: Women in Management' Catalyst. 1 March 2022. https://www.catalyst.org/research/women-in-management/.

5 Gwynn Guilford. 'The Definitive Case for Paternity Leave' Quartz. 24 September 2014. https://qz.com/266841/economic-case-for-paternity-leave.

6 'It's Good for New Moms When Dads Can Stay Home' Stanford Institute for Economic Policy Research (SIEPR). siepr.stanford.edu. 3 June 2019. https://siepr.stanford.edu/news/its-good-new-moms-when-dads-can-stay-home.

7 'Postnatal Depression' NHS. 4 August 2022. https://www.nhs.uk/mental-health/conditions/post-natal-depression/overview/.

8 M. Filippetti, A. Clarke and S. Rigato. 'The mental health crisis of expectant women in the UK: effects of the COVID-19 pandemic on prenatal mental health, antenatal attachment and social support' *BMC Pregnancy Childbirth*. 22 (68). 2022. doi:10.1186/s12884-022-04387-7.

9 'OECD Better Life Index' OECD. 2014. oecdbetterlifeindex.org. https://www.oecdbetterlifeindex.org/topics/work-life-balance/.

10 Nikolay Angelov, Per Johansson and Erica Lindahl. 'Gender Differences in Sickness Absence and the Gender Division of Family Responsibilities' IZA Discussion Papers 7379. Institute of Labor Economics (IZA). 2013. https://ideas.repec.org/p/iza/izadps/dp7379.html.

11 Terrie M. Williams. 'The Biology of Big' *Science*, 366. 6471. 2001. 1316–17. /doi/10.1126/science.aba1128 https://www. science.org/content/article/study-marathon-runners-reveals-hard-limit-human-endurance.

12 Daphna Joel, Zohar Berman, et al. 'Sex Beyond the Genitalia: The Human Brain Mosaic' *Proceedings of the National Academy of Sciences* 112 (50). 2015. 15468–73. https://doi.org/10.1073/pnas.1509654112.

13 Eyal Abraham, Talma Hendler, et al. 'Father's Brain Is Sensitive to Childcare Experiences' *Proceedings of the National Academy of Sciences* 111 (27). 2014. 9792–97. https://doi.org/10.1073/pnas.1402569111.

14 Haas, Linda, and C. Philip Hwang. 'The Impact of Taking Parental Leave on Fathers' Participation in Childcare and Relationships with Children: Lessons from Sweden' *Community, Work & Family* 11 (1). 2008. 85–104. https://doi.org/10.1080/13668800701785346.

4. Bringing Up *Børn*

1 Abigail E. Page, Matthew G. Thomas, et al. 2019. 'Testing Adaptive Hypotheses of Alloparenting in Agta Foragers' *Nature Human Behaviour* 3 (11): 1154–63. https://doi.org/10.1038/s41562-019-0679-2.

2 Sheina Lew-Levy, Stephen M. Kissler, et al. 'Who Teaches Children to Forage? Exploring the Primacy of Child to-Child Teaching Among Hadza and BaYaka Hunter-Gatherers of Tanzania and Congo' *Evolution and Human Behavior* 41 (1). 2020. 12–22. https://doi.org/10.1016/j.evolhumbehav.2019.07.003.

3 K. Libertus and D. A. Violi. 'Sit to Talk: Relation between Motor Skills and Language Development in Infancy' *Frontiers in Psychology*. 7. 2016. 475. doi: 10.3389/

fpsyg.2016.00475. PMID: 27065934; PMCID: PMC4815289.

H. C. Leonard and E. L. Hill. 'Review: The impact of motor development on typical and atypical social cognition and language: a systematic review' *Child and Adolescent Mental Health*. 19 (3). 2014. 163–170. doi: 10.1111/camh.12055. Epub 8 February 2014. PMID: 32878369.

Linda Smith and Esther Thelen. 'Development as a Dynamic System' *Trends in Cognitive Sciences*. 7. 2003. 343–8. 10.1111/1467-8721.ep10770402.

J. M. Iverson. 'Developing language in a developing body: the relationship between motor development and language development' *Journal of Child Language*, 37. 2010. 229–61.

4 'Report: Big Change Starts Small' Centre for Early Childhood. June 2021. https://centreforearlychildhood.org/report/.

5 Pasi Sahlberg, Howard Gardner and Sir Ken Robinson. 2021. *Finnish Lessons 3.0: What Can the World Learn from Educational Change in Finland?* New York: Teachers College Press, Columbia University.

6 'Income-based allowance, sibling allowance, and other allowances' Accessed 5 July 2023. https://lifeindenmark.borger.dk/family-and-children/day-care/income-based-allowance--sibling-allowance--and-other-allowances.

7 'Coram Family and Childcare Survey 2022' (n.d.) Coram Group. https://www.coram.org.uk/resource/resource-coram-family-and-childcare-survey-2022/.

'Earnings and Hours Worked, All Employees: ASHE Table 8' Office for National Statistics. (n.d.) www.ons.gov.uk. https://www.ons.gov.uk/employmentandlabourmarket/peopleinwork/earningsandworkinghours/datasets/earningsandhoursworkedallemployeesashetable8.

egibson@tuc.org.uk. 'Cost of Childcare Has Risen by

Over £2,000 a Year Since 2010' www.tuc.org.uk. 13 June 2022. https://www.tuc.org.uk/news/cost-childcare-has-risen-over-ps2000-year-2010.

8 '$10 a Day Child Care for Canadian Families' Prime Minister of Canada. 21 April 2021. https://www.pm.gc.ca/en/news/news-releases/2021/04/21/10-day-child-care-canadian-families.

9 'This Is Where Mothers Work the Longest Hours' (n.d.) World Economic Forum. https://www.weforum.org/agenda/2017/05/this-is-where-mothers-work-the-longest-hours/.

10 Michaeleen Doucleff, *Hunt, Gather, Parent: What Ancient Cultures Can Teach Us About the Lost Art of Raising Happy, Helpful Little Humans.* Avid Reader Press/Simon & Schuster, March 2021.

11 First published as John Bowlby. *Maternal Care and Mental Health.* Northvale, N.J.: Jason Aronson, 1951. Abridged and republished as the hugely influential John Bowlby and Margery Fry. *Child Care and the Growth of Love.* Based by permission of the World Health Organization on the Report 'Maternal Care and Mental Health' Abridged and edited by Margery Fry. London: Penguin Books, 1953.

12 Dina Gerdeman. 'Kids of Working Moms Grow into Happy Adults' HBS Working Knowledge. 16 July 2018. https://hbswk.hbs.edu/item/kids-of-working-moms-grow-into-happy-adults.

13 'Mothers' Part-Time Employment: Associations With Mother and Family Well-Being' Cheryl Buehler, PhD., and Marion O'Brien, PhD, University of North Carolina at Greensboro, *Journal of Family Psychology*, 25 (6).

14 Anisa Purbasari Horton. 'We Need to Stop Shaming Women for Wanting (or Not Wanting) to Return to Work'

Fast Company. 23 April 2019. https://www.fastcompany.
com/90338409/we-need-to-stop-shaming-women-for-
wanting-or-not-wanting-to-return-to-work.
15 'Danish Nursery Offers Parents Time for Making Babies'
BBC News. 13 September 2012. https://www.bbc.com/
news/world-europe-19585136.

5. No Such Thing as Bad Weather
(Just the Wrong Clothes)

1 'Just 20 Minutes of Contact with Nature Will Lower Stress
Hormone Levels, Reveals New Study' ScienceDaily. 2019.
https://www.sciencedaily.com/releases/2019/04/190404074915.
htm.

Matthew G. Frank, Laura K. Fonken, et al.
'Immunization with Mycobacterium Vaccae Induces an
Anti-Inflammatory Milieu in the CNS: Attenuation of
Stress-Induced Microglial Priming, Alarmins and
Anxiety-like Behavior' *Brain, Behavior, and Immunity* 73.
October 2018: 352–63. https://doi.org/10.1016/j.
bbi.2018.05.020.

Gregory N. Bratman, Gretchen C. Daily, et al. 'The
Benefits of Nature Experience: Improved Affect and
Cognition' *Landscape and Urban Planning* 138, June 2015:
41–50. https://doi.org/10.1016/j.landurbplan.2015.02.005.

A. Faber Taylor and F. E. Kuo. 'Children with Attention
Deficits Concentrate Better after Walk in the Park' *Journal
of Attention Disorders* 12 (5). 2009: 402–9. https://doi.
org/10.1177/1087054708323000.

Eivind Aadland, Hege Eikeland Tjomsland, et al.
'Active Learning Norwegian Preschool(Er)S (ACTNOW) –
Design of a Cluster Randomized Controlled Trial of Staff
Professional Development to Promote Physical Activity,

Motor Skills, and Cognition in Preschoolers' *Frontiers in Psychology* 11. July 2020. https://doi.org/10.3389/fpsyg.2020.01382.

2 Francesco Vitrano and Nato A. Palermo. 'Curriculum Vitae et Studiorum Informazioni Personali' 1962. https://www.asptrapani.it/upload/asp_trapani/elencodipendenti/Vitrano_Francesco_ASL06226_13192_1516.pdf.

3 Remo Frei, Kristina Heye and Caroline Roduit. 'Environmental Influences on Childhood Allergies and Asthma – the Farm Effect' *Pediatric Allergy and Immunology* 33 (6). 2022. https://doi.org/10.1111/pai.13807.

Katja Radon, Doris Windstetter, et al. 'Contact with Farm Animals in Early Life and Juvenile Inflammatory Bowel Disease: A Case-Control Study' *Pediatrics* 120 (2). 2007. 354–61. https://doi.org/10.1542/peds.2006-3624.

Michele Antonelli and Davide Donelli. 'Mud Therapy and Skin Microbiome: A Review' *International Journal of Biometeorology* 62 (11). 2018. 2037–44. https://doi.org/10.1007/s00484-018-1599-y.

Till S.Böbel, Sascha B. Hackl, et al. 'Less Immune Activation Following Social Stress in Rural vs. Urban Participants Raised with Regular or No Animal Contact, Respectively' *Proceedings of the National Academy of Sciences of the United States of America* 115 (20). 2018. 5259–64. https://doi.org/10.1073/pnas.1719866115

4 Marja I. Roslund, Riikka Puhakka, et al. 'Biodiversity Intervention Enhances Immune Regulation and Health-Associated Commensal Microbiota among Daycare Children' *Science Advances* 6 (42): eaba2578. 2020. https://doi.org/10.1126/sciadv.aba2578.

Carina Grafetstätter, Martin Gaisberger, et al. 'Does waterfall aerosol influence mucosal immunity and chronic stress? A randomized controlled clinical trial' *Journal of*

Physiological Anthropology. 36, 2017. doi:10.1186/s40101-016-0117-3.

5 Sean Clouston, Olga Morozova, and Jaymie Meliker. 'A wind speed threshold for increased outdoor transmission of coronavirus: an ecological study' *BMC Infectious Diseases*. 21, 2021. doi:10.1186/s12879-021-06796-z

6 Caoimhe Twohig-Bennett and Andy Jones, 'The Health Benefits of the Great Outdoors: A Systematic Review and Meta-analysis of Greenspace Exposure and Health Outcomes' *Environmental Research* 166. 2018. 628–37. doi:10.1016/j.envres.2018.06.030.

C. Capaldi, R. L. Dopko and J. Zelenski, 'The Relationship Between Nature Connectedness and Happiness: A Meta-analysis' *Frontiers in Psychology*, 2014. doi: 10.3389/fpsyg.2014.00976.

D. G. Pearson and T. Craig, 'The Great Outdoors? Exploring the Mental Health Benefits of Natural Environments' *Frontiers in Psychology*, 2014, 5,1178. doi:10.3389/fpsyg.2014.01178.

G. N. Bratman, J. P. Hamilton, et al., 'Nature Experience Reduces Rumination and Subgenual Prefrontal Cortex Activation' *Proceedings of the National Academy of Sciences of the United States of America* 112 (28). 2015. 8567–72. doi: 10.1073/pnas.1510459112.

R. A. Atchley, D. L. Strayer and P. Atchley, 'Creativity in the Wild: Improving Creative Reasoning Through Immersion in Natural Settings' ed. J. de Fockert, *PLoS ONE* 7 (12). 2021. e51474. doi:10.1371/journal.pone.0051474.

J. W. Zhang, P. K. Piff, R. Iyer, et al., 'An Occasion for Unselfing: Beautiful Nature Leads to Prosociality' *Journal of Environmental Psychology* 37. 2014. 61–72. doi: 10.1016/j.jenvp.2013.11.008.

F. Mayer, C. Frantz, et al., 'Why Is Nature Beneficial?

The Role of Connectedness to Nature' *Environment and Behavior* 41. 2009. 607–43. doi: 10.1177/0013916508319745.

Y. Joye and J. W. Bolderdijk, 'An Exploratory Study into the Effects of Extraordinary Nature on Emotions, Mood, and Prosociality' *Frontiers in Psychology*, 2014, 5,1577. doi:10.3389/fpsyg.2014.01577.

K. M. Korpela, T. Pasanen, et al. 'Environmental Strategies of Affect Regulation and Their Associations With Subjective Well-Being' *Frontiers in Psychology* 9. 2018. 562. doi: 10.3389/fpsyg.2018.00562.

'Spending Time in Nature Makes People Feel More Alive, Study Shows' 3 June 2010. http://www.rochester.edu/news/show.php?id=3639.

7 Damian Carrington. 'Three-Quarters of UK Children Spend Less Time Outdoors than Prison Inmates – Survey' *Guardian*. 25 March 2016. https://www.theguardian.com/environment/2016/mar/25/three-quarters-of-uk-children-spend-less-time-outdoors-than-prison-inmates-survey.

6. Foraging and Family Meals

1 'Organic Food Market: Leading Countries Based on Consumption per Capita, 2018' (n.d.) Statista. https://www.statista.com/statistics/263077/per-capita-revenue-of-organic-foods-worldwide-since-2007/.

2 Louise Kaad-Hansen. 'Facts and Figures About Danish Organics' Organic Denmark. February 2022. https://www.organicdenmark.com/facts-figures-about-danish-organics.

3 Petter Lundborg, Dan-Olof Rooth and Jesper Alex-Petersen. 'Long-Term Effects of Childhood Nutrition: Evidence from a School Lunch Reform' *Review of Economic Studies* 89 (2). 2022. 876–908. https://doi.org/10.1093/restud/rdab028.

4 Carl Baker. 2023. 'Obesity Statistics' House of Commons Library. 12 January 2023. https://commonslibrary. parliament.uk/research-briefings/sn03336/.

5 'Childhood Overweight and Obesity' Centers For Disease Control and Prevention. 30 August 2021. https://www.cdc. gov/obesity/childhood/index.html.

6 'WHO European Childhood Obesity Surveillance Initiative (COSI)' (n.d.) World Health Organization. https://www. who.int/europe/initiatives/who-european-childhood-obesity-surveillance-initiative-(cosi).

7 Jannie Nielsen, Adam Hulman, et al. 'Body Mass Index Trajectories from Childhood to Adulthood and Age at Onset of Overweight and Obesity: The Influence of Parents' Weight Status' *American Journal of Epidemiology*, July 2022. https://doi.org/10.1093/aje/kwac124.

8 'Adult Obesity Facts' Centers for Disease Control and Prevention. 11 February 2021. https://www.cdc.gov/obesity/ data/adult.html.

9 Reynalda Cordova, Nathalie Kliemann, et al. 'Consumption of Ultra-Processed Foods Associated with Weight Gain and Obesity in Adults: A Multi-National Cohort Study' *Clinical Nutrition* 40 (9). 2021. 5079–88. https://doi.org/10.1016/j. clnu.2021.08.009.

10 Christine Frithioff-Bøjsøe, Morten Asp Vonsild Lund, et al. 'Early Detection of Childhood Overweight and Related Complications in a Danish Population-Based Cohort Aged 2–8 Years' *Obesity Research & Clinical Practice* 16 (3). 2022. 228–34. https://doi.org/10.1016/j.orcp.2022.04.001.

11 'Country Profiles on Nutrition, Physical Activity and Obesity in the 53 WHO European Region Member States: Methodology and Summary' (n.d.) www.who.int. https:// www.who.int/europe/publications/i/item/9789289050036.

7. Singing, *Samfundssind* and the Social Brain

1 Nick Alan Joseph Stewart and Adam Jonathan Lonsdale. 'It's Better Together: The Psychological Benefits of Singing in a Choir' *Psychology of Music* 44 (6). 2016. 1240–54. https://doi.org/10.1177/0305735615624976.

   Jason R. Keeler, Edward A. Roth, et al. 2015. 'The Neurochemistry and Social Flow of Singing: Bonding and Oxytocin' *Frontiers in Human Neuroscience* 9. September 2015. https://doi.org/10.3389/fnhum.2015.00518.

2 Alain Cohn, Michel André Maréchal, et al. 'Civic Honesty Around the Globe' *Science* 365 (6448). 2019. 70–73. https://doi.org/10.1126/science.aau8712.

3 'Parents Should Avoid Pressuring Young Children over Grades, ASU Study Says' *ASU News*. 28 November 2016. https://news.asu.edu/20161128-discoveries-parents-should-avoid-pressuring-young-children-over-grades-asu-study-says.

4 Soyoung Q. Park, Thorsten Kahnt, et al. 'A Neural Link between Generosity and Happiness' *Nature Communications* 8: 15964. 2017. https://doi.org/10.1038/ncomms15964.

5 Kirstie Brewer. 'The Day Iceland's Women Went on Strike' *BBC News*, 23 October 2015. https://www.bbc.com/news/magazine-34602822.

6 'Iceland Holds Funeral for First Glacier Lost to Climate Change' *Guardian*. 19 August 2019. https://www.theguardian.com/world/2019/aug/19/iceland-holds-funeral-for-first-glacier-lost-to-climate-change.

7 'Made with Love: Greta Thunberg on Apple Podcasts' (n.d.) Apple Podcasts. Accessed 7 July 2023. https://podcasts.apple.com/gb/podcast/greta-thunberg/id1671846653?i=1000603841617.

8 Nanna Gelebo, David Sandberg, et al. 'Cost of Living

Crisis: Nordic Consumer Sentiment 2022' BCG Global. 17 November 2022. https://www.bcg.com/publications/2022/nordic-cost-of-living-crisis-consumer-sentiment-report.

9 Jo Arne Marvik. '*Ny Rapport: Ein Av Tre Hushaldningar Har Fått Ein Dårlegare Økonomi Sidan Januar*' NRK. 29 July 2022. https://www.nrk.no/norge/ny-rapport_-ein-av-tre-hushaldningar-har-fatt-ein-darlegare-okonomi-sidan-januar-1.16052465.

'Sweden Has a Poverty Problem: The Social Stores Offering Food at Rock-Bottom Prices' *Guardian*. 5 December 2022. https://www.theguardian.com/world/2022/dec/05/sweden-has-a-poverty-problem-the-social-stores-offering-food-at-rock-bottom-prices.

Simon Johnson, 'Analysis: Sweden's Cost of Living Crisis Spooks Voters ahead of Election' Reuters, 5 September 2022, https://www.reuters.com/world/swedens-cost-living-crisis-spooks-voters-ahead-election-2022-09-02/.

8. Show, Don't Tell: Discipline – Danish Style

1 Daniel J. Siegel and Tina Payne Bryson. *The Whole-Brain Child: 12 Revolutionary Strategies to Nurture Your Child's Developing Mind*. New York: Bantam Books. 2012.

2 Jesper Juul. *Your Competent Child*. Balboa Press. 2011.

3 Aksel Sandemose and Eugene Gay-Tifft. *A Fugitive Crosses His Tracks*. New York, A.A. Knopf. 1936.

4 Jesper Juul. *Your Competent Child*. Balboa Press. 2011. 155.

5 Michael Potegal and Dorothy Einon. 'Aggressive Behaviors in Adult Rats Deprived of Playfighting Experience as Juveniles' *Developmental Psychobiology* 22 (2). 159–72. 1989. https://doi.org/10.1002/dev.420220206.

9. Play (Well)

1 Stuart L. Brown and Christopher C. Vaughan. *Play: How It Shapes the Brain, Opens the Imagination, and Invigorates the Soul*. New York: Avery. 2009. Chapter 1.

2 'Learning Through Play: Increasing Impact, Reducing Inequality' (n.d.) philea.issuelab.org. Accessed 7 July 2023. https://philea.issuelab.org/resource/learning-through-play-increasing-impact-reducing-inequality.html.

3 K. R. Ginsburg. 'The Importance of Play in Promoting Healthy Child Development and Maintaining Strong Parent-Child Bonds' *PEDIATRICS* 119 (1). 182–91. 2017. https://doi.org/10.1542/peds.2006-2697.

4 Sandra L. Hofferth and John F. Sandberg. 'Changes in American Children's Time, 1981–1997' *Advances in Life Course Research* 6. 2001. 193–229. https://doi.org/10.1016/s1040-2608(01)80011-3.

5 Kazuaki Nagata. 'Four-Day Workweek Boosted Productivity by 40%, Microsoft Japan Experiment Shows' *Japan Times*. 5 November 2019. https://www.japantimes.co.jp/news/2019/11/05/business/microsoft-japan-says-four-day-workweek-boosted-productivity-40/.

6 Eleanor Ainge Roy. 'Work Less, Get More: New Zealand Firm's Four-Day Week an "Unmitigated Success"' *Guardian*. 18 July 2018. https://www.theguardian.com/world/2018/jul/19/work-less-get-more-new-zealand-firms-four-day-week-an-unmitigated-success.

7 Valerie Strauss. 'Delaying Kindergarten until Age 7 Offers Key Benefits to Kids – Study (Research by Thomas Dee)' Stanford Graduate School of Education. 8 October 2015. https://ed.stanford.edu/in-the-media/delaying-kindergarten-until-age-7-offers-key-benefits-kids-study-research-thomas-dee.

Thomas Dee and Hans Henrik Sievertsen. 'The Gift of

Time? School Starting Age and Mental Health' National Bureau of Economic Research. October 2015. https://doi.org/10.3386/w21610.

8 Michigan State University. 'Nearly one million children in U.S. potentially misdiagnosed with ADHD, study finds' ScienceDaily. www.sciencedaily.com/releases/2010/08/100817103342.htm Accessed 7 July 2023.

9 Timothy J. Layton, Michael L. Barnett, Tanner R. Hicks and Anupam B. Jena. 'Attention Deficit–Hyperactivity Disorder and Month of School Enrollment' *New England Journal of Medicine* 379 (22). 2018. 2122–30. https://doi.org/10.1056/nejmoa1806828.

10 Pasi Sahlberg and William Doyle. *Let the Children Play: Why More Play Will Save Our Schools and Help Children Thrive*. New York: Oxford University Press. 2019. 158.

11 'About | Project Zero' (n.d.) Project Zero. Harvard Graduate School of Education. https://pz.harvard.edu/who-we-are/about.

12 Floriane Laroche. 'Parents Spend a Total of 1,300 Hours Playing with Their Kids during Their First Five Years' Digitalhub. 28 September 2022. https://swnsdigital.com/uk/2022/09/parents-spend-a-total-of-1300-hours-playing-with-their-kids-during-their-first-five-years/.

13 'Serve and Return' Center on the Developing Child, Harvard University. 2021. https://developingchild.harvard.edu/science/key-concepts/serve-and-return/.

14 'What Do Children Have to Say About Play?' Lego Foundation, results of LEGO® Play Well Study 2022. https://learningthroughplay.com/explore-the-research/what-do-children-have-to-say-about-play.

15 'Engaging Young Children in Play' (n.d.) Lego Foundation. Accessed 6 July 2023. https://learningthroughplay.com/explore-the-research/engaging-young-children-in-play.

10. Risk (aka Viking Health and Safety)

1 Gunnar Breivik. *Sug I Magen Og Livskvalitet*. 2001.
2 Gunnar Breivik. 'The Quest for Excitement and the Safe Society' June, 2007. 24–38. https://doi.org/10.4324/9780203698570-8.
3 'Learning the Ropes: Why Germany Is Building Risk into Its Playgrounds' *Guardian*. 24 October 2021. https://www.theguardian.com/world/2021/oct/24/why-germany-is-building-risk-into-its-playgrounds.
4 'Resources' Play Safety Forum. 4 March 2015. https://playsafetyforum.wordpress.com/resources/.
5 Sue Dremann. 'Palo Alto School District Sued for Negligence over Kindergartener's Broken Leg' Palo Alto Online. 3 August 2023. Accessed 23 August 2023. https://www.paloaltoonline.com/news/2023/08/03/palo-alto-school-district-sued-for-negligence-over-kindergarteners-broken-leg.
6 'Global Peace Index' Vision of Humanity. 2023. https://www.visionofhumanity.org/maps/#/.

11. Digital Blind Spot

1 'Online Games Gamble with Children's Data' Danish Society of Engineers' Working Group on Ethics and Technology & DataEthics.eu. March 2021. https://dataethics.eu/wp-content/uploads/GameTechEnglish Version.pdf.
2 Richard Jenkins. 'Children Spend Twice as Long Looking at Screens than Playing Outside, Study Finds' *Independent*. 26 October 2018. https://www.independent.co.uk/life-style/children-screens-play-outside-computer-phone-time-healthy-games-a8603411.html.
3 'Children and Parents: Media Use and Attitudes Report

2022' Ofcom. 31 March 2022. https://www.ofcom.org.uk/
research-and-data/media-literacy-research/childrens/
children-and-parents-media-use-and-attitudes-report-2022.

4 Anne Cathrine Joergensen, Katrine Strandberg-Larsen, et
al. 'Spinal Pain in Pre-Adolescence and the Relation with
Screen Time and Physical Activity Behavior' *BMC
Musculoskeletal Disorders* 22 (1). 2021. 393. https://doi.
org/10.1186/s12891-021-04263-z.

5 Jeremy J. Walsh, Joel D. Barnes, et al. 'Associations
between 24 Hour Movement Behaviours and Global
Cognition in US Children: A Cross-Sectional Observational
Study' *The Lancet Child & Adolescent Health* 2 (11). 2018.
783–91. https://doi.org/10.1016/s2352-4642(18)30278-5.

6 Joshua Foreman, Arief Tjitra Salim, et al. 'Association
Between Digital Smart Device Use and Myopia: A
Systematic Review and Meta-Analysis' *The Lancet Digital
Health* 3 (12). 2021. https://doi.org/10.1016/s2589-
7500(21)00135-7.

7 'What Do Children Have to Say About Play?' (n.d.) Lego
Foundation. Accessed 3 July 2023. https://
learningthroughplay.com/explore-the-research/what-do-
children-have-to-say-about-play.

8 Linn Elise Jakhelln. '*Barn Leker Mindre Ute I Nærområdet*'
Norsk Friluftsliv. 5 May 2022. https://norskfriluftsliv.no/
barn-leker-mindre-ute-i-naeromradet/.

9 Jessica Mudditt. 'Why Short-Sightedness is on the Rise'
BBC. 5 October 2022. https://www.bbc.com/future/
article/20220927-can-you-prevent-short-sightedness-in-kids.

10 Naomi Schaefer Riley. 'Opinion | America's Real Digital
Divide' *New York Times*, 11 February 2018, https://www.
nytimes.com/2018/02/11/opinion/america-digital-divide.html.

11 '*Demokratisk Kontrol Med Tech Giganternes
Forretningsmodeller* – Delafrapportering Fra Regeringens

Ekspertgruppe Om Tech-Giganter' (n.d.) Accessed 23 June 2023. https://em.dk/media/19630/anbefalinger-fra-tech-ekspertgruppe.pdf.

'*Regeringens Ekspertgruppe Om Tech-Giganter Udgiver Første Rapport Med Konkrete Anbefalinger*' (n.d.) www. medieraadet.dk. Accessed 7 July 2023. https://www. medieraadet.dk/medieradet/regeringens-ekspertgruppe-om-tech-giganter-udgiver-foerste-rapport-med-konkrete.

12 '*Tech-Giganterne Skal Begrænses: Regeringen Vil Beskytte Børn Bedre*' (n.d.) em.dk. Accessed 23 June 2023. https://em.dk/nyhedsarkiv/2023/juni/tech-giganterne-skal-begraenses-regeringen-vil-beskytte-boern-bedre/.

13 '*Anbefalinger Om Børn, Unges Og Forældres Brug Af Skærm*' (n.d.) www.sst.dk. Accessed 23 June 2023. https://www. sst.dk/da/Opgaver/Forebyggelse/Indsatser/Fokusomraader/Sundhed-og-digitale-medier/Skaermbrug-0-15-aar.

14 '*Pædagoger Ser Ikke Skærmproblem I Dagtilbud*' 2023. DR. 5 June 2023. https://www.dr.dk/nyheder/politik/paedagoger-ser-ikke-skaermproblem-i-dagtilbud.

15 'Empathy: College Students Don't Have as Much as They Used To' *University of Michigan News*. 27 May 2010. https://news.umich.edu/empathy-college-students-don-t-have-as-much-as-they-used-to/.

16 '*To Timer Foran Skærmen Dagligt Kan Skade Dit Barns Indlæring*' 2018. DR. 1 October 2018. https://www.dr.dk/nyheder/viden/kroppen/timer-foran-skaermen-dagligt-kan-skade-dit-barns-indlaering.

17 '*Sådan Påvirker Telefoner Relationen Mellem Forældre Og Børn*' 2018. NOPA. 24 September 2018. https://nordicparenting.dk/nyt-studie-viser-hvordan-telefoner-paavirker-relationen-mellem-foraeldre-og-boern/.

18 Twitter post. Adam Grant. Twitter. 15 May 2023. Accessed

23 June 2023. https://twitter.com/AdamMGrant/status/16581
21692416204801?lang=en.

19 'Study out from Sapien Labs Links Age of First
Smartphone to Mental Wellbeing' Sapien Labs. 14 May
2023. Accessed 23 June 2023. https://sapienlabs.org/whats_
new/study-out-from-sapien-labs-links-age-of-first-smart
phone-to-mental-wellbeing/.

20 Jon Haidt and Zach Rausch. 'Kids Who Get Smartphones
Earlier Become Adults with Worse Mental Health' After
Babel. 15 May 2023. https://jonathanhaidt.substack.com/p/
sapien-smartphone-report.

12. The New Norse Sagas

1 'Great Lives, Astrid Lindgren, Creator of Pippi
Longstocking' (n.d.) BBC Radio 4. Accessed 6 July 2023.
https://www.bbc.co.uk/programmes/m001c6gv.

2 'The Relationship Between Empathy and Reading Fiction:
Separate Roles for Cognitive and Affective Components'
Journal of European Psychology Students 5 (3). 2014. 9–18.
https://doi.org/10.5334/jeps.ca.

3 Janice McCabe, Emily Fairchild, et al. 'Gender in
Twentieth-Century Children's Books' *Gender & Society* 25
(2). 2011. 197–226. https://doi.org/10.1177/0891243211398358.

13. Schooltime (Barely)

1 Carl Cullinane and Rebecca Montacute. 'Life Lessons' 11
October 2017. Sutton Trust. https://www.suttontrust.com/
our-research/life-lessons-workplace-skills/.

2 Nancy Carlsson-Paige, Geralyn Bywater McLaughlin and
Joan Almon. 'Reading Instruction in Kindergarten: Little to

Gain and Much to Lose' ERIC, Institution of Education
Sciences. January 2015. https://eric.ed.gov/?id=ED609172.

Sebastian P. Suggate, Elizabeth A. Schaughency and
Elaine Reese. 'Children Learning to Read Later Catch up
to Children Reading Earlier' *Early Childhood Research
Quarterly* 28 (1). 2013. 33–48. https://doi.org/10.1016/j.
ecresq.2012.04.004.

3 Sebastian P. Suggate. 'School Entry Age and Reading
Achievement in the 2006 Programme for International
Student Assessment (PISA)' *International Journal of
Educational Research* 48 (3). 2009. 151–61. https://doi.
org/10.1016/j.ijer.2009.05.001.

4 'PISA 2018 Results' OECD. 2018. https://www.oecd.org/
pisa/publications/pisa-2018-results.htm.

5 '2018 Database – PISA' OECD. 2018. https://www.oecd.
org/pisa/data/2018database/.

6 Charlotte Edmond. 'These Are the Countries Where
Children Are Most Satisfied with Their Lives' World
Economic Forum. 4 September 2020. https://www.weforum.
org/agenda/2020/09/child-well-being-health-happiness-
unicef-report/.

7 D. Hofkins, S. Northen and Robin John Alexander.
Introducing the Cambridge Primary Review. *York Research
Database*. Cambridge: University of Cambridge, Faculty of
Education. 2009. https://pure.york.ac.uk/portal/en/
publications/introducing-the-cambridge-primary-review.

8 Frank Martela, Bent Greve, et al. 'The Nordic
Exceptionalism: What Explains Why the Nordic Countries
Are Constantly Among the Happiest in the World' *World
Happiness Report 2020*. January 2020. 128–45. https://
worldhappiness.report/ed/2020/#read.

14. *God Ferie!* Holidaying Like a Viking

1 '*Norska Ägandet Av Svenska Fritidshus Störst*' (n.d.) Statistiska Centralbyrån. Accessed 3 July 2023. https://www.scb.se/ hitta-statistik/statistik-efter-amne/boende-byggande-och-bebyggelse/bostadsbyggande-och-ombyggnad/ bostadsbestand/pong/statistiknyhet/utlandskt-agande-och-utlandssvenskars-agande-av-fritidshus-i-sverige-2021/.

2 M. P. White, S. Pahl, et al. 'The "Blue Gym": What Can Blue Space Do for You and What Can You Do for Blue Space?' *Journal of the Marine Biological Association of the United Kingdom* 96 (1). 2016. 5–12. https://doi.org/10.1017/ S0025315415002209.

3 Salvatore Bimonte and Valeria Faralla. 'Happiness and Nature-Based Vacations' *Annals of Tourism Research* 46. May 2014. 176–78. https://doi.org/10.1016/j. annals.2014.02.002.

4 Nelly A. Papalambros, Giovanni Santostasi, et al. 'Acoustic Enhancement of Sleep Slow Oscillations and Concomitant Memory Improvement in Older Adults' *Frontiers in Human Neuroscience* 11. March 2017. https://doi.org/10.3389/ fnhum.2017.00109.

 Steven Morris. 'A Stroll by the Sea Will Help You Sleep Longer, Study Finds' *Guardian*, 16 September 2015. https://www.theguardian.com/uk-news/2015/ sep/17/a-stroll-by-the-sea-will-help-you-sleep-longer-study-finds.

15. Let's Get Physical

1 Guy Martin. 'How to Get Naked in Iceland: New "Spa Etiquette" Tourist Video is Viral Comedy Gold' *Forbes*. 1 March 2016. Accessed 3 July 2023. https://www.forbes.com/

sites/guymartin/2016/03/01/how-to-get-naked-in-iceland-spa-
etiquette-tourist-video-gudmundur/?sh=750f0d233635.

2 'Sauna Culture in Finland' (n.d.) UNESCO. https://ich.
unesco.org/en/RL/sauna-culture-in-finland-01596.

3 'Gelotophobia: Living a Life in Fear of Laughter' BBC
News. 26 June 2014. http://www.bbc.co.uk/news/health-
27323470.

4 Denmark Active Healthy Kids Global Alliance. (n.d.)
Accessed 3 July 2023. https://www.activehealthykids.org/
denmark/.

5 Helen Russell. 'Porn Belongs in the Classroom, Says Danish
Professor' *Guardian*. 16 March 2015. https://www.
theguardian.com/culture/2015/mar/16/pornography-belongs-
classroom-professor-denmark.

16. Teen Viking

1 Margit Warburg. 'Graduation in Denmark: Secular Ritual
and Civil Religion' *Journal of Ritual Studies* 23 (2). 2009.
31–42. http://www.jstor.org/stable/44368808.

2 *Spotlight on Adolescent Health and Well-Being. Findings from
the 2017/2018 Health Behaviour in School-Aged Children
(HBSC) Survey in Europe and Canada. International Report.
Volume 2. Key Data. Apps.who.int*. World Health
Organization. Regional Office for Europe. 2020 https://apps.
who.int/iris/handle/10665/332104.

3 Frederik Kraglund, Thomas Deleuran, et al. 'Decreasing
Incidence of Alcohol-Related Liver Disease in Denmark: A
25-Year Nationwide Study' *Clinical Epidemiology 13. 2021.*
1–11. https://doi.org/10.2147/clep.s287870.

4 Harshad Devarbhavi, Sumeet K. Asrani, et al. 'Global
Burden of Liver Disease: 2023 Update' *Journal of*

Hepatology 79 (2). 2023. 516–37. https://doi.org/10.1016/j.jhep.2023.03.017.

Epilogue

1 Jeremy Stahl. 'Sweden's Bizarre Tradition of Watching Donald Duck Cartoons on Christmas Eve' *Slate* magazine. 22 December 2009. https://slate.com/culture/2009/12/sweden-s-bizarre-tradition-of-watching-donald-duck-kalle-anka-cartoons-on-christmas-eve.html.
2 Carl Frey and Michael Osborne. 'The Future of Employment: How Susceptible Are Jobs to Computerisation?' *Technological Forecasting and Social Change* 114. January 2017. 254–80. https://doi.org/10.1016/j.techfore.2016.08.019.
3 Julia Isaacs, Isabel V. Sawhill and Ron Haskins. 'Getting Ahead or Losing Ground: Economic Mobility in America' Brookings. 20 February 2008. https://www.brookings.edu/articles/getting-ahead-or-losing-ground-economic-mobility-in-america/.

Index

education: approach to behavioural issues, 228–9; business schools, 275; children with diagnoses/challenges, 229; cooking taught in schools, 98–9; corporal punishment, 204; and digital technology, 189, 194, 195; *Efterskoler*, 272–5; and equality in Nordic countries, 63–5, 73, 102, 220, 228–32, 273–5; *folkeskole* (state school), 218, 273; free school meals, 97–8, 100; free-thinking/anti-authoritarian basis in Denmark, 219–25, 230–2, 233, 273–4, 291–2, 296; *fri for mobberi* ('free from bullying' programme), 115; *friskole* (private school), 218–19, 273; global comparisons, 224–5, 231–2; graduation Danish style, 266–71, 276, 277, 280, 281, 283–4; *gymnasium* school, 223, 266–71, 273, 275–6, 278; homework as minimal in Nordic countries, 222, 225, 233; late teaching of literacy skills, 1, 221–2, 223–4, 225; *legepatruljen* (play patrol), 118–19; length of school day, 230; monthly *spise og lege* ('eat and play'), 227; as not competitive/grade-focused, 220, 222–5, 230, 232; parents as 'collaborators' in Denmark, 226–7; pedagogy of play, 159; problems in Danish system, 229; and public speaking/oracy skills, 221, 233; school starting age, 59, 219, 230, 291–2; school trips to view dissections, 217–18; sex education, 258–62; 'spontaneous dissection day', 216–17; teacher autonomy, 230–1, 233; teacher training in Finland, 230–1; teaching about *fællesskab* ("community"), 123; they/them pronouns in Denmark, 208–10; tolerance/social

skills as important, 61, 67, 115, 135–6, 147, 195–6, 227–8; trade/technical education, 275 *see also* childcare/early-years education

Egebæk, Pernille Ane, 259

Emilia (Finnish Scout leader), 180, 221, 254

environmental politics, 31, 32, 81, 111, 116, 123

equality: and education/childcare, 63–5, 73, 102, 154, 220, 228–32, 273–5; in Finland, 32, 229–31; global structural inequalities, 32, 39; and happiness, 39, 40, 47, 232; Tove Jansson's belief in, 208–9; levels of in Nordic countries, 5, 10, 39, 40, 47–53, 63–5, 68–9, 73, 115–16, 123, 229–32; and movement towards individualisation, 39, 73, 119, 123–4; and parenting, 53–4, 101–2, 130, 134–5; and play, 154 *see also* gender equality

Erb, Karin, 21

Faber, Phillip, 112–13

family life: adoption process in Denmark, 21; and Christmas, 286–91, 294–300; dinner together round the table, 100–2, 107–8, 142; and holidays, 235, 236–7, 238–9, 241–50, 251; as private responsibility in US/UK, 124–5; same-sex couples, 10, 11; and *samfundssind*, 119–20, 124–5; single mothers, 11, 21–2, 23–5, 27–8; types of in Nordic countries, 10–11, 27 *see also* parenting Danishly

farming tradition, 46, 103, 162, 178, 188, 193, 217, 303, 304–5

Faroe Isles, 9*

Ferrell, Will, 238

fertility treatment: anonymous vs

INDEX

351